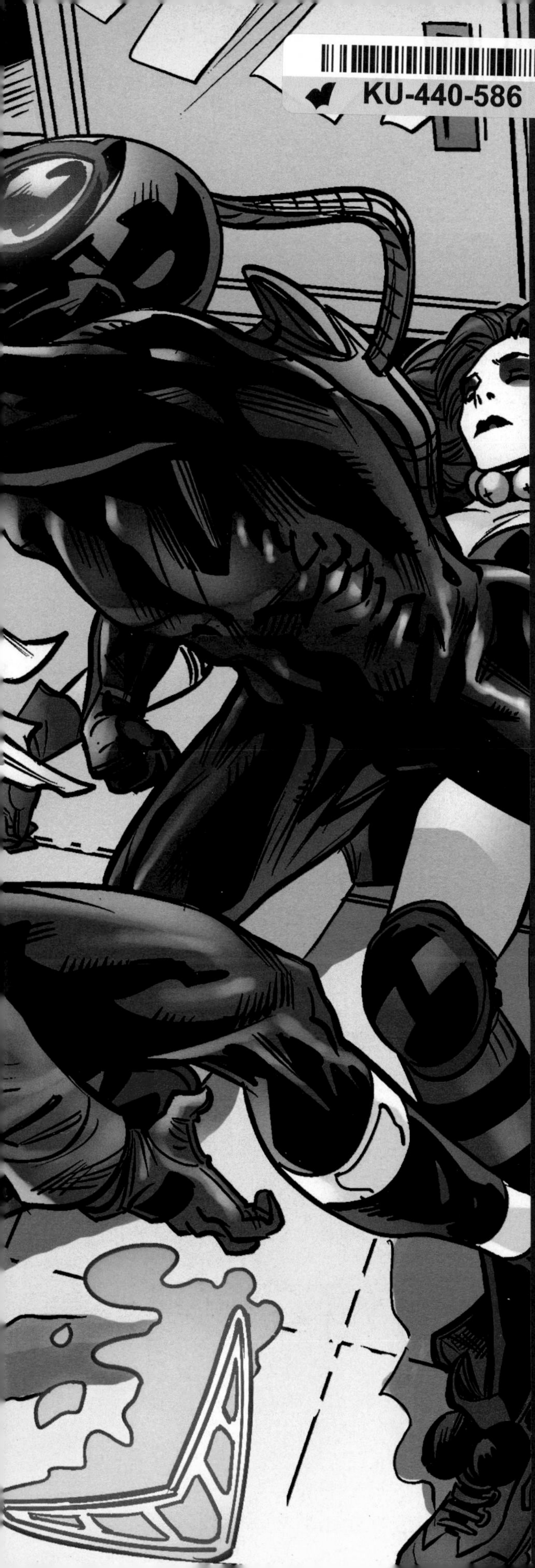

NEW SUICIDE SQUAD

VOLUME 3
FREEDOM

WRITTEN BY
SEAN RYAN
BRIAN BUCCELLATO
MIKE W. BARR

ART BY
PHILIPPE BRIONES
VIKTOR BOGDANOVIC
RICHARD FRIEND
DIOGENES NEVES

COLOR BY
BLOND
MICHAEL SPICER
CARRIE STRACHAN

LETTERS BY
DAVE SHARPE
CLEM ROBINS
SAIDA TEMOFONTE

COLLECTION COVER ART BY
JUAN FERREYRA

AMANDA WALLER CREATED BY
JOHN OSTRANDER AND
JOHN BYRNE

DEADSHOT CO-CREATED BY
LEW SAYRE SCHWARTZ

KATANA CREATED BY
MIKE W. BARR AND
JIM APARO

ANDY KHOURI ALEX ANTONE KRISTY QUINN Editors – Original Series
HARVEY RICHARDS JESSICA CHEN Associate Editors – Original Series
BRITTANY HOLZHERR Assistant Editor – Original Series
JEB WOODARD Group Editor – Collected Editions
LIZ ERICKSON Editor – Collected Edition
STEVE COOK Design Director – Books
DAMIAN RYLAND Publication Design

BOB HARRAS Senior VP – Editor-in-Chief, DC Comics

DIANE NELSON President
DAN DIDIO and JIM LEE Co-Publishers
GEOFF JOHNS Chief Creative Officer
AMIT DESAI Senior VP – Marketing & Global Franchise Management
NAIRI GARDINER Senior VP – Finance
SAM ADES VP – Digital Marketing
BOBBIE CHASE VP – Talent Development
MARK CHIARELLO Senior VP – Art, Design & Collected Editions
JOHN CUNNINGHAM VP – Content Strategy
ANNE DEPIES VP – Strategy Planning & Reporting
DON FALLETTI VP – Manufacturing Operations
LAWRENCE GANEM VP – Editorial Administration & Talent Relations
ALISON GILL Senior VP – Manufacturing & Operations
HANK KANALZ Senior VP – Editorial Strategy & Administration
JAY KOGAN VP – Legal Affairs
DEREK MADDALENA Senior VP – Sales & Business Development
JACK MAHAN VP – Business Affairs
DAN MIRON VP – Sales Planning & Trade Development
NICK NAPOLITANO VP – Manufacturing Administration
CAROL ROEDER VP – Marketing
EDDIE SCANNELL VP – Mass Account & Digital Sales
COURTNEY SIMMONS Senior VP – Publicity & Communications
JIM (SKI) SOKOLOWSKI VP – Comic Book Specialty & Newsstand Sales
SANDY YI Senior VP – Global Franchise Management

NEW SUICIDE SQUAD VOLUME 3: FREEDOM

DC Comics, 2900 West Alameda Avenue, Burbank, CA 91505.
Printed by RR Donnelley, Salem, VA, USA. 6/24/16. First Printing.
ISBN: 978-1-4012-6264-8

Library of Congress Cataloging-in-Publication Data

Names: Ryan, Sean, 1982- author. | Briones, Philippe, 1970- illustrator. |
Blond, illustrator.
Title: New Suicide Squad. Volume 3, Freedom / written by Sean Ryan ; art by
Philippe Briones ; color by Blond.
Other titles: Freedom
Description: Burbank, CA : DC Comics, [2016]
Identifiers: LCCN 2016018855 | ISBN 9781401262648 (paperback)
Subjects: LCSH: Comic books, strips, etc. | BISAC: COMICS & GRAPHIC NOVELS /
Superheroes.
Classification: LCC PN6728.S825 R95 2016 | DDC 741.5/973—dc23
LC record available at https://lccn.loc.gov/2016018855

PEFC Certified

Printed on paper from
sustainably managed
forests and controlled
sources

PEFC/29-31-75   www.pefc.org

FT
Pbk

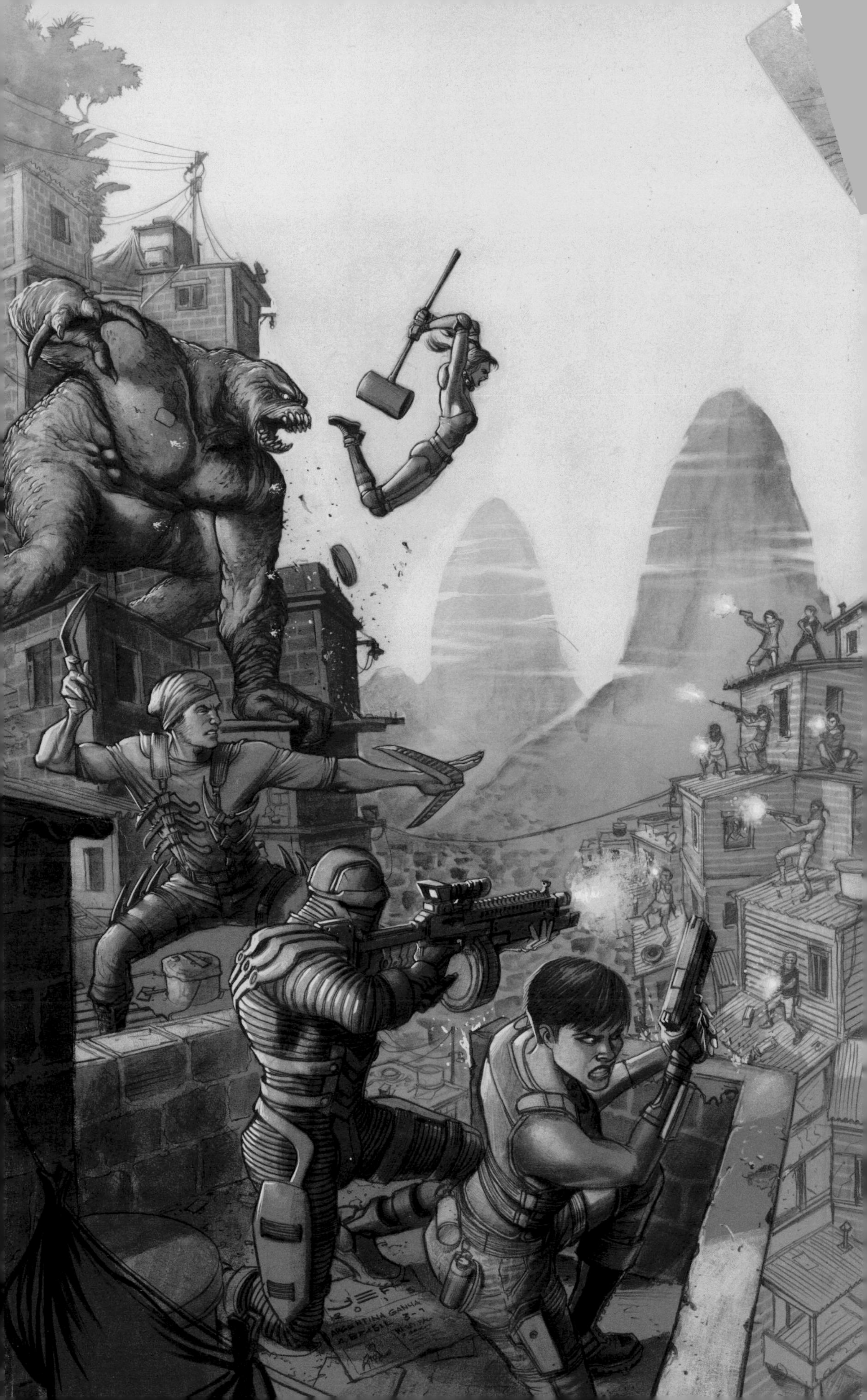

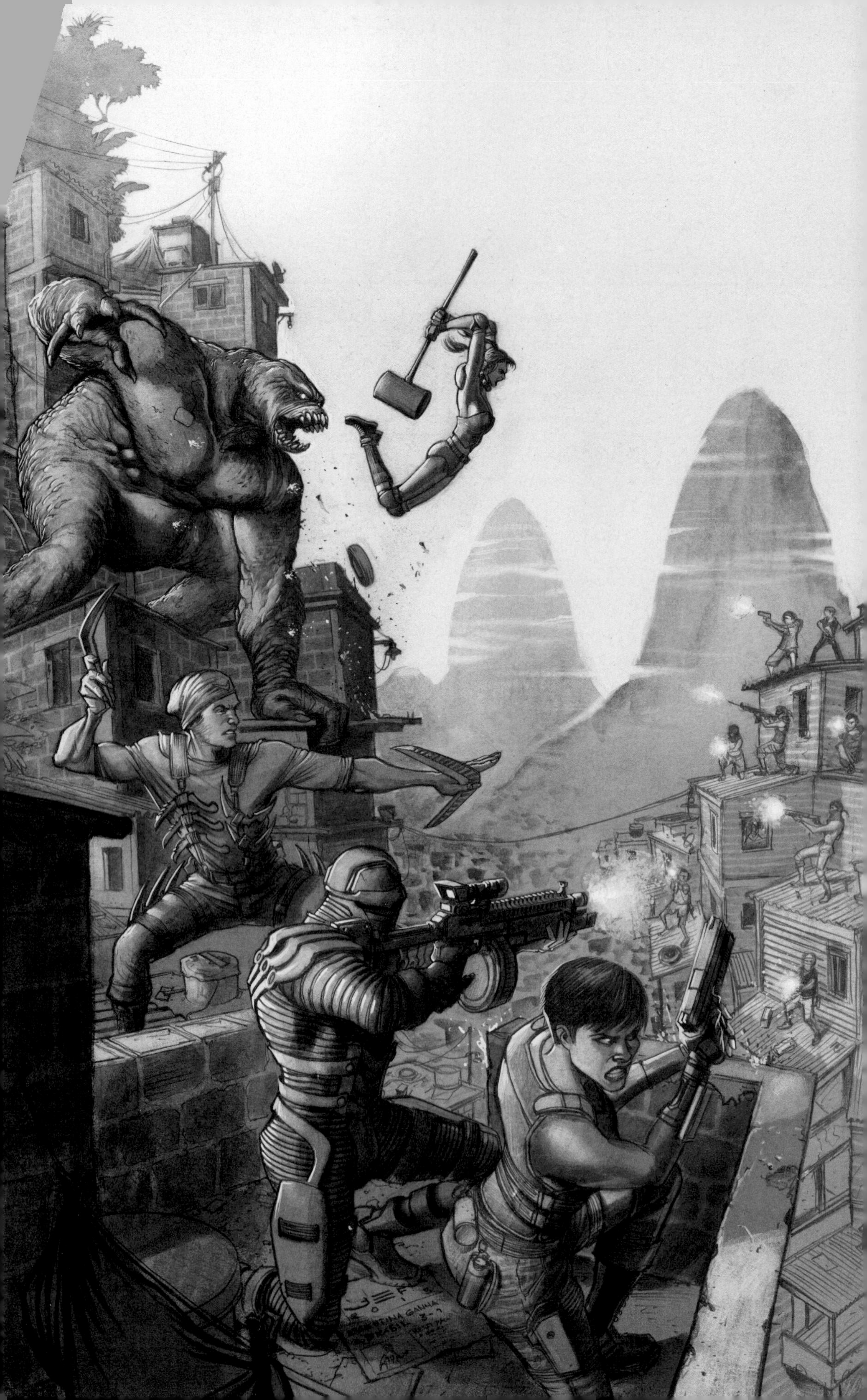

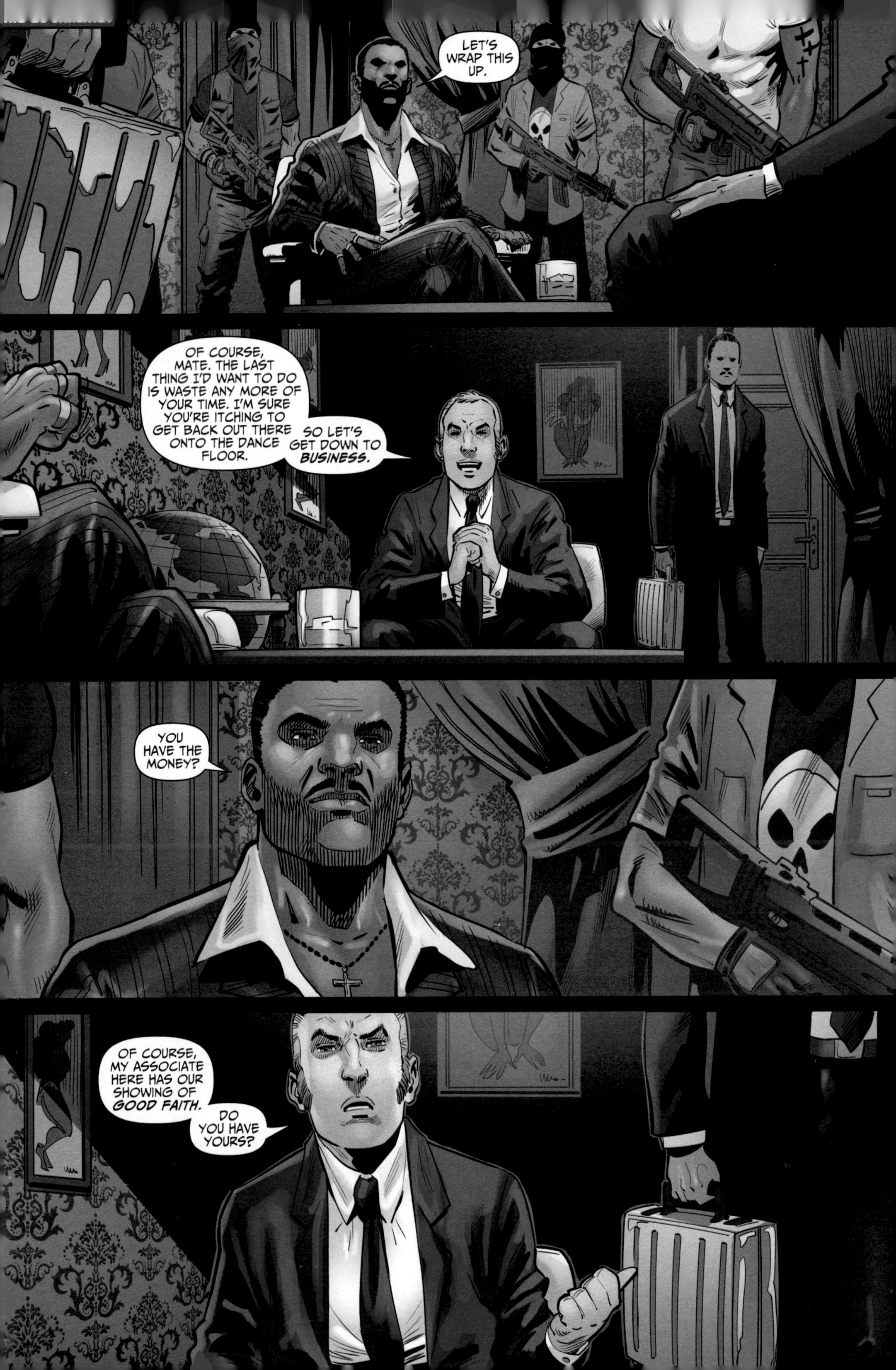
LET'S WRAP THIS UP.
OF COURSE, MATE. THE LAST THING I'D WANT TO DO IS WASTE ANY MORE OF YOUR TIME. I'M SURE YOU'RE ITCHING TO GET BACK OUT THERE ONTO THE DANCE FLOOR.
SO LET'S GET DOWN TO BUSINESS.
YOU HAVE THE MONEY?
OF COURSE, MY ASSOCIATE HERE HAS OUR SHOWING OF GOOD FAITH.
DO YOU HAVE YOURS?

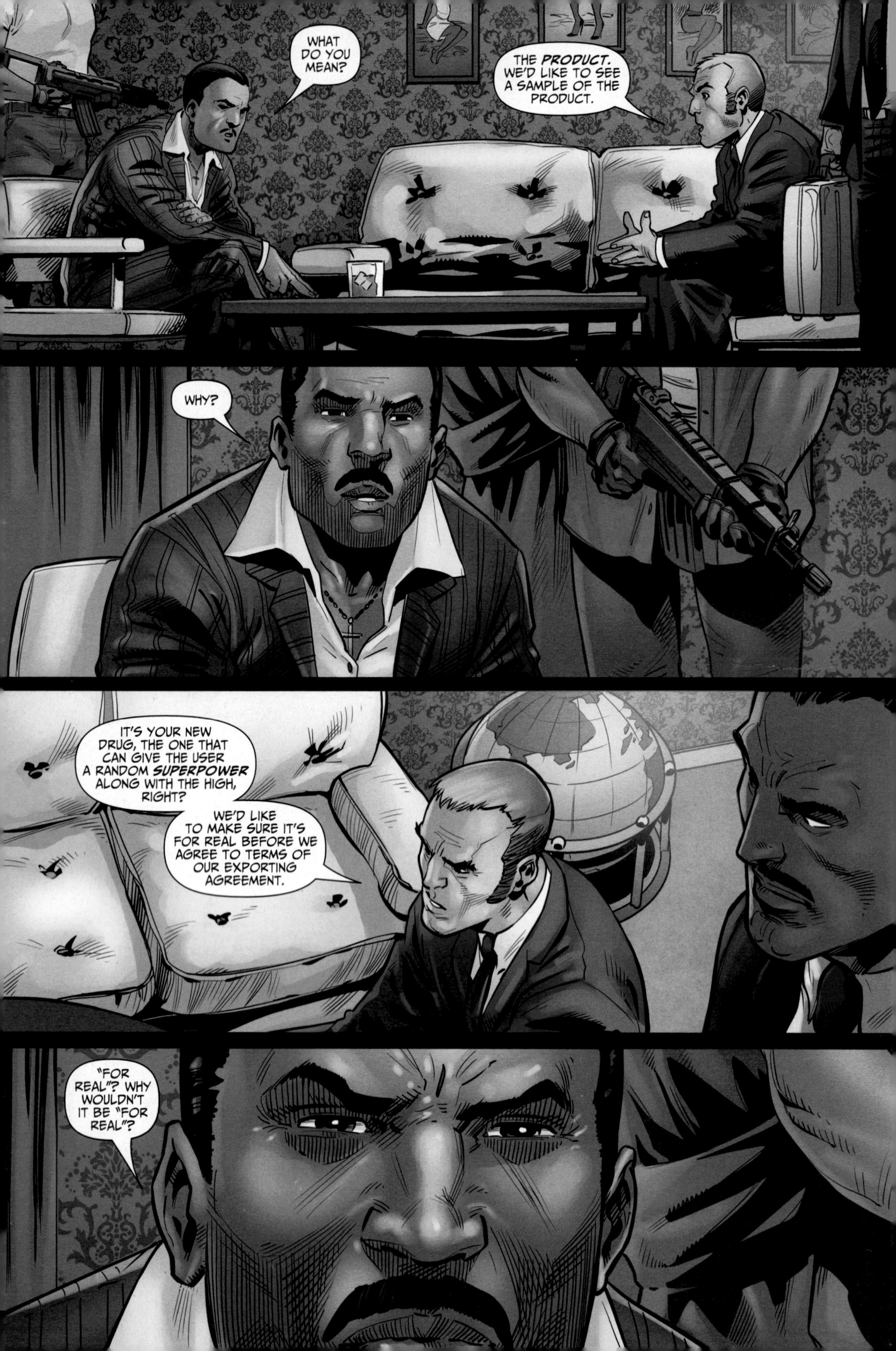
WHAT DO YOU MEAN?
THE PRODUCT. WE'D LIKE TO SEE A SAMPLE OF THE PRODUCT.
WHY?
IT'S YOUR NEW DRUG, THE ONE THAT CAN GIVE THE USER A RANDOM SUPERPOWER ALONG WITH THE HIGH, RIGHT?
WE'D LIKE TO MAKE SURE IT'S FOR REAL BEFORE WE AGREE TO TERMS OF OUR EXPORTING AGREEMENT.
"FOR REAL"? WHY WOULDN'T IT BE "FOR REAL"?

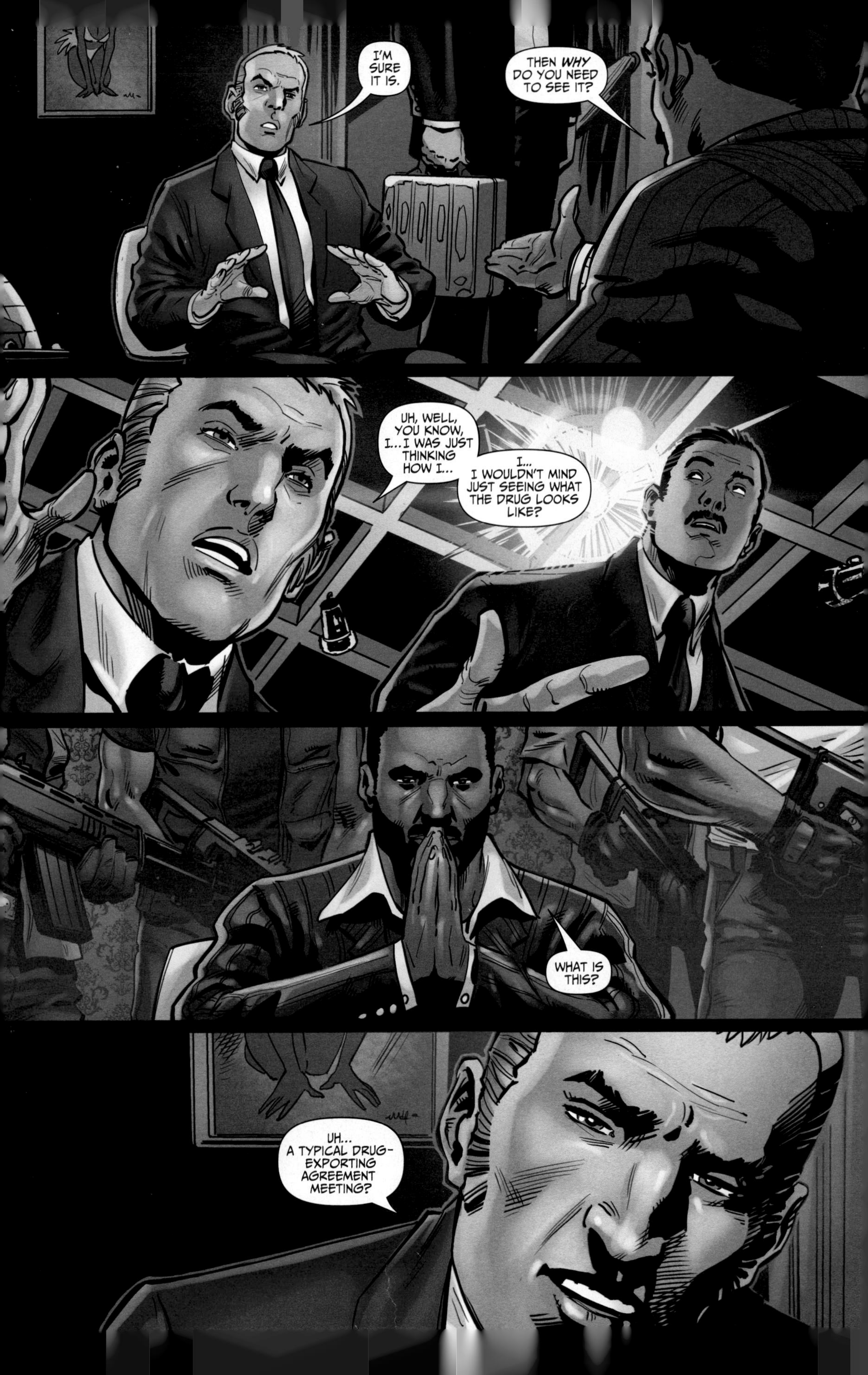
I'M SURE IT IS.
THEN WHY DO YOU NEED TO SEE IT?
UH, WELL, YOU KNOW, I...I WAS JUST THINKING HOW I...
I... I WOULDN'T MIND JUST SEEING WHAT THE DRUG LOOKS LIKE?
WHAT IS THIS?
UH... A TYPICAL DRUG-EXPORTING AGREEMENT MEETING?

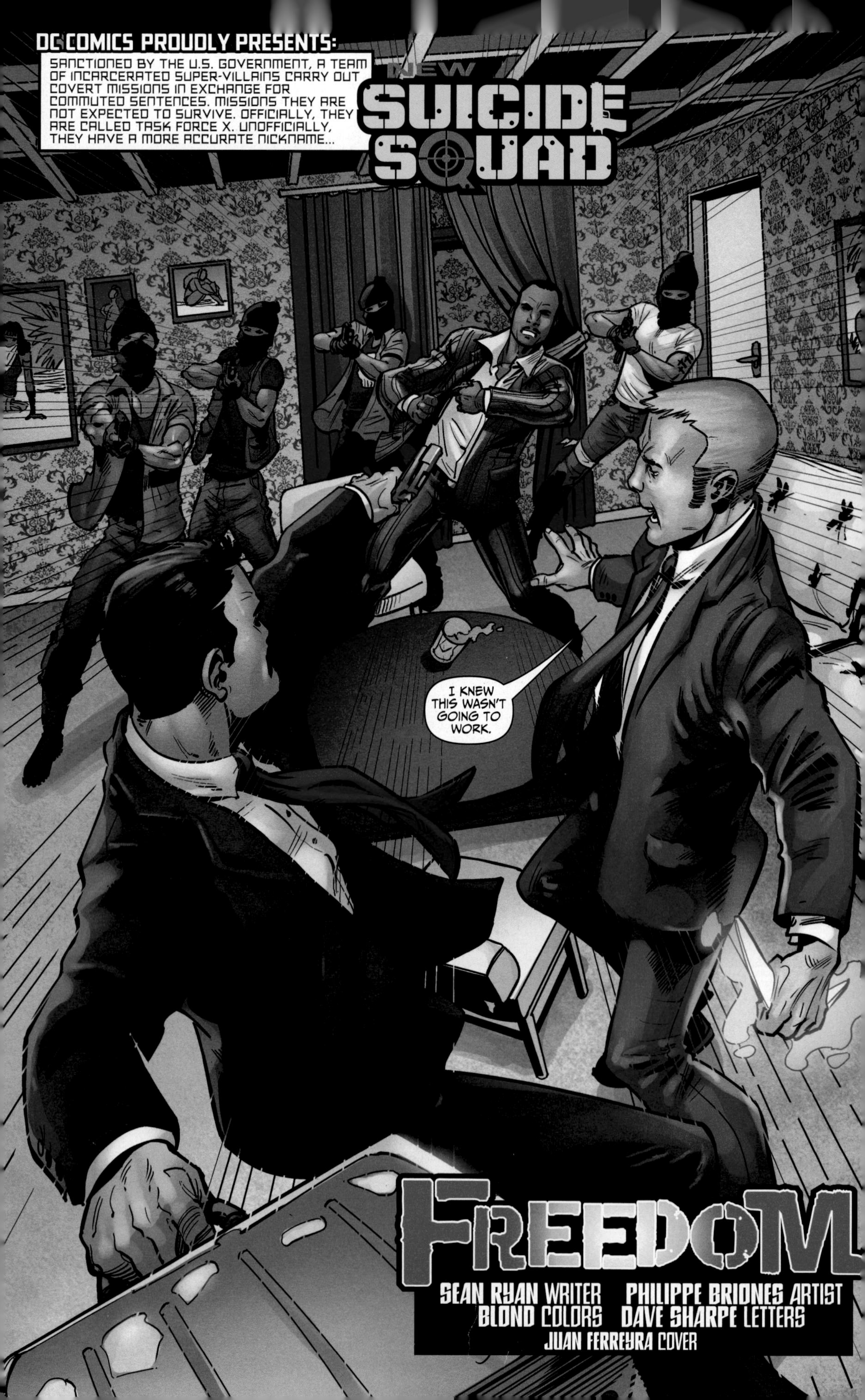
DC COMICS PROUDLY PRESENTS:
SANCTIONED BY THE U.S. GOVERNMENT, A TEAM OF INCARCERATED SUPER-VILLAINS CARRY OUT COVERT MISSIONS IN EXCHANGE FOR COMMUTED SENTENCES. MISSIONS THEY ARE NOT EXPECTED TO SURVIVE. OFFICIALLY, THEY ARE CALLED TASK FORCE X. UNOFFICIALLY, THEY HAVE A MORE ACCURATE NICKNAME...
NEW SUICIDE SQUAD
I KNEW THIS WASN'T GOING TO WORK.
FREEDOM
SEAN RYAN WRITER PHILIPPE BRIONES ARTIST
BLOND COLORS DAVE SHARPE LETTERS
JUAN FERREYRA COVER

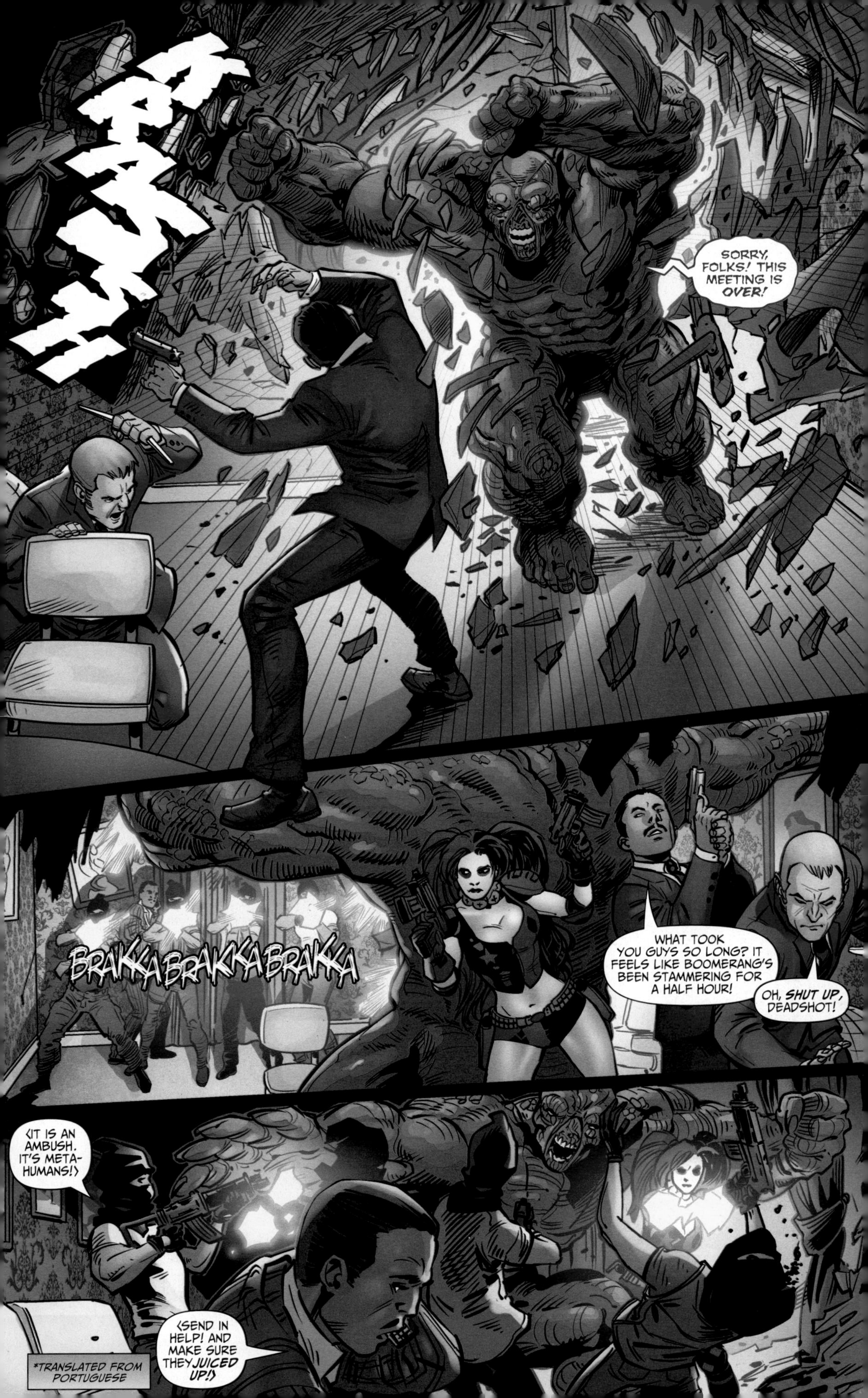
KRAKK
SORRY, FOLKS! THIS MEETING IS OVER!
BRAKKA BRAKKA BRAKKA
WHAT TOOK YOU GUYS SO LONG? IT FEELS LIKE BOOMERANG'S BEEN STAMMERING FOR A HALF HOUR!
OH, SHUT UP, DEADSHOT!
‹IT IS AN AMBUSH. IT'S META-HUMANS!›
‹SEND IN HELP! AND MAKE SURE THEY JUICED UP!›
*TRANSLATED FROM PORTUGUESE

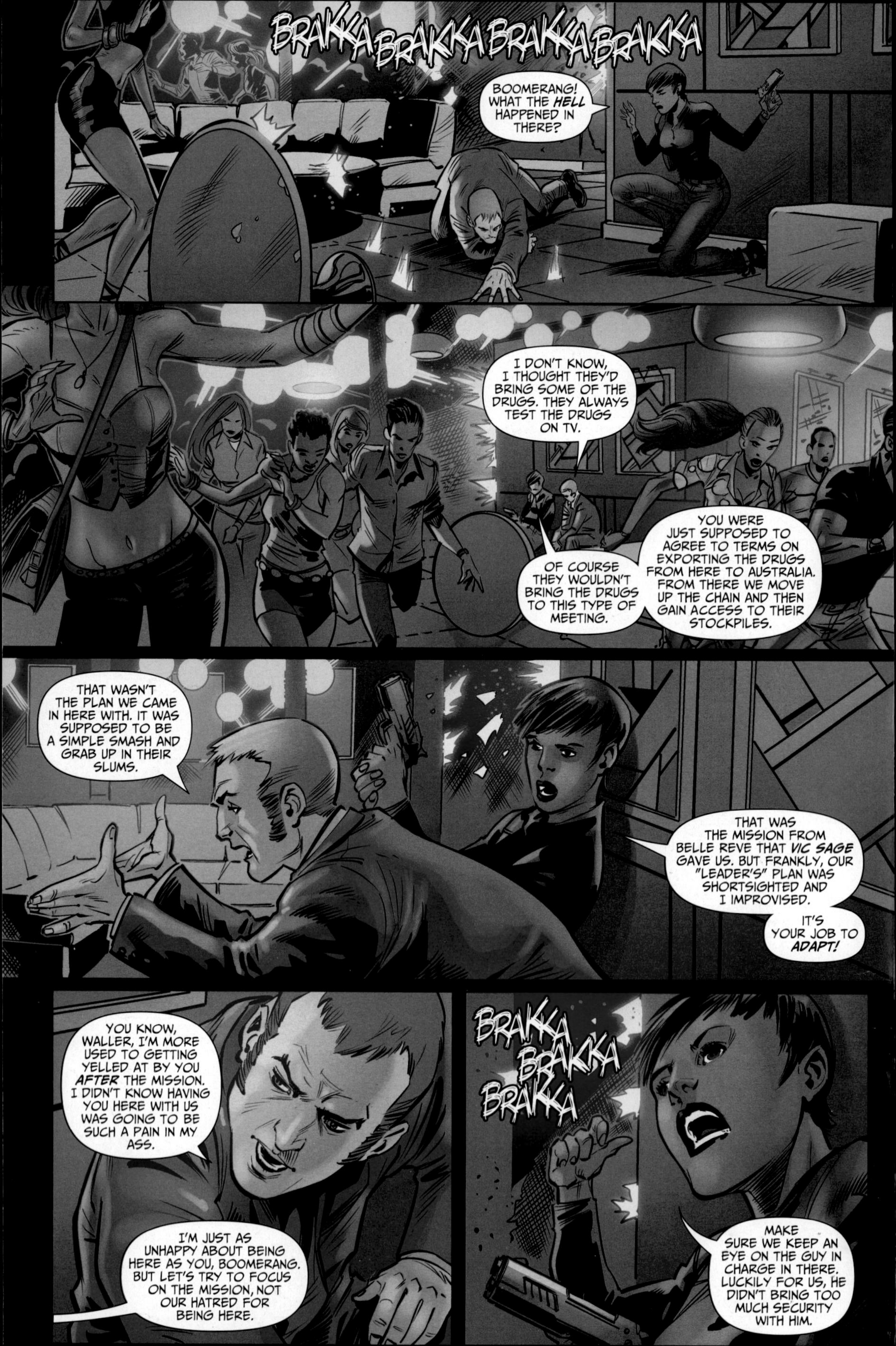
BRAKKA BRAKKA BRAKKA BRAKKA
BOOMERANG! WHAT THE HELL HAPPENED IN THERE?
I DON'T KNOW, I THOUGHT THEY'D BRING SOME OF THE DRUGS. THEY ALWAYS TEST THE DRUGS ON TV.
OF COURSE THEY WOULDN'T BRING THE DRUGS TO THIS TYPE OF MEETING.
YOU WERE JUST SUPPOSED TO AGREE TO TERMS ON EXPORTING THE DRUGS FROM HERE TO AUSTRALIA. FROM THERE WE MOVE UP THE CHAIN AND THEN GAIN ACCESS TO THEIR STOCKPILES.
THAT WASN'T THE PLAN WE CAME IN HERE WITH. IT WAS SUPPOSED TO BE A SIMPLE SMASH AND GRAB UP IN THEIR SLUMS.
THAT WAS THE MISSION FROM BELLE REVE THAT VIC SAGE GAVE US. BUT FRANKLY, OUR "LEADER'S" PLAN WAS SHORTSIGHTED AND I IMPROVISED.
IT'S YOUR JOB TO ADAPT!
YOU KNOW, WALLER, I'M MORE USED TO GETTING YELLED AT BY YOU AFTER THE MISSION. I DIDN'T KNOW HAVING YOU HERE WITH US WAS GOING TO BE SUCH A PAIN IN MY ASS.
I'M JUST AS UNHAPPY ABOUT BEING HERE AS YOU, BOOMERANG. BUT LET'S TRY TO FOCUS ON THE MISSION, NOT OUR HATRED FOR BEING HERE.
BRAKKA BRAKKA BRAKKA
MAKE SURE WE KEEP AN EYE ON THE GUY IN CHARGE IN THERE. LUCKILY FOR US, HE DIDN'T BRING TOO MUCH SECURITY WITH HIM.

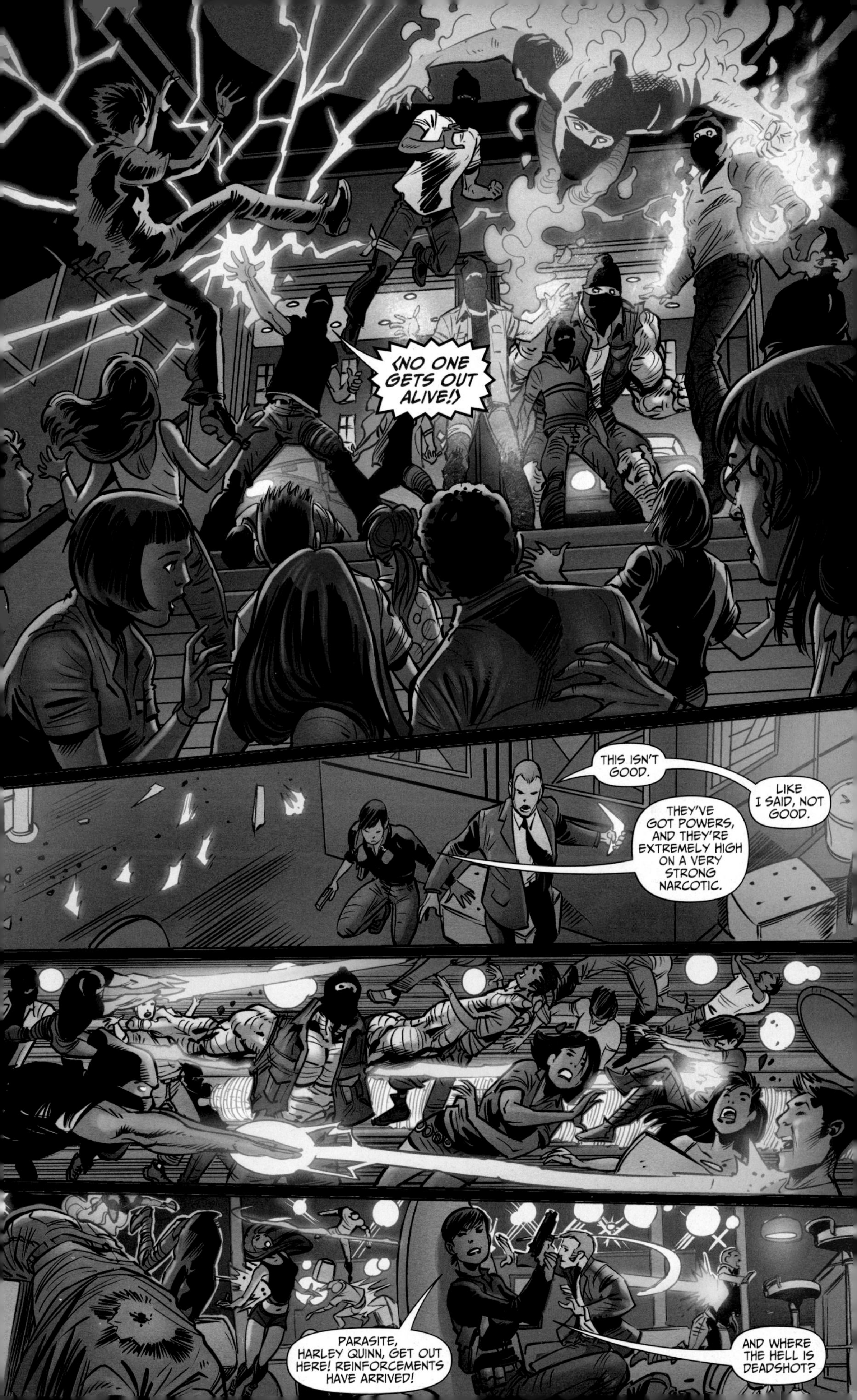
⟨NO ONE GETS OUT ALIVE!⟩
THIS ISN'T GOOD.
THEY'VE GOT POWERS, AND THEY'RE EXTREMELY HIGH ON A VERY STRONG NARCOTIC.
LIKE I SAID, NOT GOOD.
PARASITE, HARLEY QUINN, GET OUT HERE! REINFORCEMENTS HAVE ARRIVED!
AND WHERE THE HELL IS DEADSHOT?

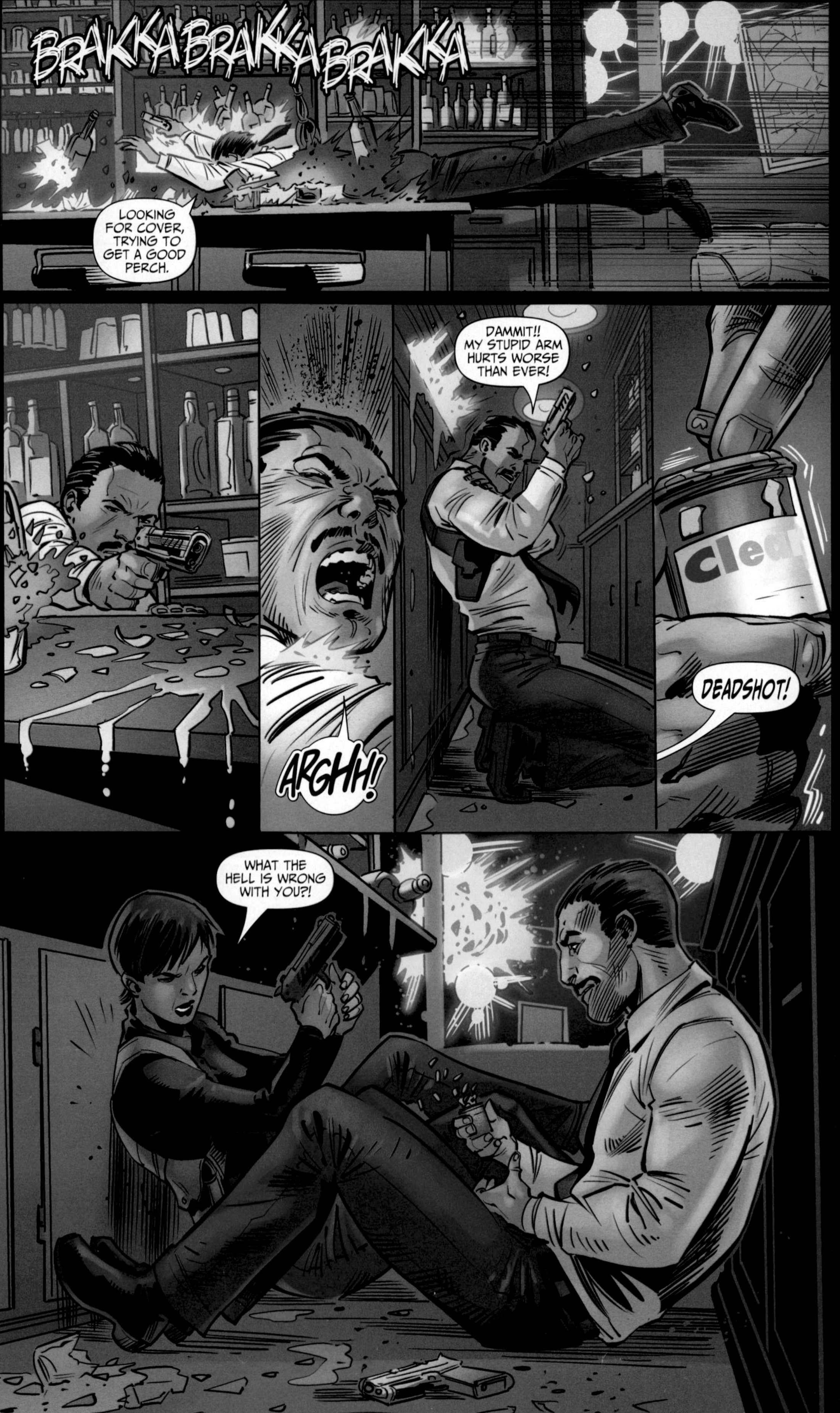
BRAKKA BRAKKA BRAKKA
LOOKING FOR COVER, TRYING TO GET A GOOD PERCH.
ARGHH!
DAMMIT!! MY STUPID ARM HURTS WORSE THAN EVER!
Clea
DEADSHOT!
WHAT THE HELL IS WRONG WITH YOU?!

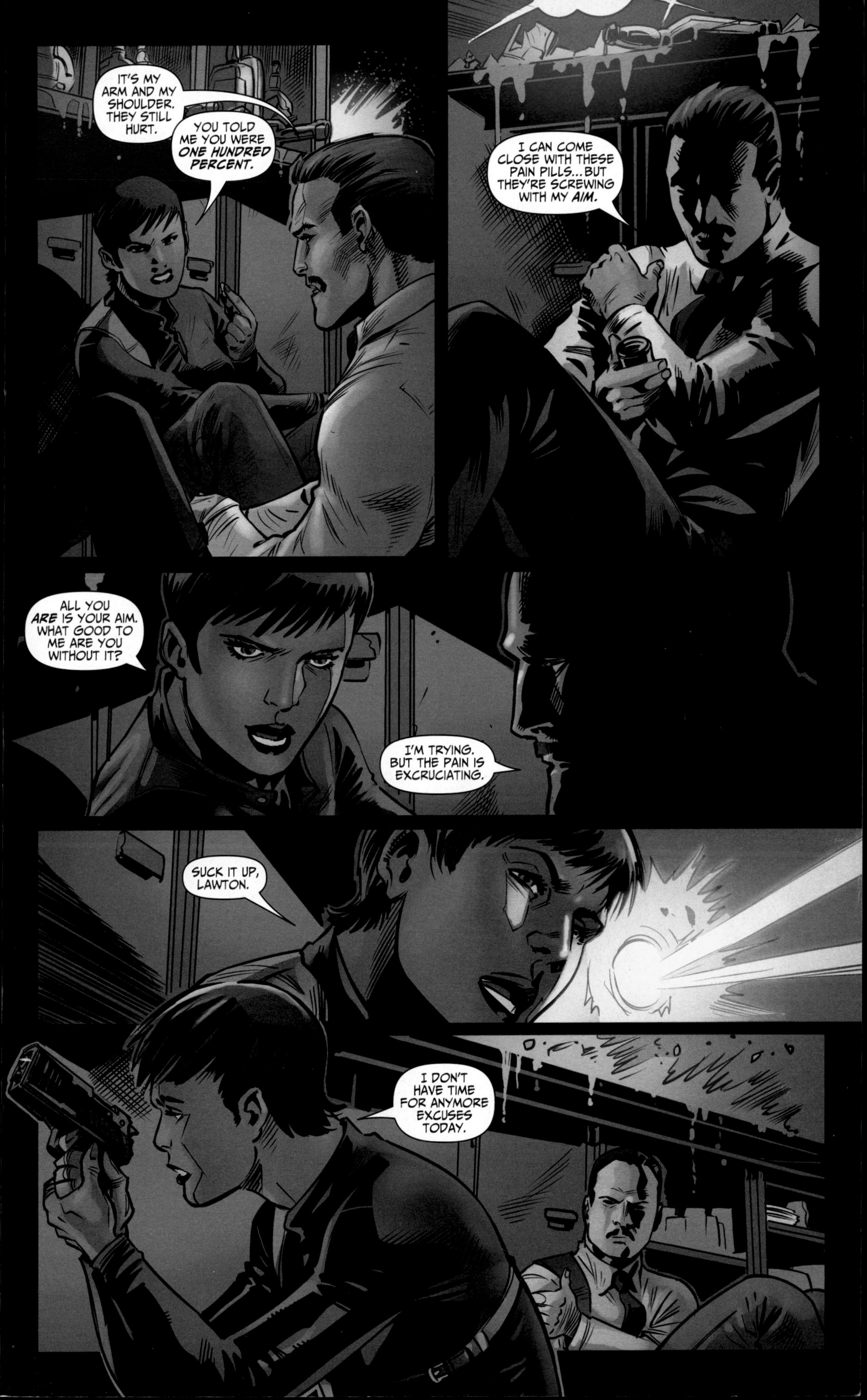
IT'S MY ARM AND MY SHOULDER. THEY STILL HURT.
YOU TOLD ME YOU WERE *ONE HUNDRED PERCENT.*
I CAN COME CLOSE WITH THESE PAIN PILLS...BUT THEY'RE SCREWING WITH MY *AIM.*
ALL YOU *ARE* IS YOUR AIM. WHAT GOOD TO ME ARE YOU WITHOUT IT?
I'M TRYING. BUT THE PAIN IS EXCRUCIATING.
SUCK IT UP, LAWTON.
I DON'T HAVE TIME FOR ANYMORE EXCUSES TODAY.

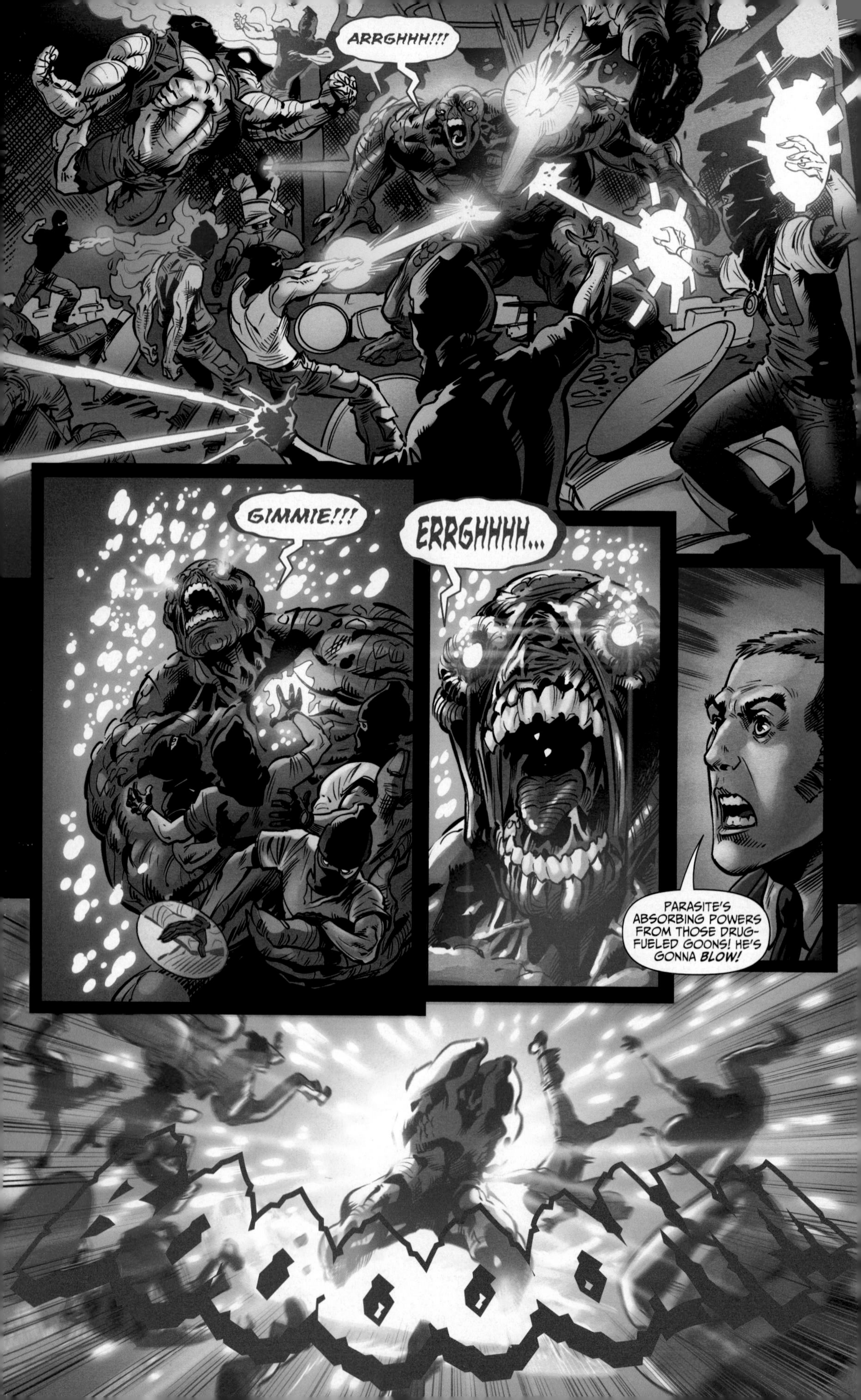
ARRGHHH!!!
GIMMIE!!!
ERRGHHHH...
PARASITE'S ABSORBING POWERS FROM THOSE DRUG-FUELED GOONS! HE'S GONNA BLOW!

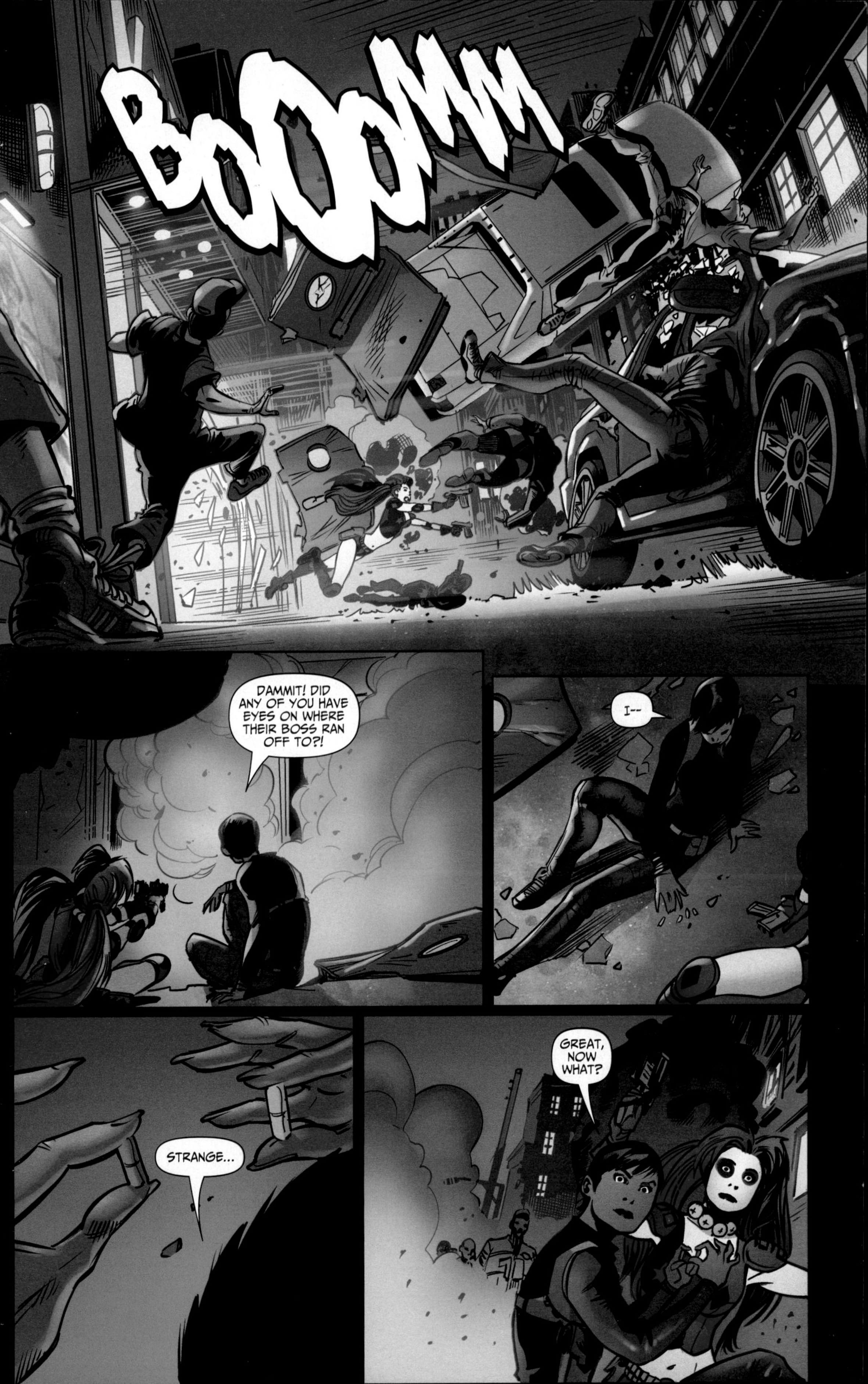
BOOOMM
DAMMIT! DID ANY OF YOU HAVE EYES ON WHERE THEIR BOSS RAN OFF TO?!
I--
STRANGE...
GREAT, NOW WHAT?

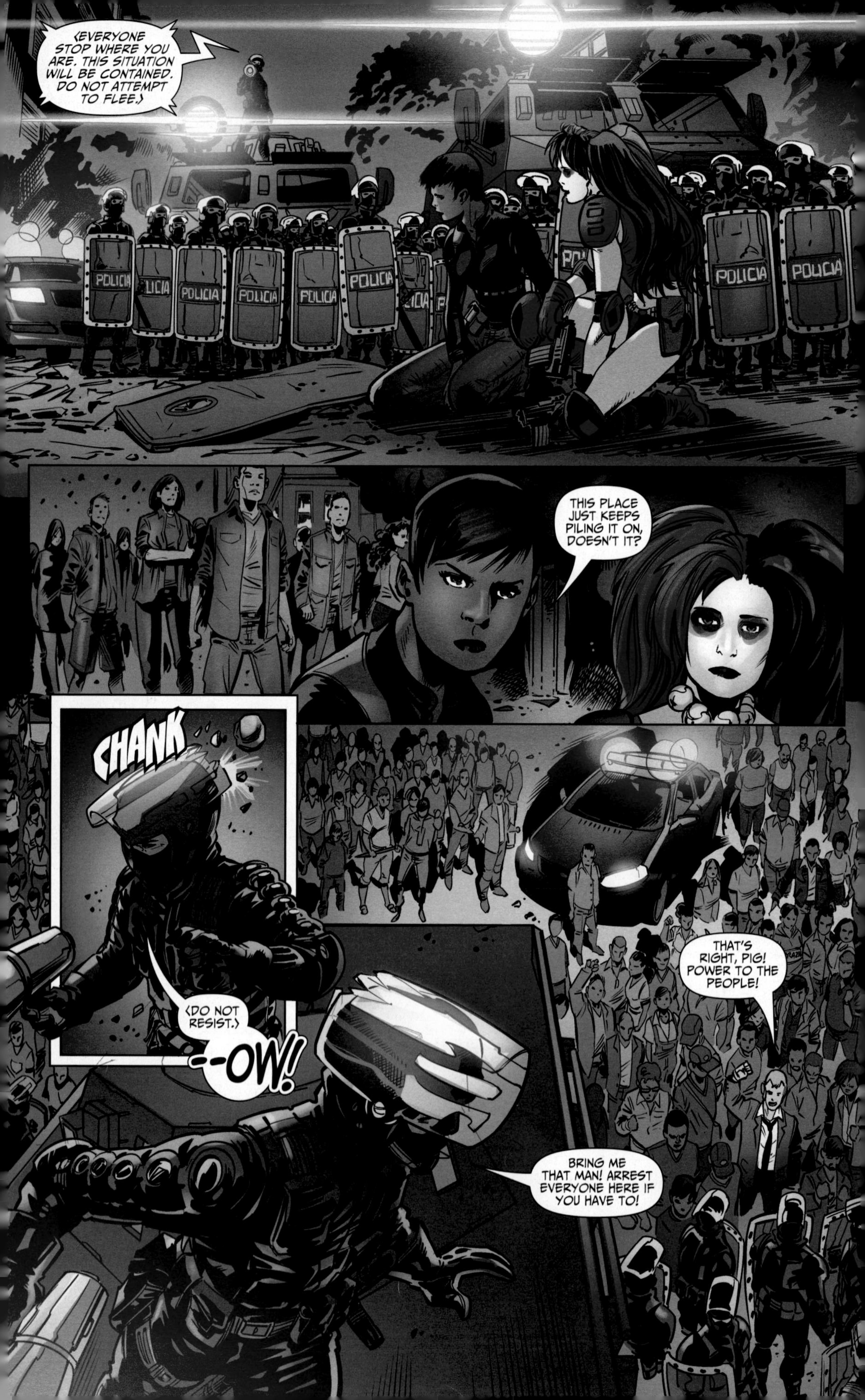
<EVERYONE STOP WHERE YOU ARE. THIS SITUATION WILL BE CONTAINED. DO NOT ATTEMPT TO FLEE.>
POLICIA
THIS PLACE JUST KEEPS PILING IT ON, DOESN'T IT?
CHANK
<DO NOT RESIST.>
--OW!
THAT'S RIGHT, PIG! POWER TO THE PEOPLE!
BRING ME THAT MAN! ARREST EVERYONE HERE IF YOU HAVE TO!

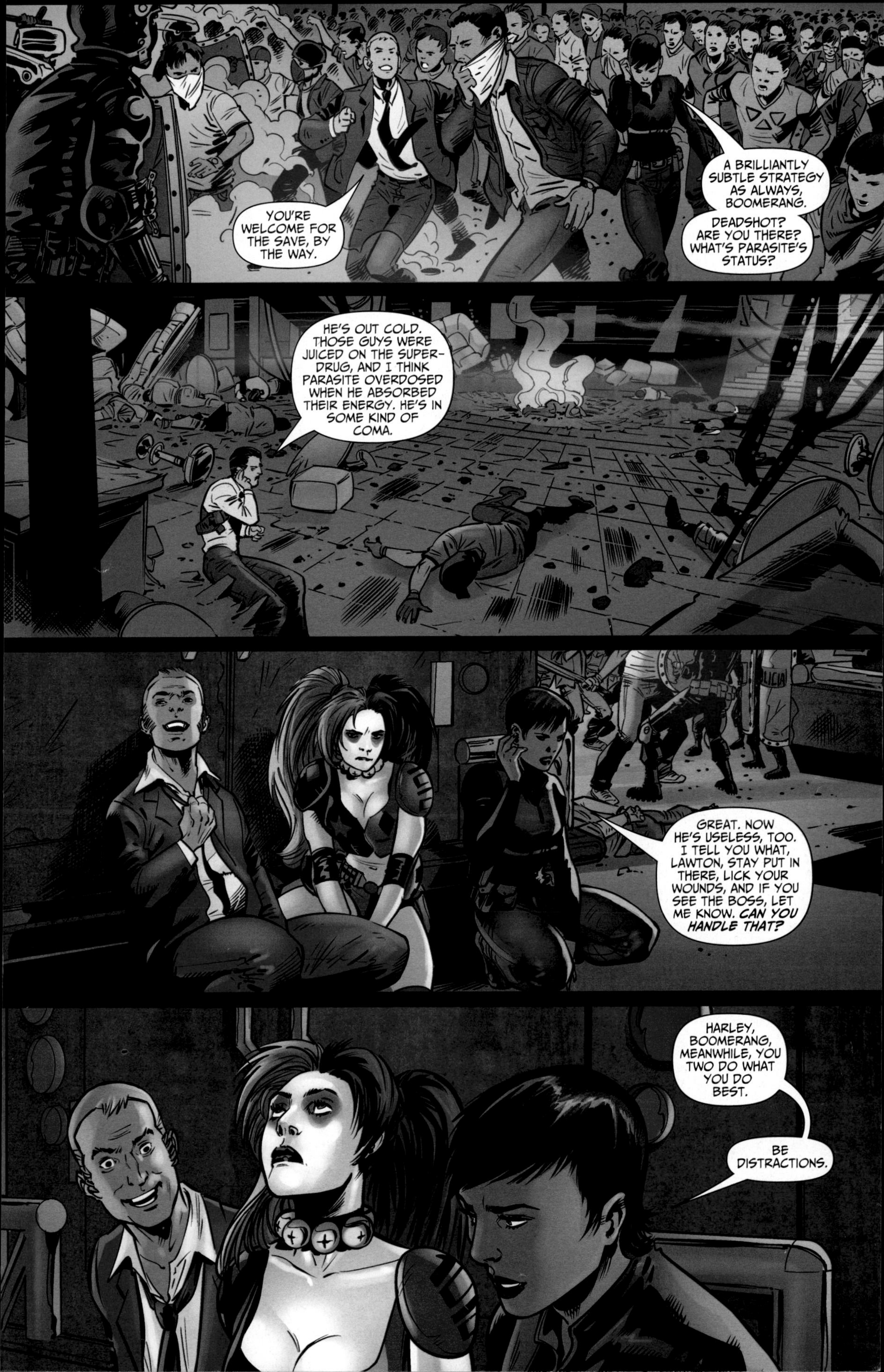
YOU'RE WELCOME FOR THE SAVE, BY THE WAY.
A BRILLIANTLY SUBTLE STRATEGY AS ALWAYS, BOOMERANG.
DEADSHOT? ARE YOU THERE? WHAT'S PARASITE'S STATUS?
HE'S OUT COLD. THOSE GUYS WERE JUICED ON THE SUPER-DRUG, AND I THINK PARASITE OVERDOSED WHEN HE ABSORBED THEIR ENERGY. HE'S IN SOME KIND OF COMA.
GREAT. NOW HE'S USELESS, TOO. I TELL YOU WHAT, LAWTON, STAY PUT IN THERE, LICK YOUR WOUNDS, AND IF YOU SEE THE BOSS, LET ME KNOW. ***CAN YOU HANDLE THAT?***
HARLEY, BOOMERANG, MEANWHILE, YOU TWO DO WHAT YOU DO BEST.
BE DISTRACTIONS.

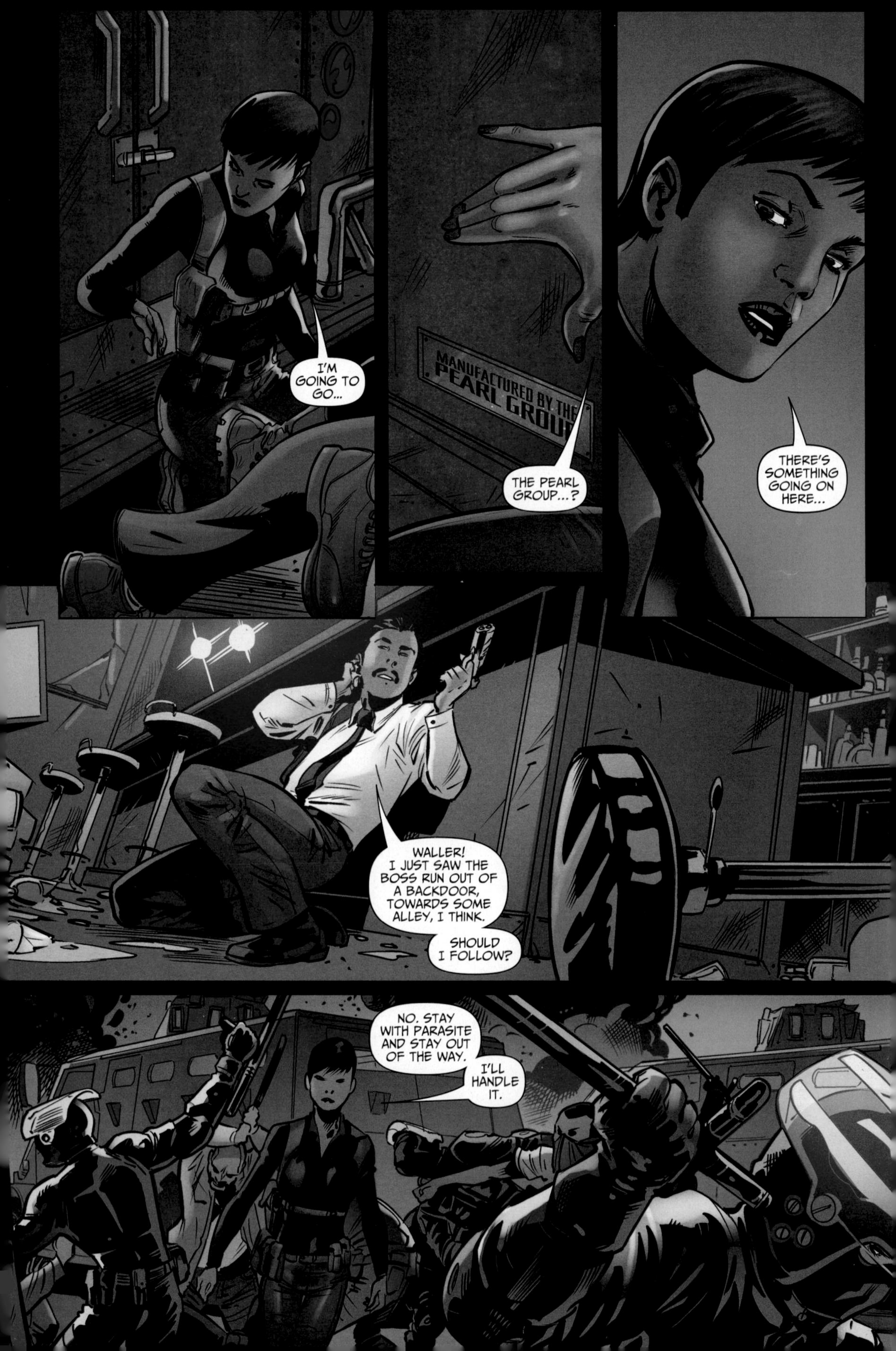
I'M GOING TO GO...
MANUFACTURED BY THE PEARL GROUP
THE PEARL GROUP...?
THERE'S SOMETHING GOING ON HERE...
WALLER! I JUST SAW THE BOSS RUN OUT OF A BACKDOOR, TOWARDS SOME ALLEY, I THINK.
SHOULD I FOLLOW?
NO. STAY WITH PARASITE AND STAY OUT OF THE WAY.
I'LL HANDLE IT.

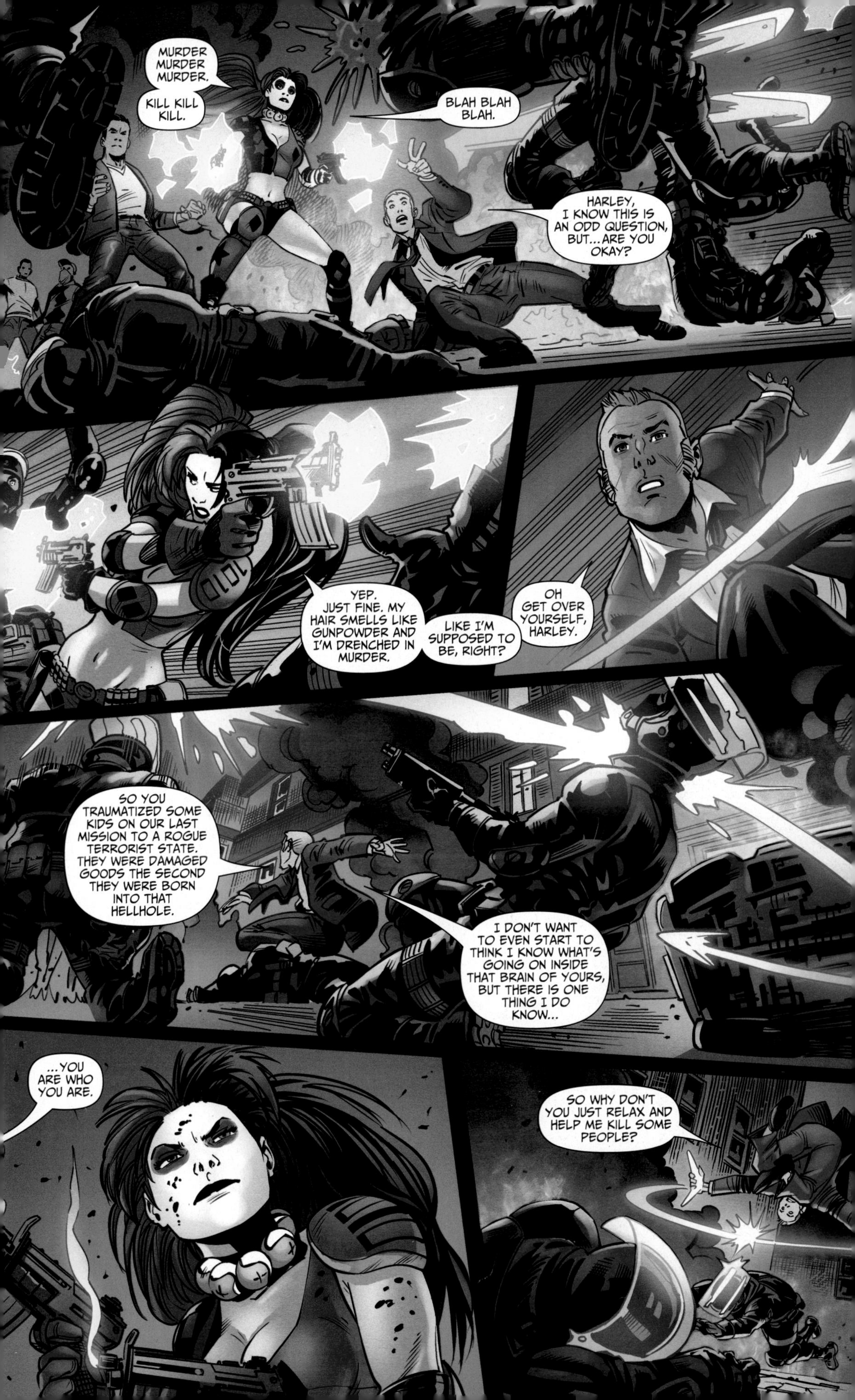
MURDER MURDER MURDER.
KILL KILL KILL.
BLAH BLAH BLAH.
HARLEY, I KNOW THIS IS AN ODD QUESTION, BUT...ARE YOU OKAY?
YEP. JUST FINE. MY HAIR SMELLS LIKE GUNPOWDER AND I'M DRENCHED IN MURDER.
LIKE I'M SUPPOSED TO BE, RIGHT?
OH GET OVER YOURSELF, HARLEY.
SO YOU TRAUMATIZED SOME KIDS ON OUR LAST MISSION TO A ROGUE TERRORIST STATE. THEY WERE DAMAGED GOODS THE SECOND THEY WERE BORN INTO THAT HELLHOLE.
I DON'T WANT TO EVEN START TO THINK I KNOW WHAT'S GOING ON INSIDE THAT BRAIN OF YOURS, BUT THERE IS ONE THING I DO KNOW...
...YOU ARE WHO YOU ARE.
SO WHY DON'T YOU JUST RELAX AND HELP ME KILL SOME PEOPLE?

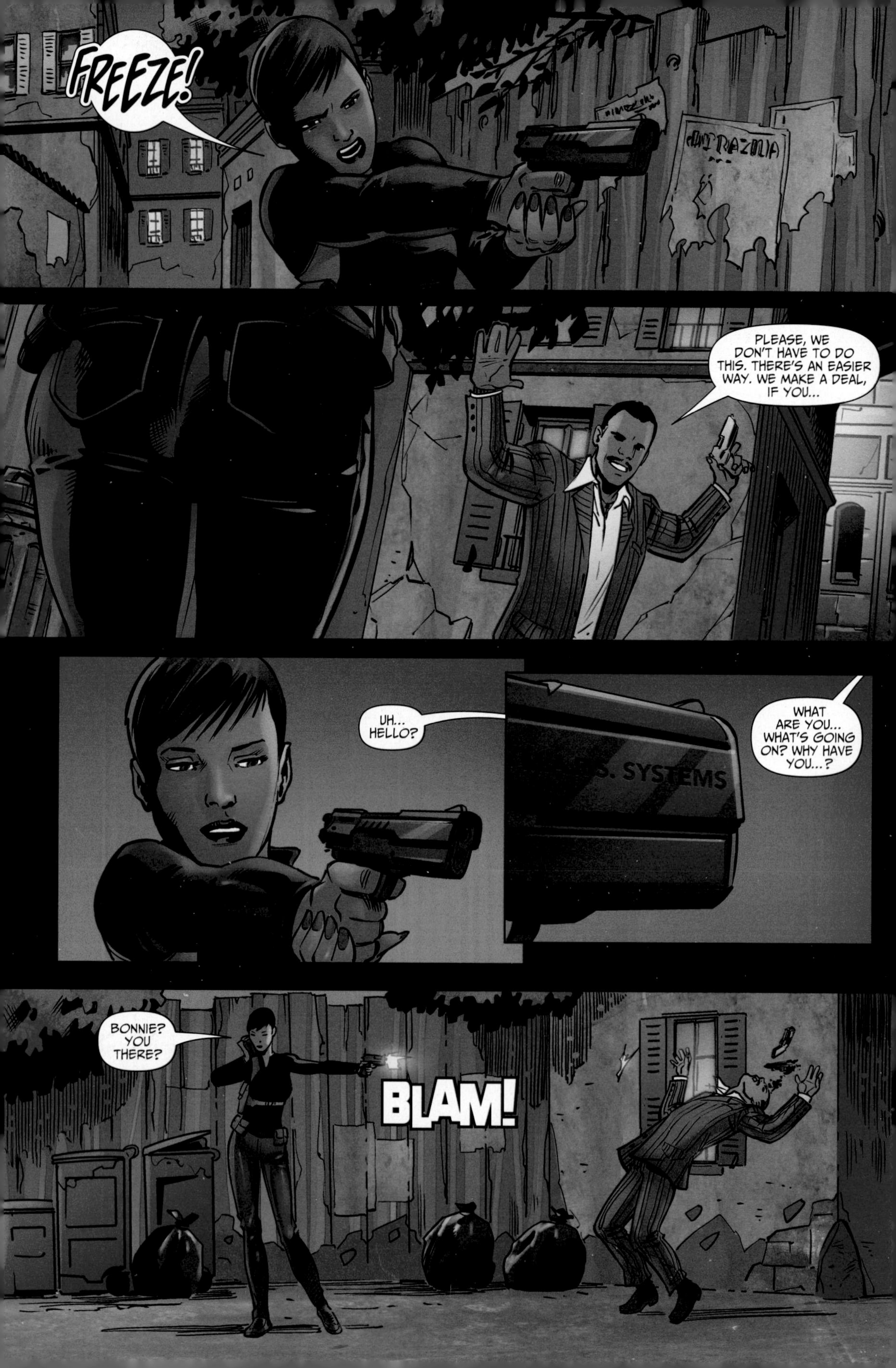
FREEZE!
PLEASE, WE DON'T HAVE TO DO THIS. THERE'S AN EASIER WAY. WE MAKE A DEAL, IF YOU...
UH... HELLO?
S. SYSTEMS
WHAT ARE YOU... WHAT'S GOING ON? WHY HAVE YOU...?
BONNIE? YOU THERE?
BLAM!

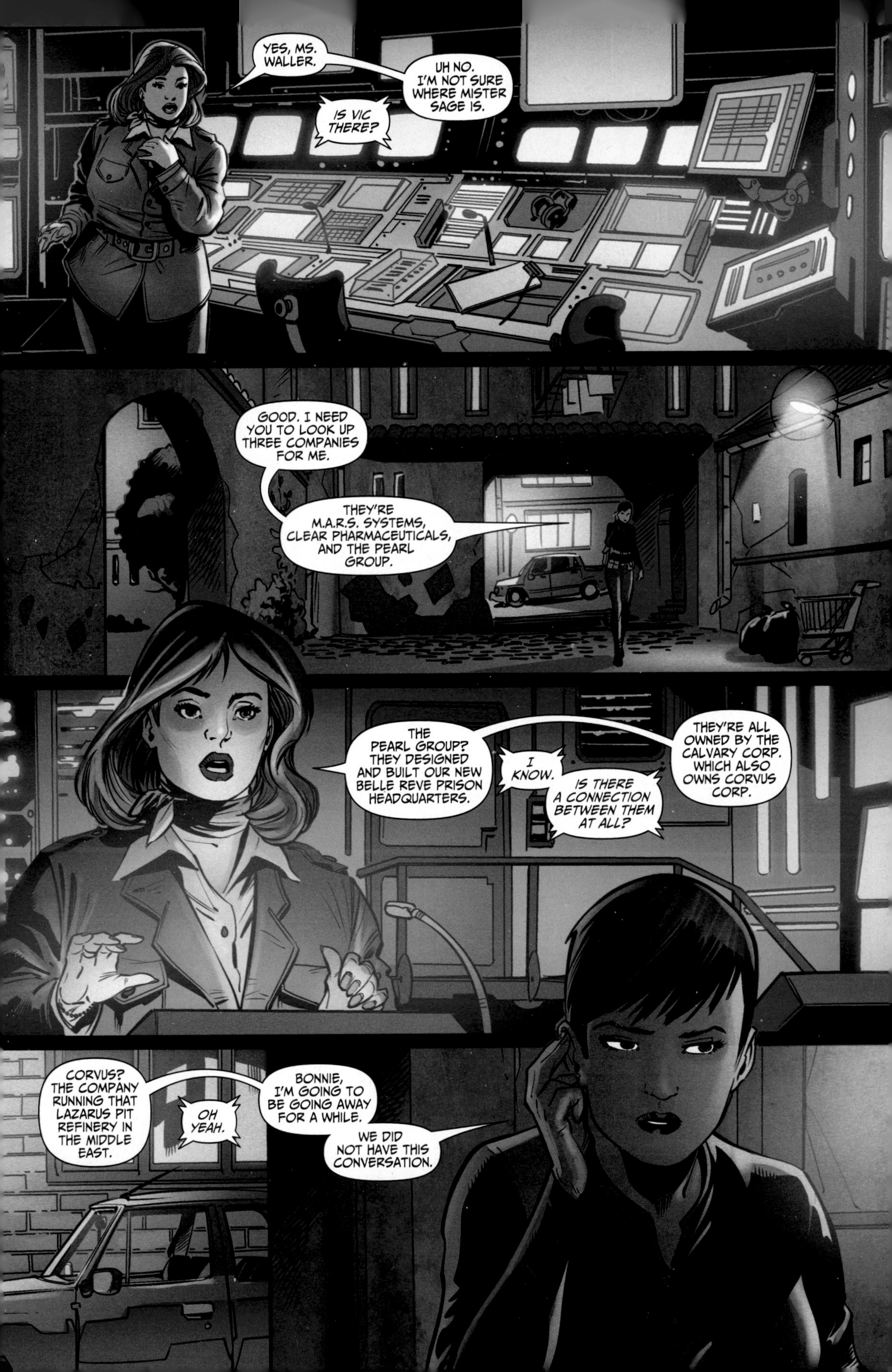
YES, MS. WALLER.
IS VIC THERE?
UH NO. I'M NOT SURE WHERE MISTER SAGE IS.
GOOD. I NEED YOU TO LOOK UP THREE COMPANIES FOR ME.
THEY'RE M.A.R.S. SYSTEMS, CLEAR PHARMACEUTICALS, AND THE PEARL GROUP.
THE PEARL GROUP? THEY DESIGNED AND BUILT OUR NEW BELLE REVE PRISON HEADQUARTERS.
I KNOW.
IS THERE A CONNECTION BETWEEN THEM AT ALL?
THEY'RE ALL OWNED BY THE CALVARY CORP. WHICH ALSO OWNS CORVUS CORP.
CORVUS? THE COMPANY RUNNING THAT LAZARUS PIT REFINERY IN THE MIDDLE EAST.
OH YEAH.
BONNIE, I'M GOING TO BE GOING AWAY FOR A WHILE.
WE DID NOT HAVE THIS CONVERSATION.

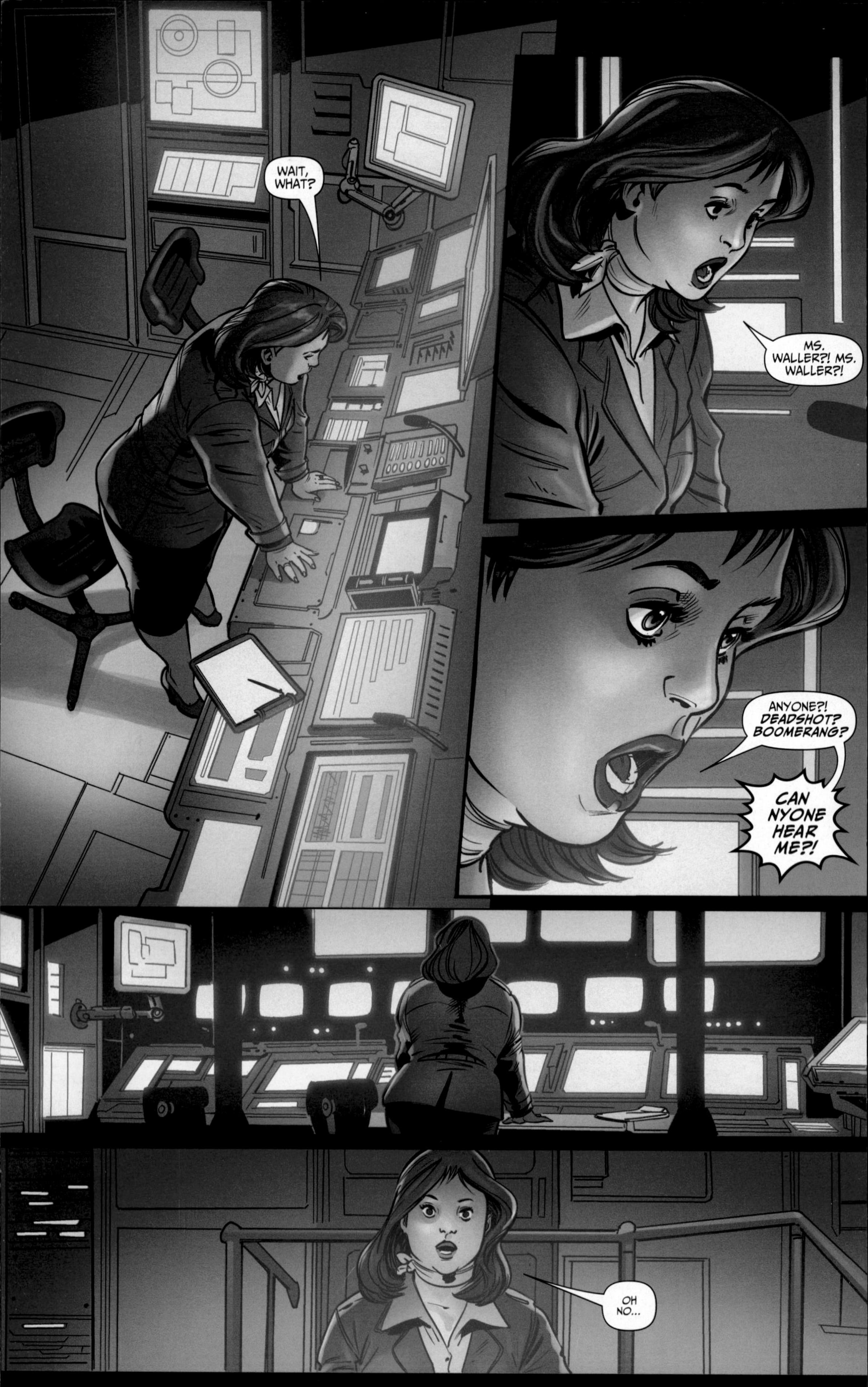
WAIT, WHAT?
MS. WALLER?! MS. WALLER?!
ANYONE?! DEADSHOT? BOOMERANG?
CAN NYONE HEAR ME?!
OH NO...

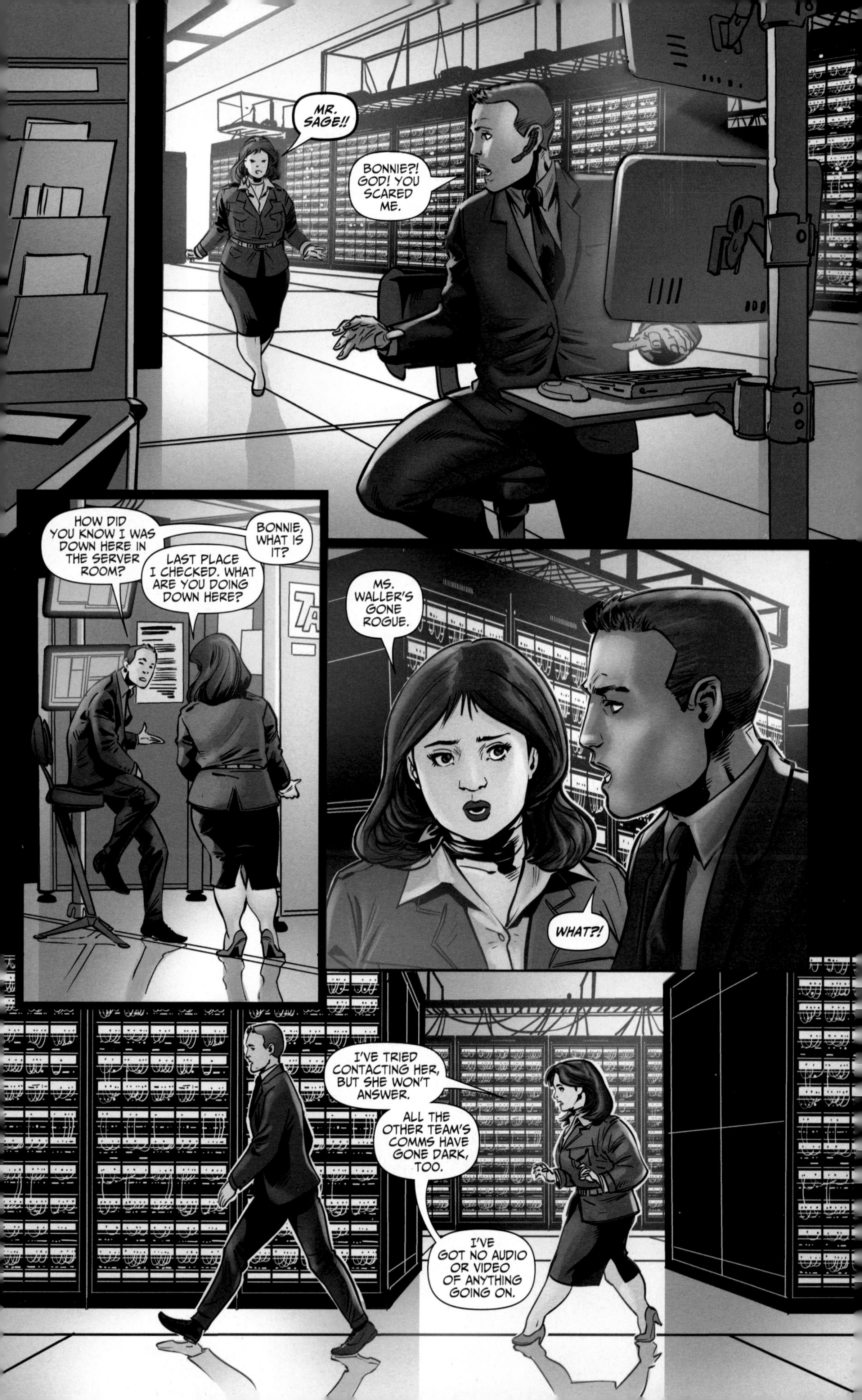
MR. SAGE!!
BONNIE?! GOD! YOU SCARED ME.
HOW DID YOU KNOW I WAS DOWN HERE IN THE SERVER ROOM?
LAST PLACE I CHECKED. WHAT ARE YOU DOING DOWN HERE?
BONNIE, WHAT IS IT?
MS. WALLER'S GONE ROGUE.
WHAT?!
I'VE TRIED CONTACTING HER, BUT SHE WON'T ANSWER.
ALL THE OTHER TEAM'S COMMS HAVE GONE DARK, TOO.
I'VE GOT NO AUDIO OR VIDEO OF ANYTHING GOING ON.

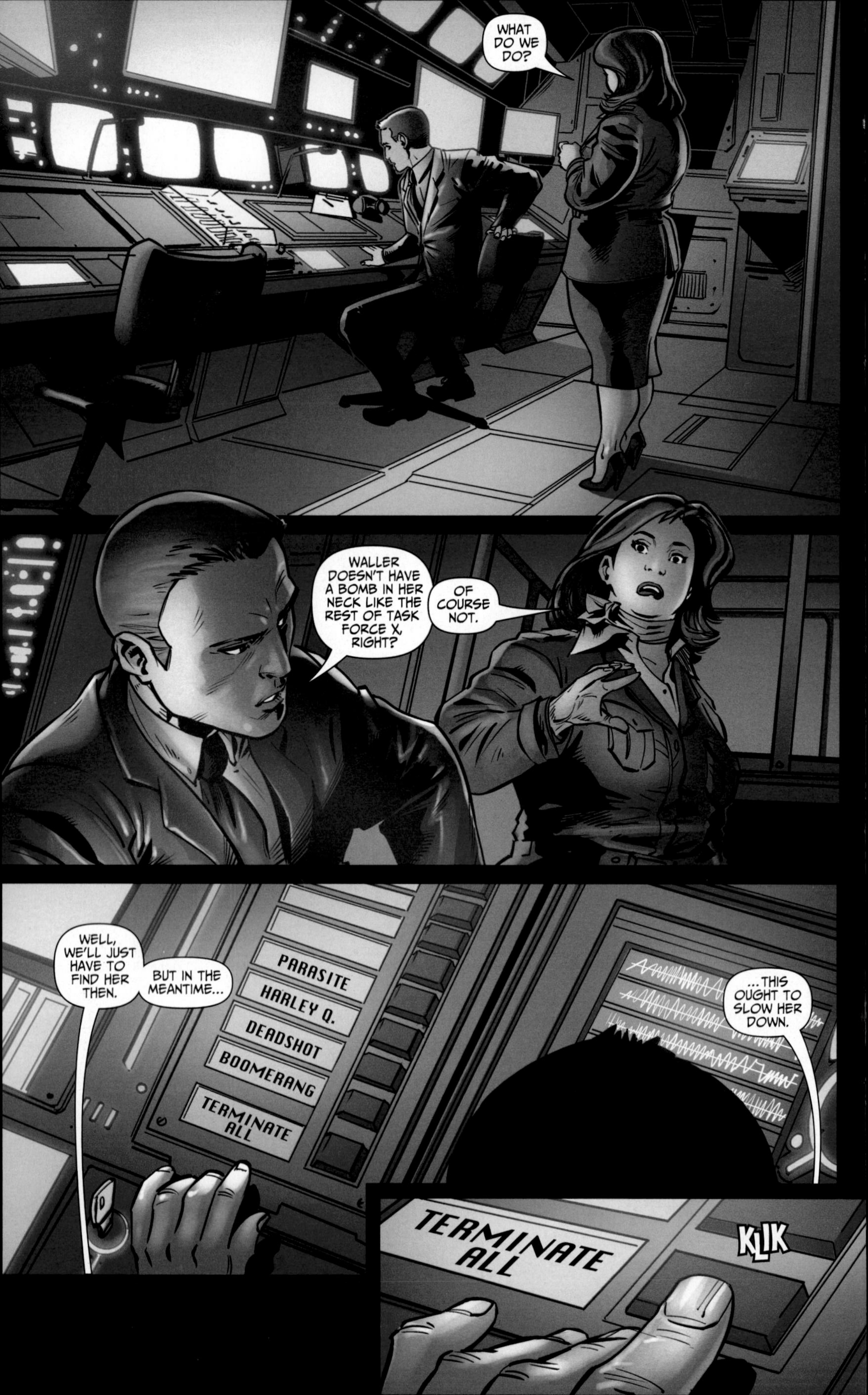
WHAT DO WE DO?
WALLER DOESN'T HAVE A BOMB IN HER NECK LIKE THE REST OF TASK FORCE X, RIGHT?
OF COURSE NOT.
WELL, WE'LL JUST HAVE TO FIND HER THEN.
BUT IN THE MEANTIME...
PARASITE
HARLEY Q.
DEADSHOT
BOOMERANG
TERMINATE ALL
...THIS OUGHT TO SLOW HER DOWN.
TERMINATE ALL
KLIK

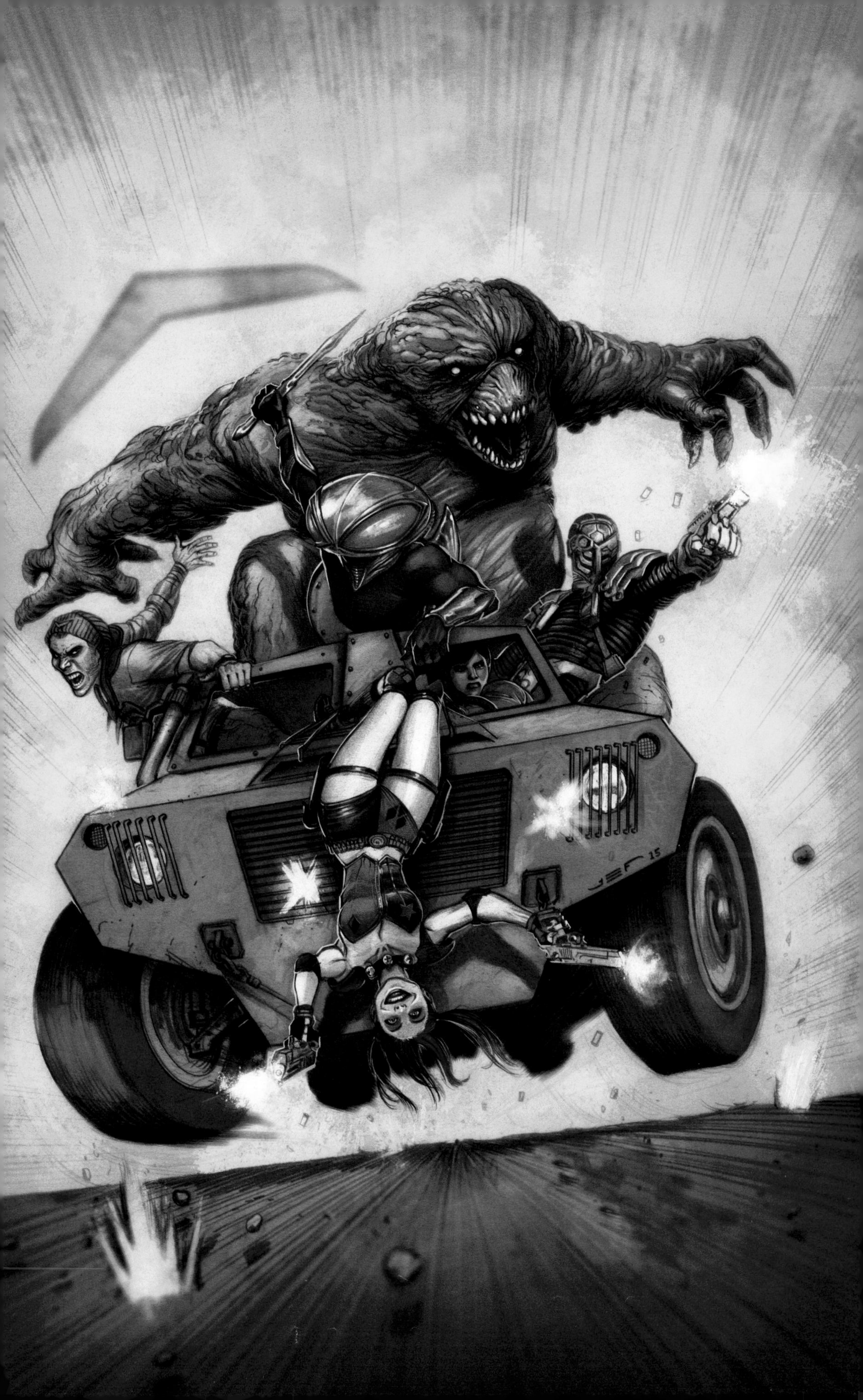

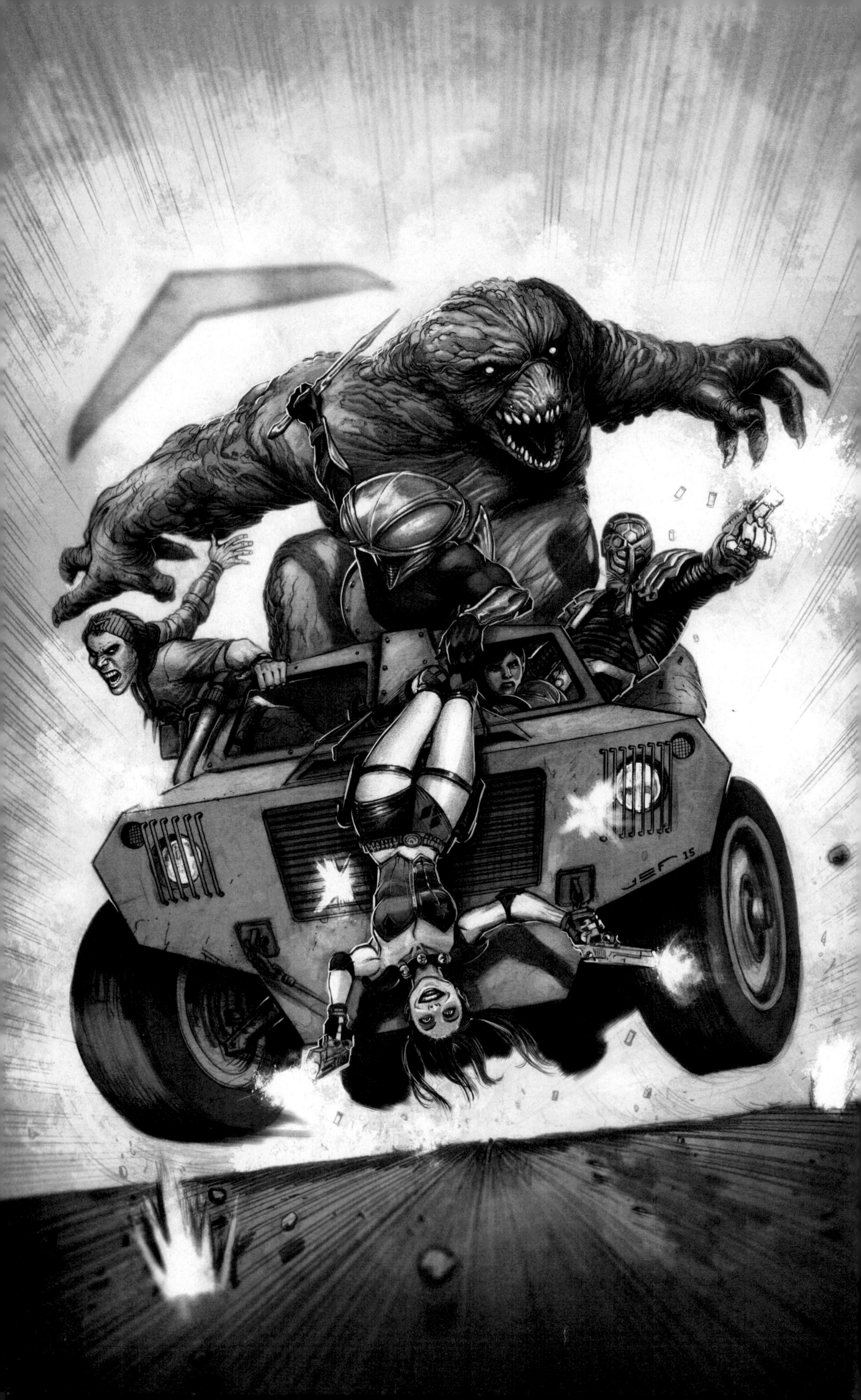

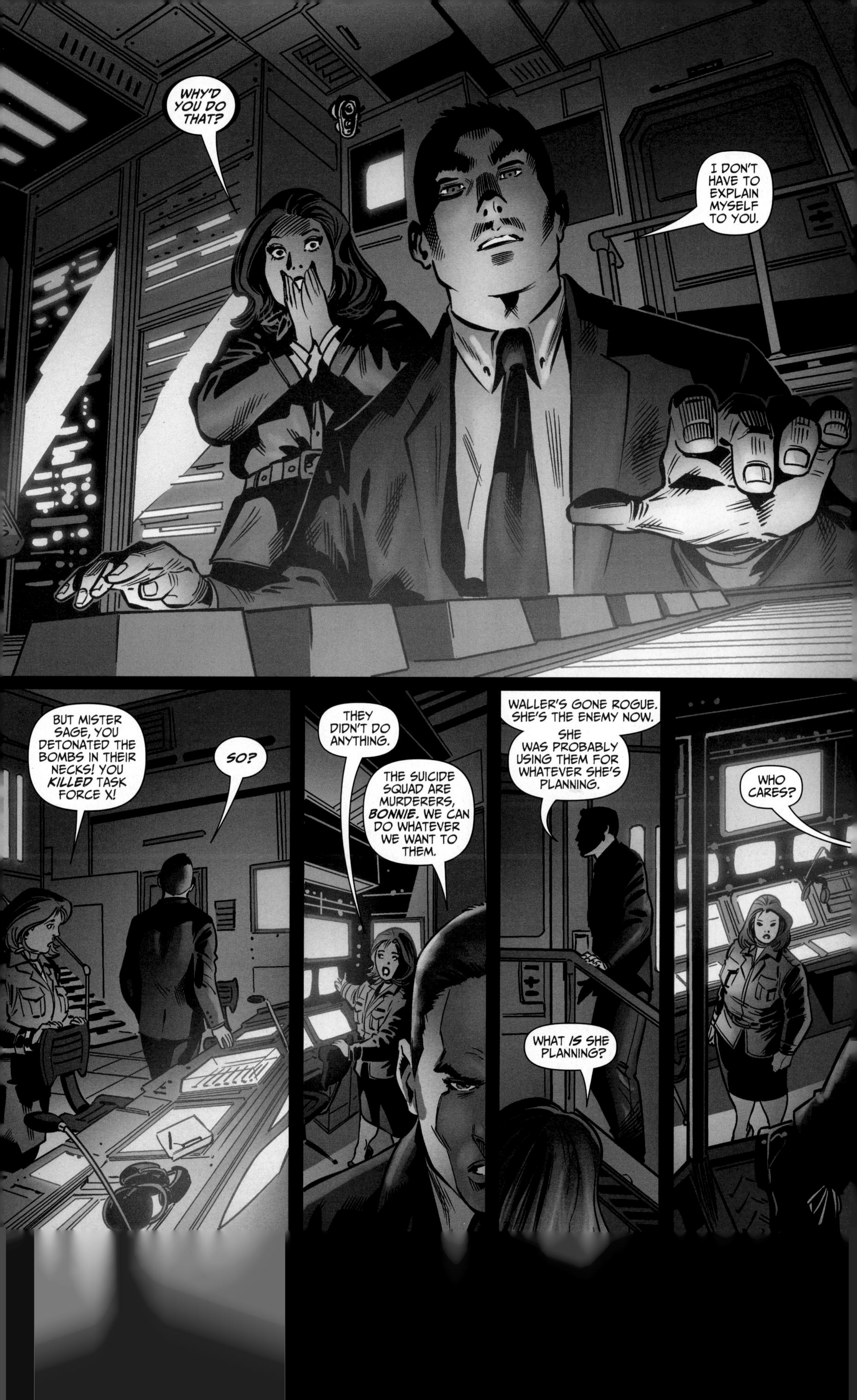
WHY'D YOU DO THAT?
I DON'T HAVE TO EXPLAIN MYSELF TO YOU.
BUT MISTER SAGE, YOU DETONATED THE BOMBS IN THEIR NECKS! YOU KILLED TASK FORCE X!
SO?
THEY DIDN'T DO ANYTHING.
THE SUICIDE SQUAD ARE MURDERERS, BONNIE. WE CAN DO WHATEVER WE WANT TO THEM.
WALLER'S GONE ROGUE. SHE'S THE ENEMY NOW.
SHE WAS PROBABLY USING THEM FOR WHATEVER SHE'S PLANNING.
WHAT IS SHE PLANNING?
WHO CARES?

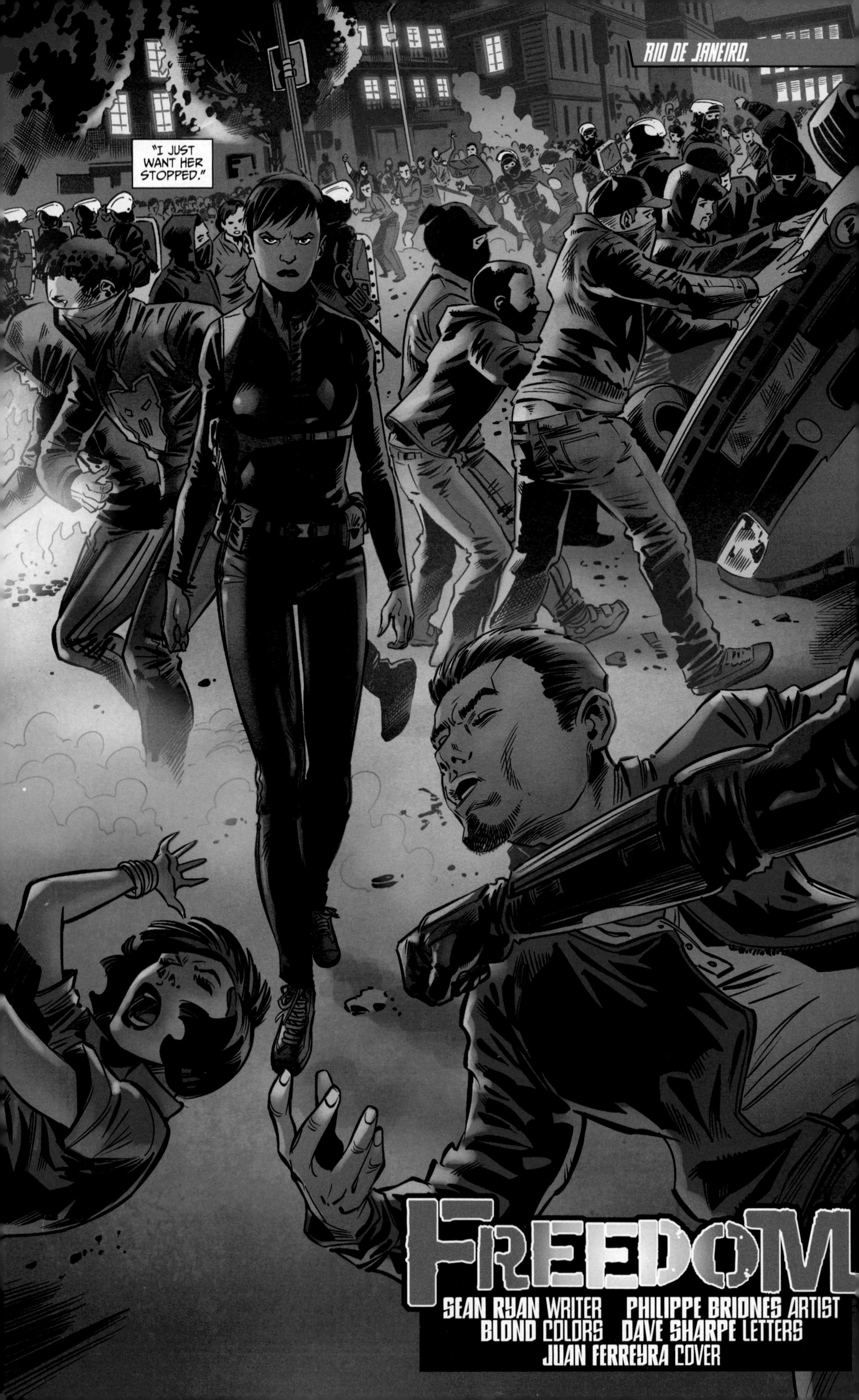
RIO DE JANEIRO.
"I JUST WANT HER STOPPED."
FREEDOM
SEAN RYAN WRITER PHILIPPE BRIONES ARTIST
BLOND COLORS DAVE SHARPE LETTERS
JUAN FERREYRA COVER

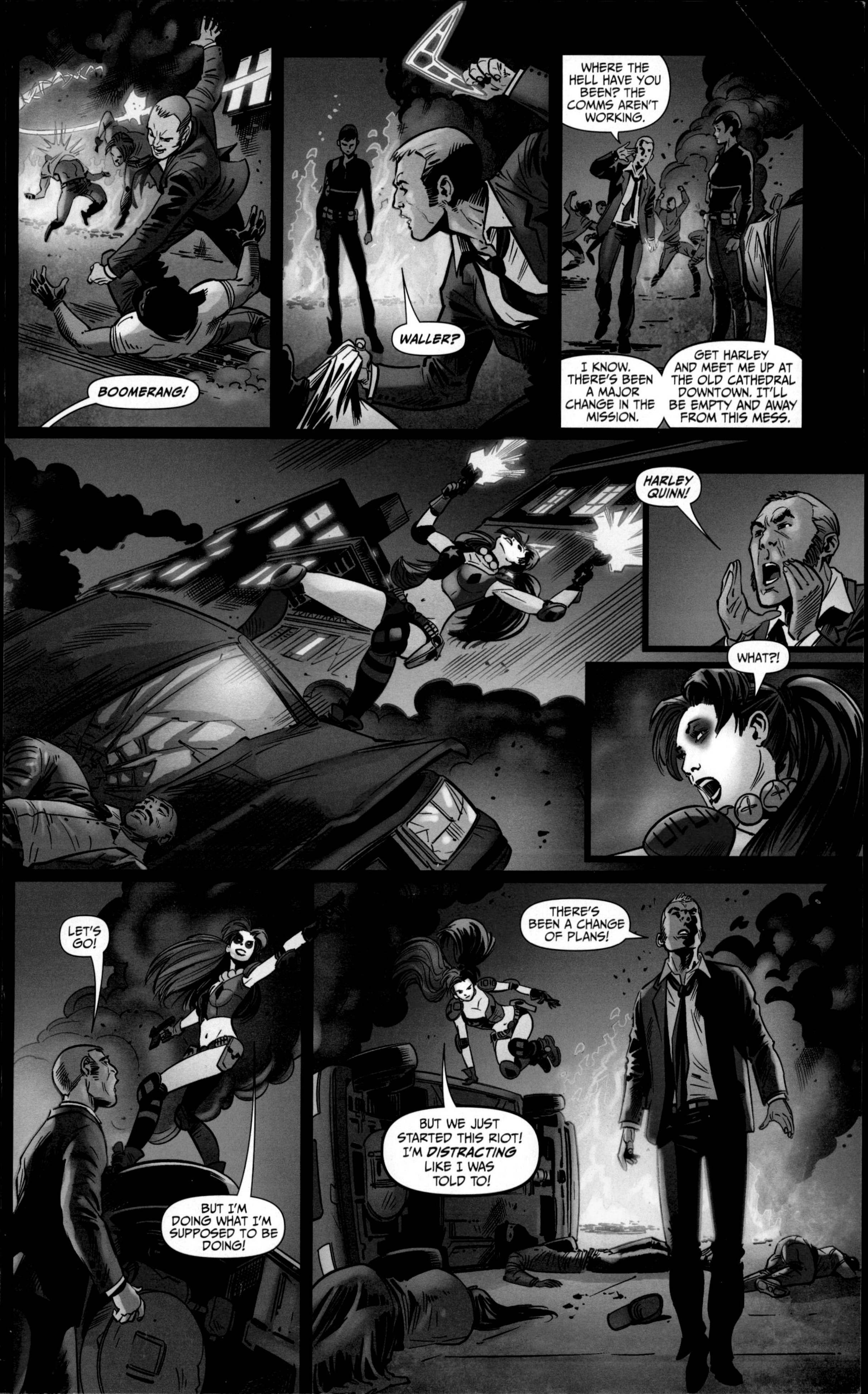
BOOMERANG!
WALLER?
WHERE THE HELL HAVE YOU BEEN? THE COMMS AREN'T WORKING.
I KNOW. THERE'S BEEN A MAJOR CHANGE IN THE MISSION.
GET HARLEY AND MEET ME UP AT THE OLD CATHEDRAL DOWNTOWN. IT'LL BE EMPTY AND AWAY FROM THIS MESS.
HARLEY QUINN!
WHAT?!
LET'S GO!
BUT I'M DOING WHAT I'M SUPPOSED TO BE DOING!
THERE'S BEEN A CHANGE OF PLANS!
BUT WE JUST STARTED THIS RIOT! I'M DISTRACTING LIKE I WAS TOLD TO!

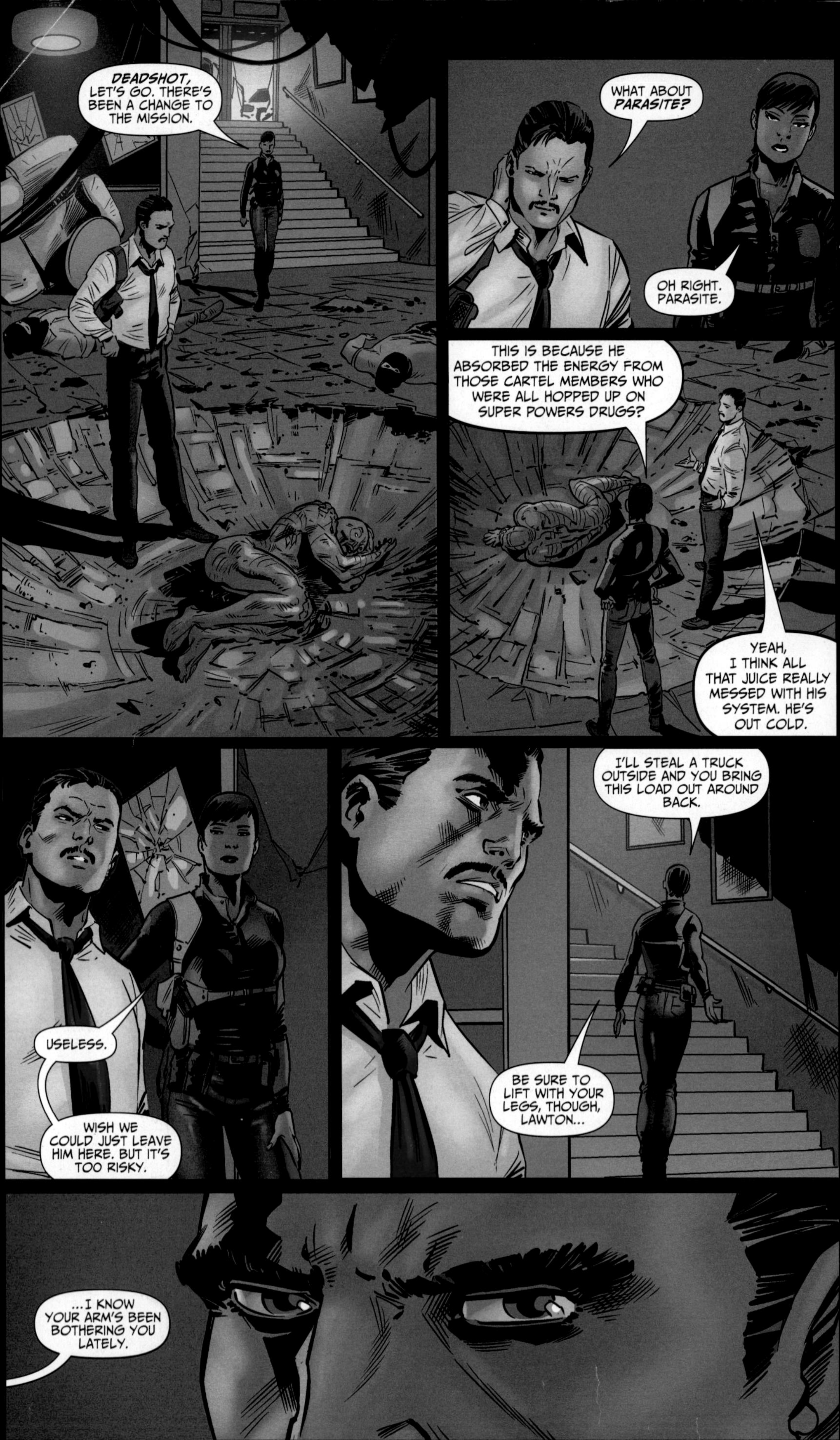
DEADSHOT, LET'S GO. THERE'S BEEN A CHANGE TO THE MISSION.
WHAT ABOUT PARASITE?
OH RIGHT. PARASITE.
THIS IS BECAUSE HE ABSORBED THE ENERGY FROM THOSE CARTEL MEMBERS WHO WERE ALL HOPPED UP ON SUPER POWERS DRUGS?
YEAH, I THINK ALL THAT JUICE REALLY MESSED WITH HIS SYSTEM. HE'S OUT COLD.
USELESS.
WISH WE COULD JUST LEAVE HIM HERE. BUT IT'S TOO RISKY.
I'LL STEAL A TRUCK OUTSIDE AND YOU BRING THIS LOAD OUT AROUND BACK.
BE SURE TO LIFT WITH YOUR LEGS, THOUGH, LAWTON...
...I KNOW YOUR ARM'S BEEN BOTHERING YOU LATELY.

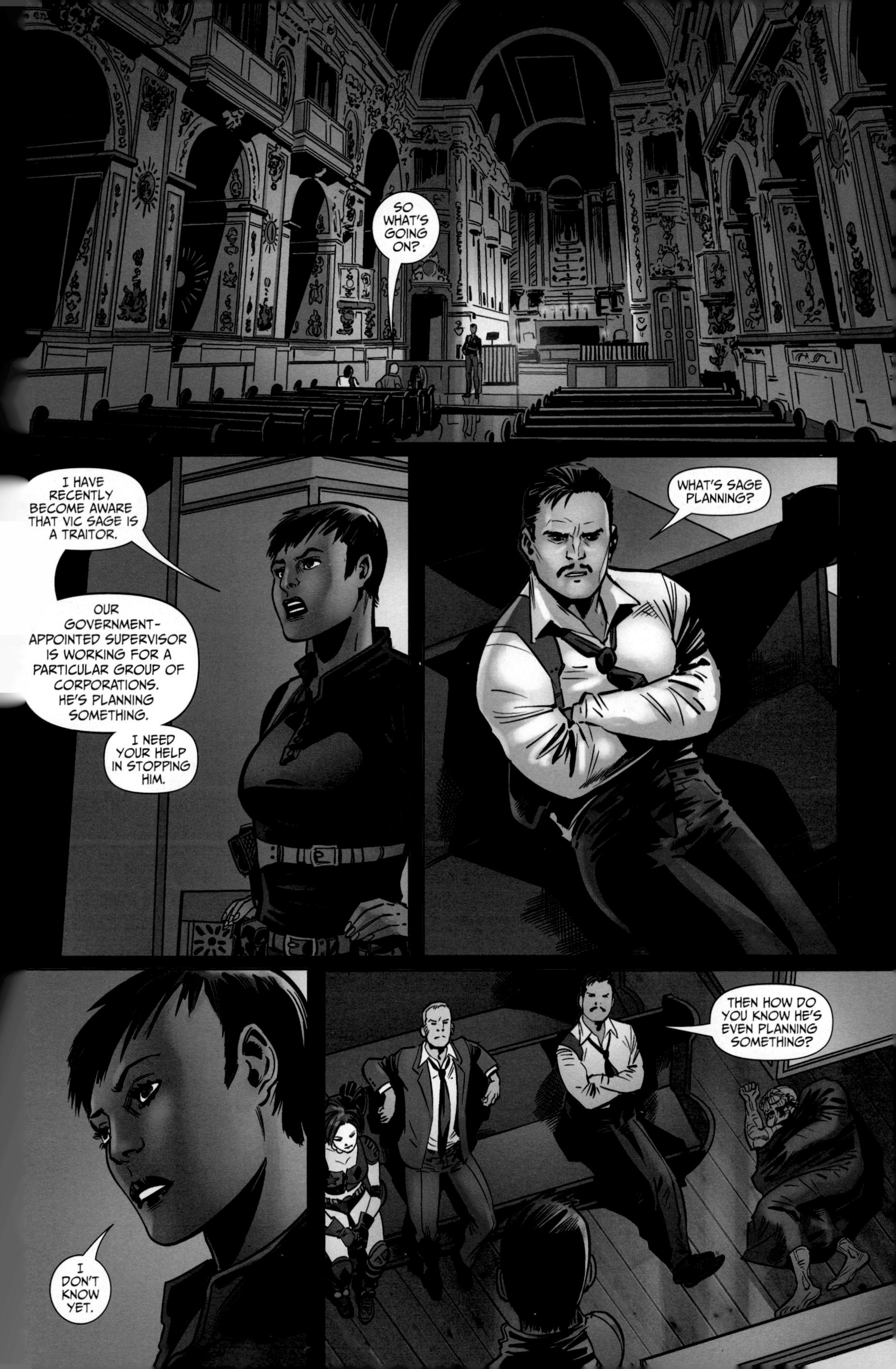
SO WHAT'S GOING ON?
I HAVE RECENTLY BECOME AWARE THAT VIC SAGE IS A TRAITOR.
OUR GOVERNMENT-APPOINTED SUPERVISOR IS WORKING FOR A PARTICULAR GROUP OF CORPORATIONS. HE'S PLANNING SOMETHING.
I NEED YOUR HELP IN STOPPING HIM.
WHAT'S SAGE PLANNING?
I DON'T KNOW YET.
THEN HOW DO YOU KNOW HE'S EVEN PLANNING SOMETHING?

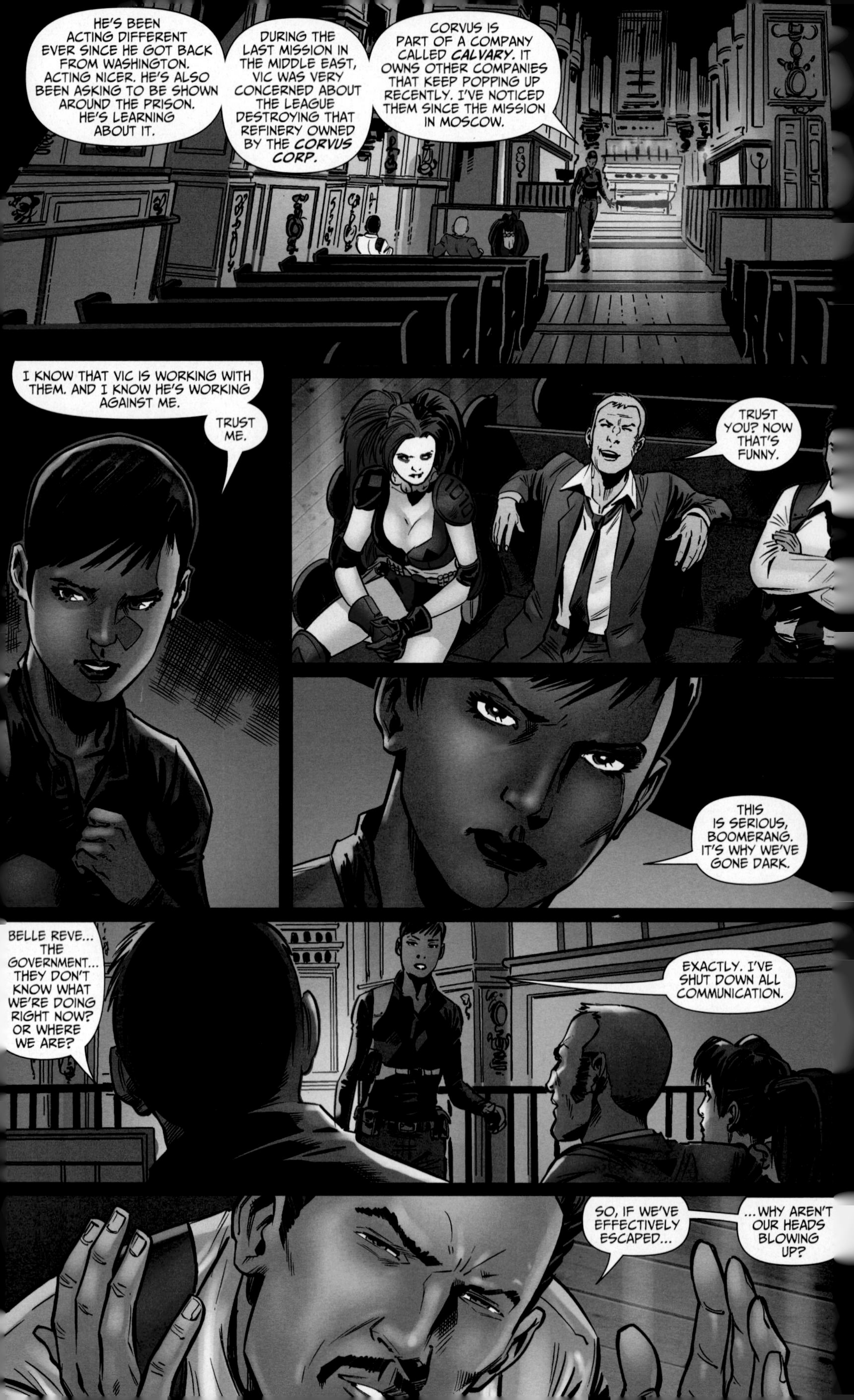
HE'S BEEN ACTING DIFFERENT EVER SINCE HE GOT BACK FROM WASHINGTON. ACTING NICER. HE'S ALSO BEEN ASKING TO BE SHOWN AROUND THE PRISON. HE'S LEARNING ABOUT IT.
DURING THE LAST MISSION IN THE MIDDLE EAST, VIC WAS VERY CONCERNED ABOUT THE LEAGUE DESTROYING THAT REFINERY OWNED BY THE CORVUS CORP.
CORVUS IS PART OF A COMPANY CALLED CALVARY. IT OWNS OTHER COMPANIES THAT KEEP POPPING UP RECENTLY. I'VE NOTICED THEM SINCE THE MISSION IN MOSCOW.
I KNOW THAT VIC IS WORKING WITH THEM. AND I KNOW HE'S WORKING AGAINST ME.
TRUST ME.
TRUST YOU? NOW THAT'S FUNNY.
THIS IS SERIOUS, BOOMERANG. IT'S WHY WE'VE GONE DARK.
BELLE REVE... THE GOVERNMENT... THEY DON'T KNOW WHAT WE'RE DOING RIGHT NOW? OR WHERE WE ARE?
EXACTLY. I'VE SHUT DOWN ALL COMMUNICATION.
SO, IF WE'VE EFFECTIVELY ESCAPED...
...WHY AREN'T OUR HEADS BLOWING UP?

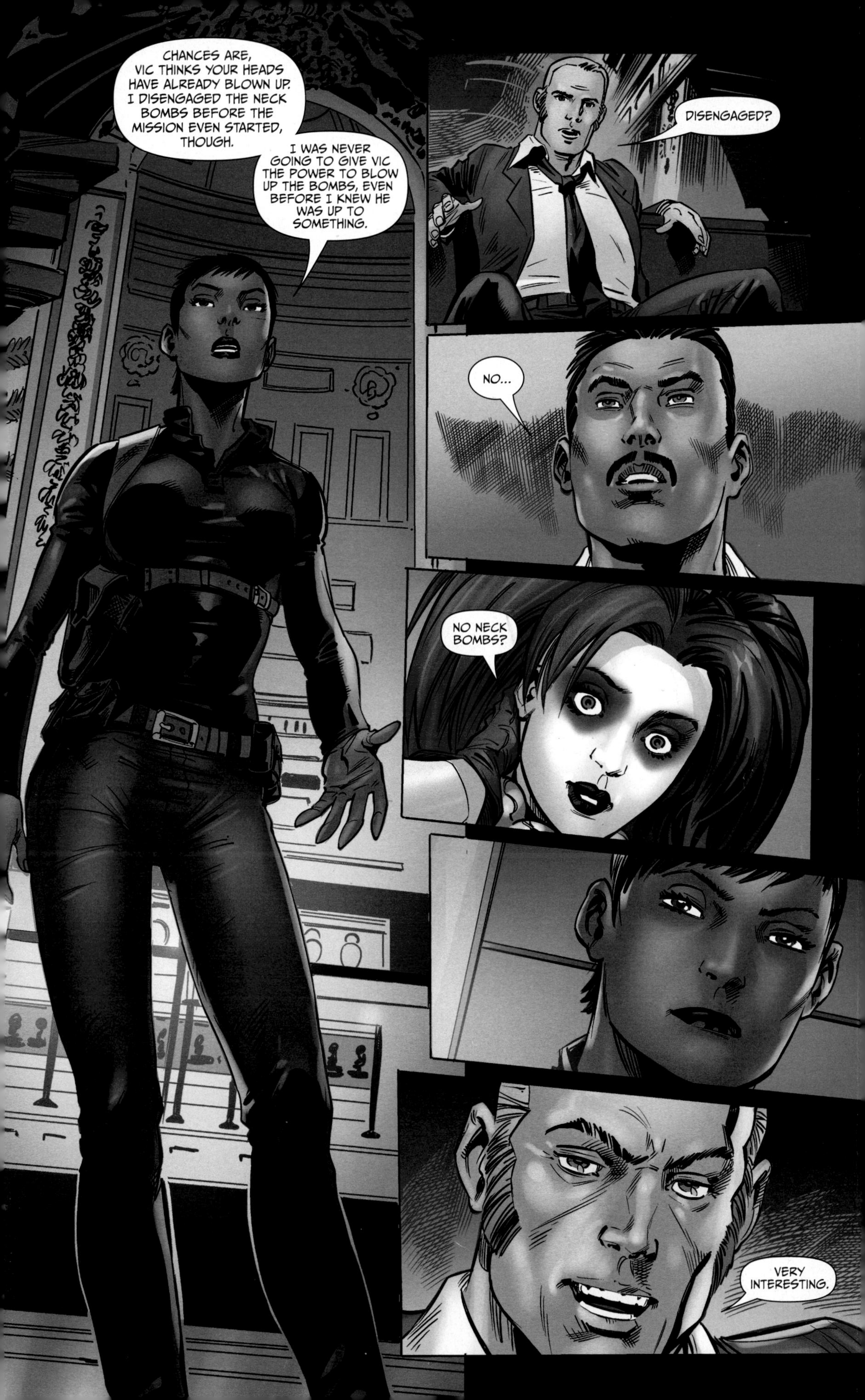
CHANCES ARE, VIC THINKS YOUR HEADS HAVE ALREADY BLOWN UP. I DISENGAGED THE NECK BOMBS BEFORE THE MISSION EVEN STARTED, THOUGH.
I WAS NEVER GOING TO GIVE VIC THE POWER TO BLOW UP THE BOMBS, EVEN BEFORE I KNEW HE WAS UP TO SOMETHING.
DISENGAGED?
NO...
NO NECK BOMBS?
VERY INTERESTING.

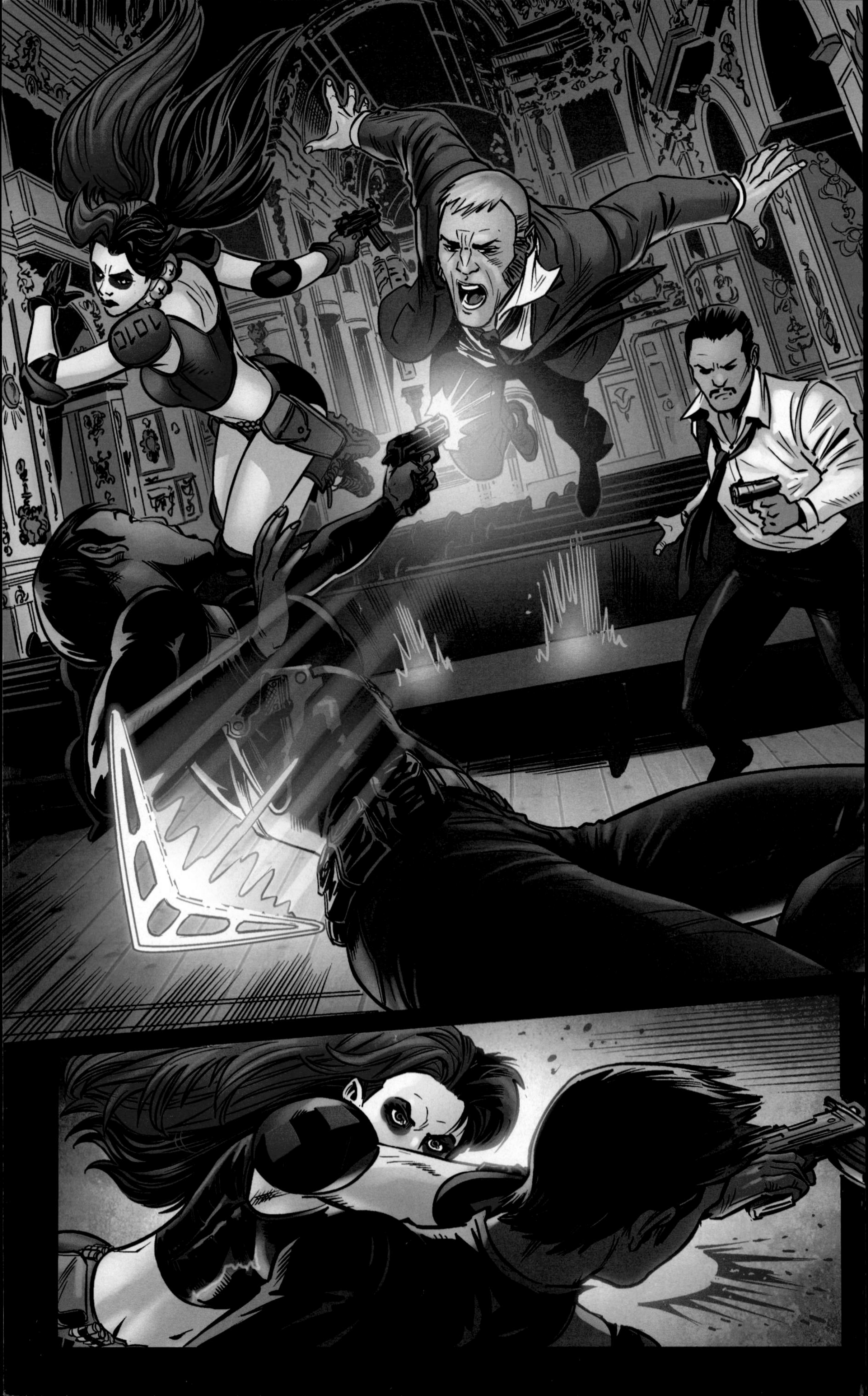

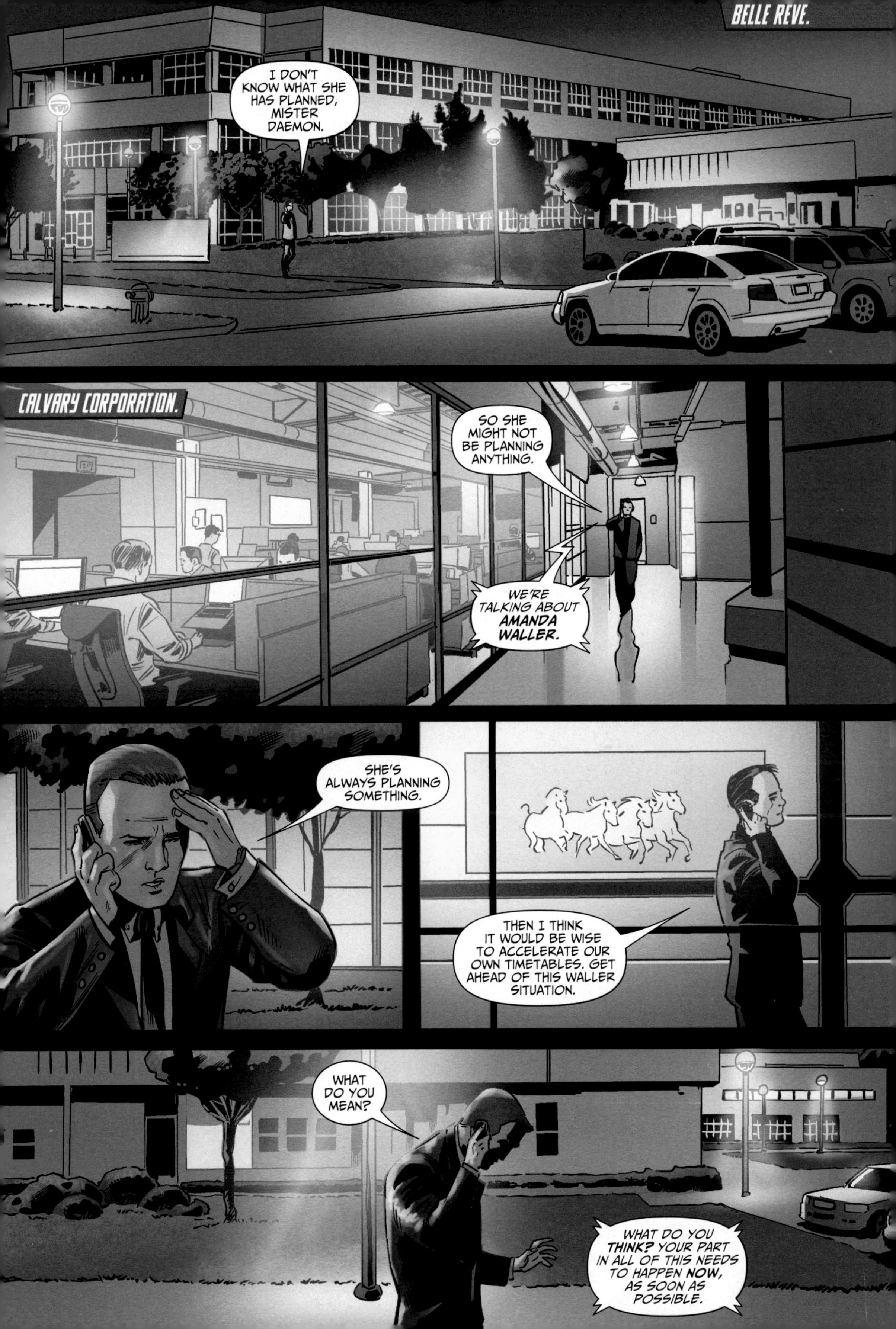
BELLE REVE.
I DON'T KNOW WHAT SHE HAS PLANNED, MISTER DAEMON.
CALVARY CORPORATION.
SO SHE MIGHT NOT BE PLANNING ANYTHING.
WE'RE TALKING ABOUT **AMANDA WALLER.**
SHE'S ALWAYS PLANNING SOMETHING.
THEN I THINK IT WOULD BE WISE TO ACCELERATE OUR OWN TIMETABLES. GET AHEAD OF THIS WALLER SITUATION.
WHAT DO YOU MEAN?
*WHAT DO YOU **THINK?** YOUR PART IN ALL OF THIS NEEDS TO HAPPEN **NOW,** AS SOON AS POSSIBLE.*

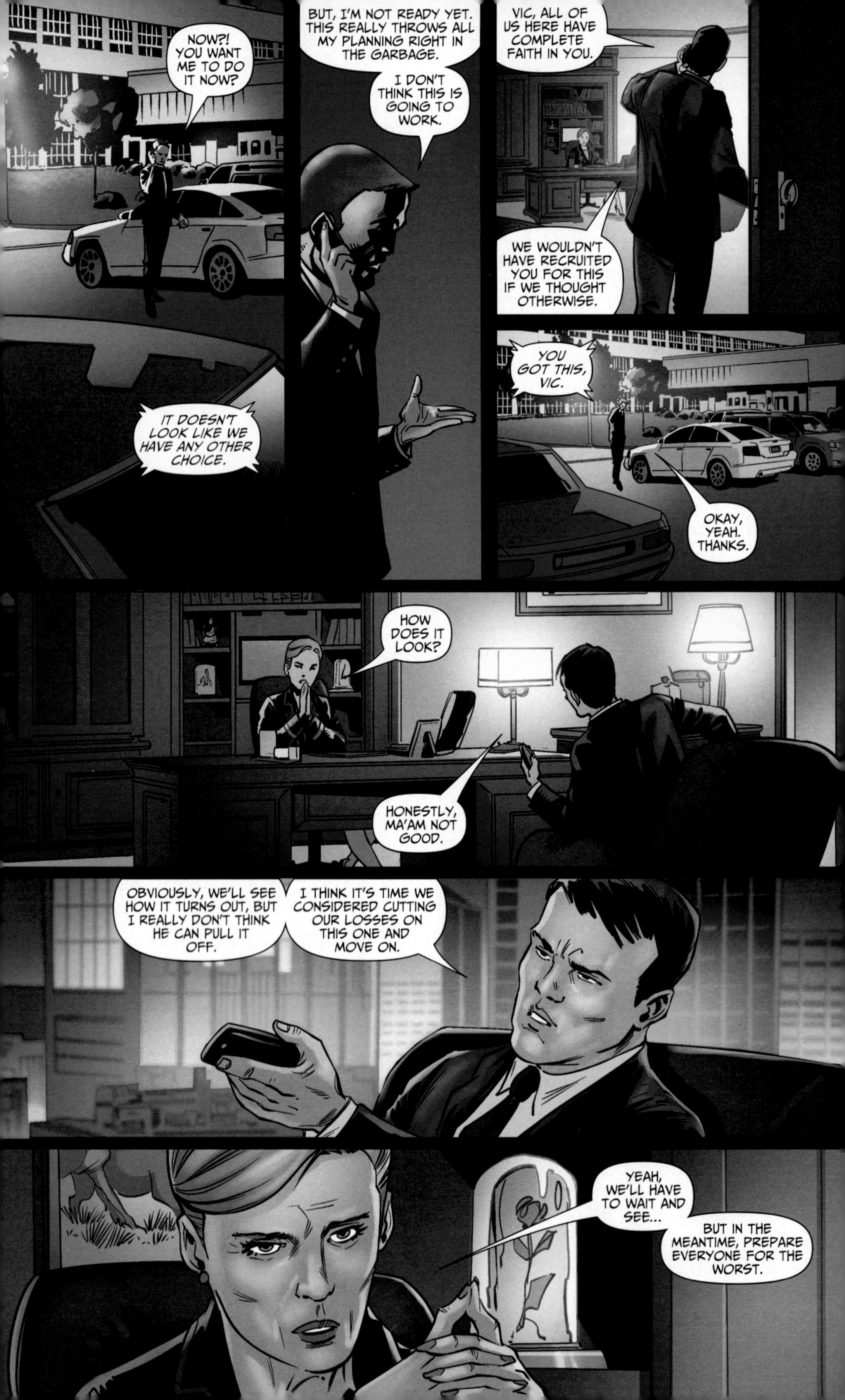
NOW?! YOU WANT ME TO DO IT NOW?
BUT, I'M NOT READY YET. THIS REALLY THROWS ALL MY PLANNING RIGHT IN THE GARBAGE.
I DON'T THINK THIS IS GOING TO WORK.
VIC, ALL OF US HERE HAVE COMPLETE FAITH IN YOU.
WE WOULDN'T HAVE RECRUITED YOU FOR THIS IF WE THOUGHT OTHERWISE.
IT DOESN'T LOOK LIKE WE HAVE ANY OTHER CHOICE.
YOU GOT THIS, VIC.
OKAY, YEAH. THANKS.
HOW DOES IT LOOK?
HONESTLY, MA'AM NOT GOOD.
OBVIOUSLY, WE'LL SEE HOW IT TURNS OUT, BUT I REALLY DON'T THINK HE CAN PULL IT OFF.
I THINK IT'S TIME WE CONSIDERED CUTTING OUR LOSSES ON THIS ONE AND MOVE ON.
YEAH, WE'LL HAVE TO WAIT AND SEE...
BUT IN THE MEANTIME, PREPARE EVERYONE FOR THE WORST.

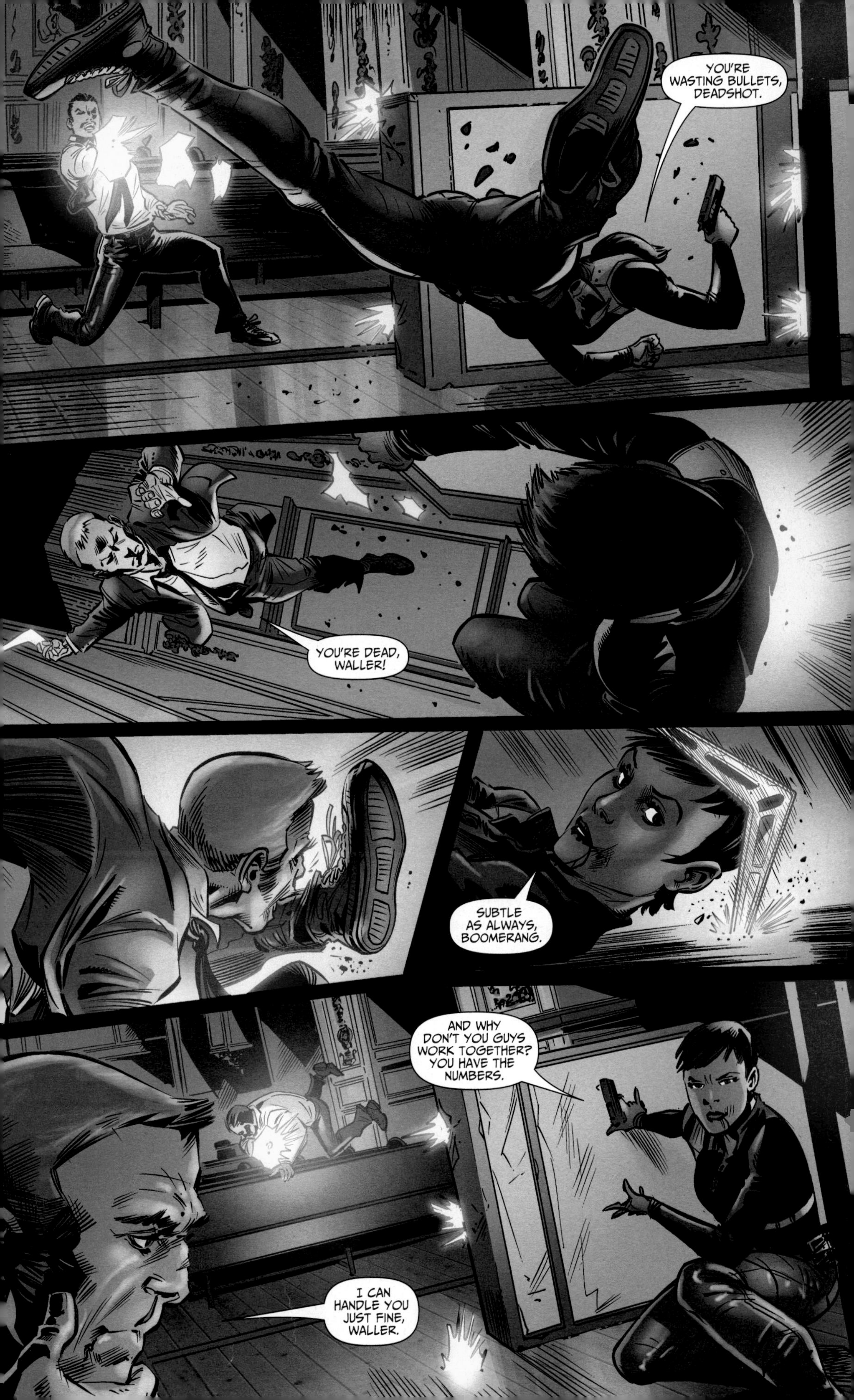
YOU'RE WASTING BULLETS, DEADSHOT.
YOU'RE DEAD, WALLER!
SUBTLE AS ALWAYS, BOOMERANG.
AND WHY DON'T YOU GUYS WORK TOGETHER? YOU HAVE THE NUMBERS.
I CAN HANDLE YOU JUST FINE, WALLER.

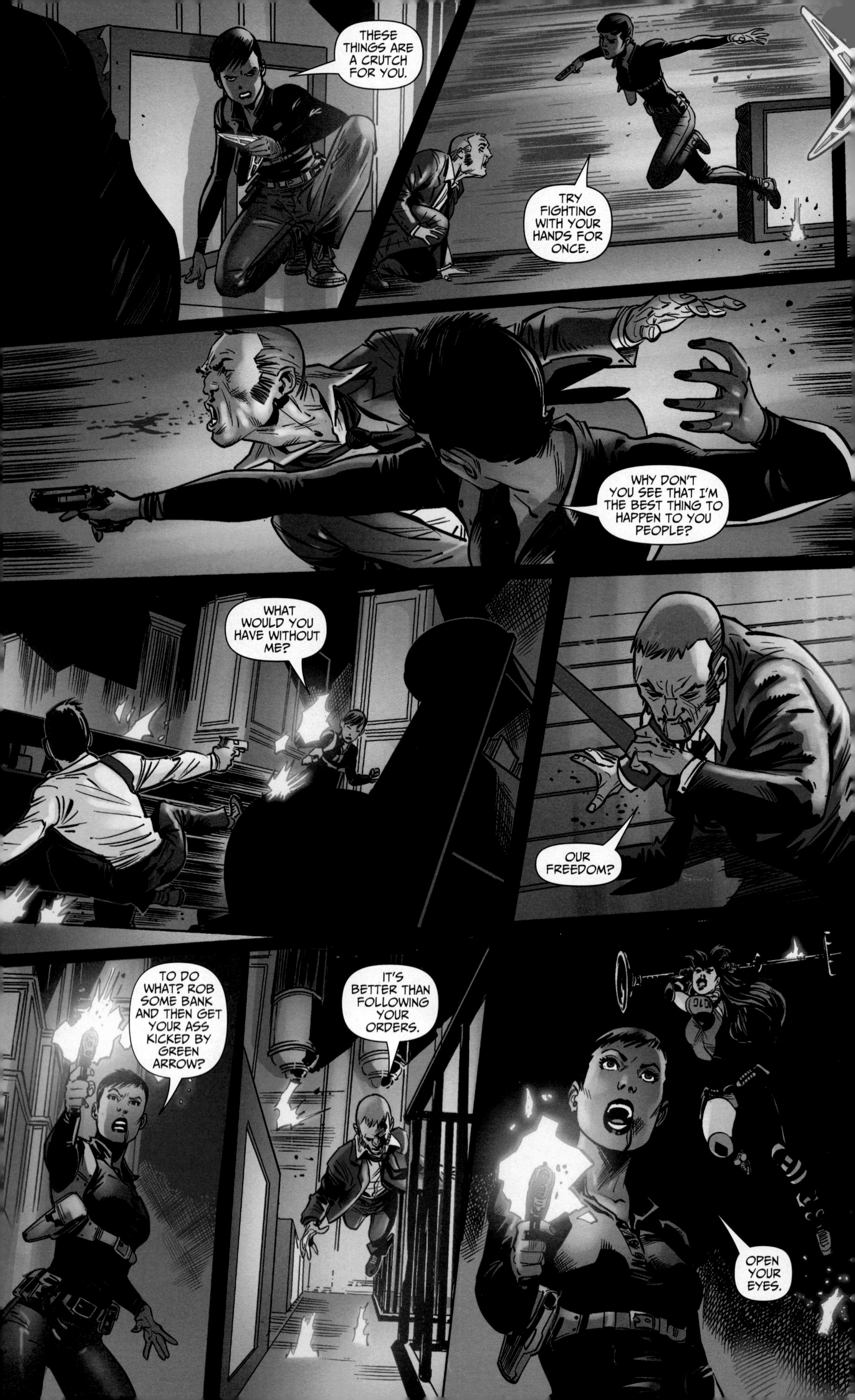
THESE THINGS ARE A CRUTCH FOR YOU.
TRY FIGHTING WITH YOUR HANDS FOR ONCE.
WHY DON'T YOU SEE THAT I'M THE BEST THING TO HAPPEN TO YOU PEOPLE?
WHAT WOULD YOU HAVE WITHOUT ME?
OUR FREEDOM?
TO DO WHAT? ROB SOME BANK AND THEN GET YOUR ASS KICKED BY GREEN ARROW?
IT'S BETTER THAN FOLLOWING YOUR ORDERS.
OPEN YOUR EYES.

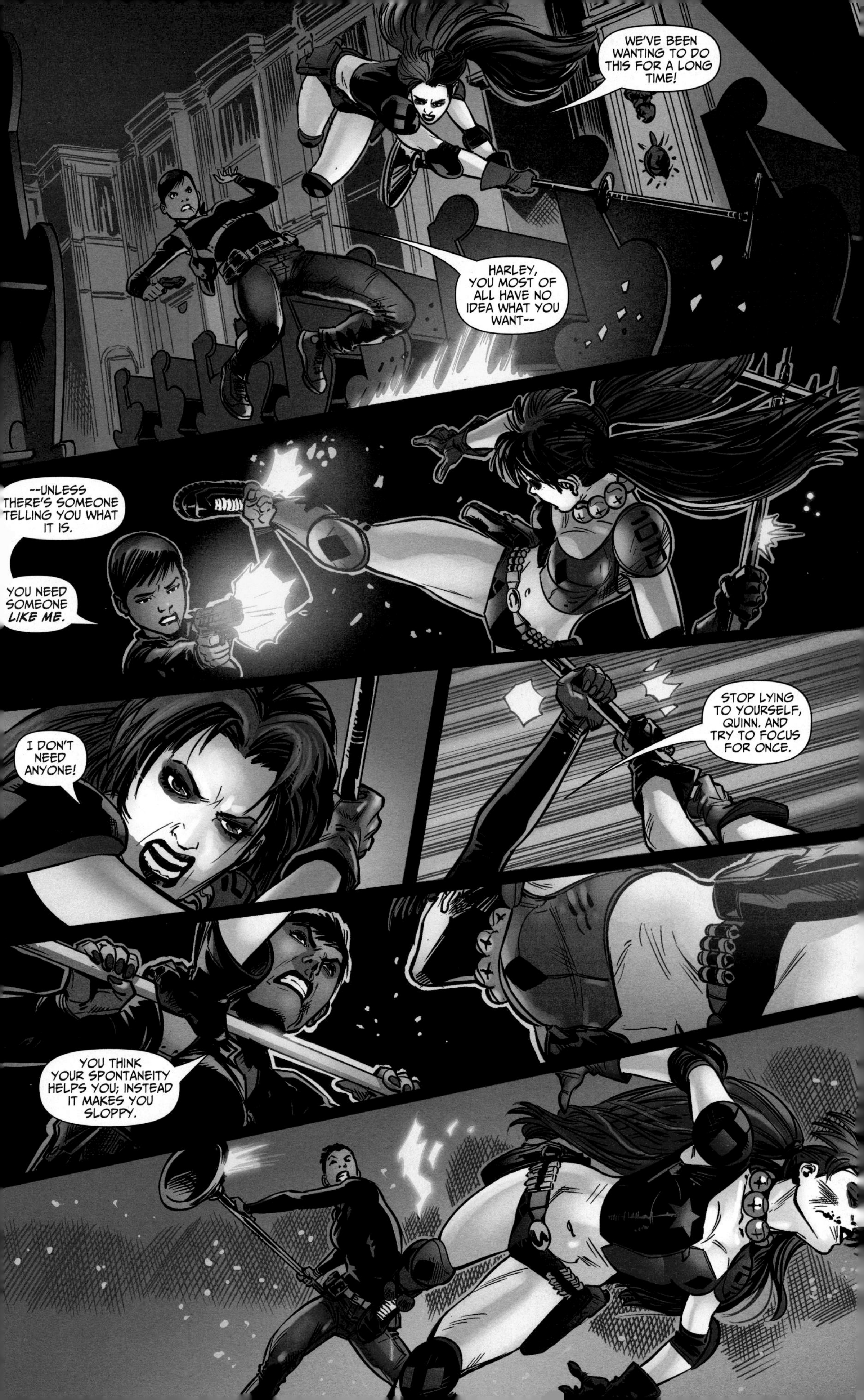
WE'VE BEEN WANTING TO DO THIS FOR A LONG TIME!
HARLEY, YOU MOST OF ALL HAVE NO IDEA WHAT YOU WANT--
--UNLESS THERE'S SOMEONE TELLING YOU WHAT IT IS.
YOU NEED SOMEONE *LIKE ME.*
I DON'T NEED ANYONE!
STOP LYING TO YOURSELF, QUINN. AND TRY TO FOCUS FOR ONCE.
YOU THINK YOUR SPONTANEITY HELPS YOU; INSTEAD IT MAKES YOU SLOPPY.

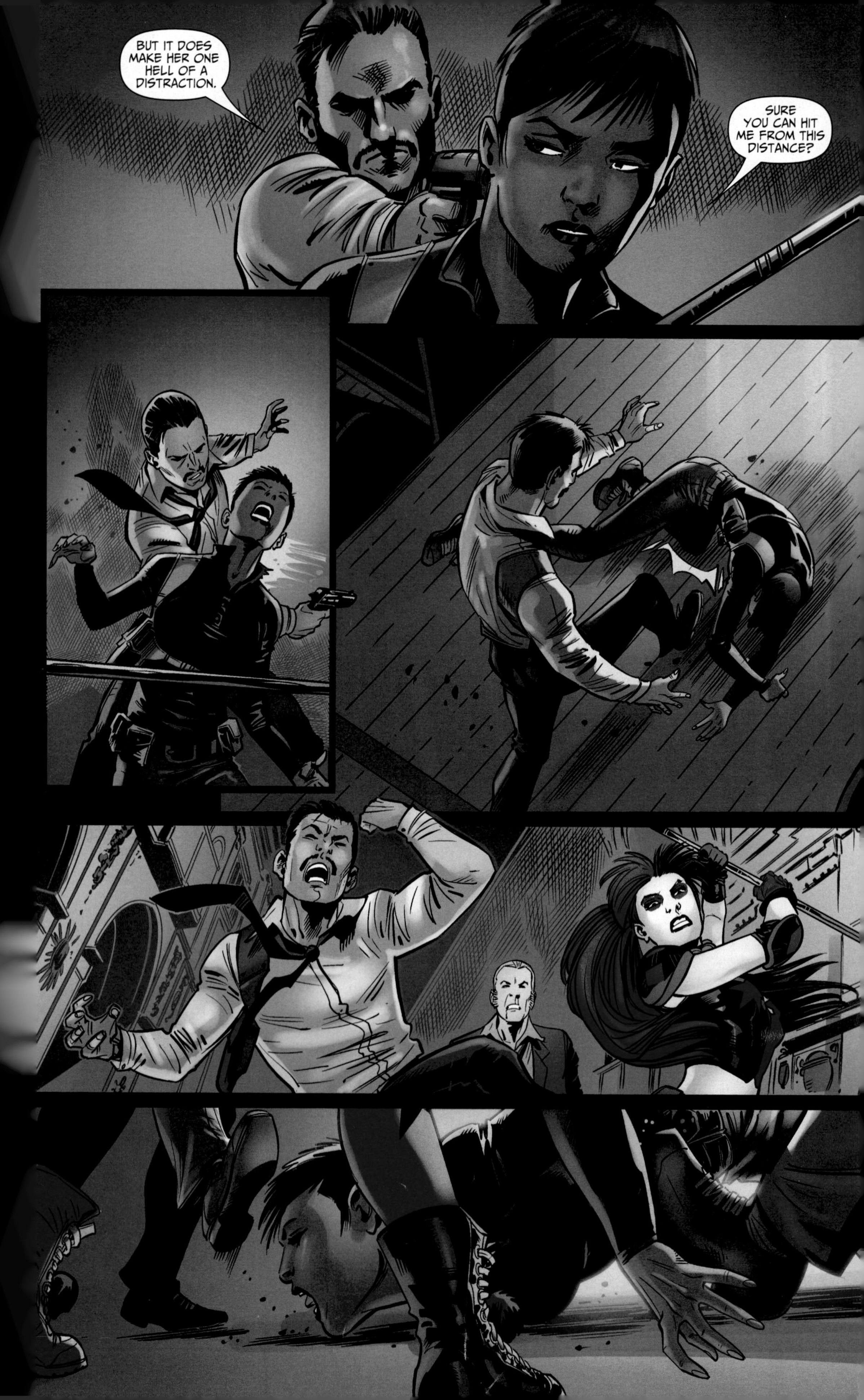
BUT IT DOES MAKE HER ONE HELL OF A DISTRACTION.
SURE YOU CAN HIT ME FROM THIS DISTANCE?

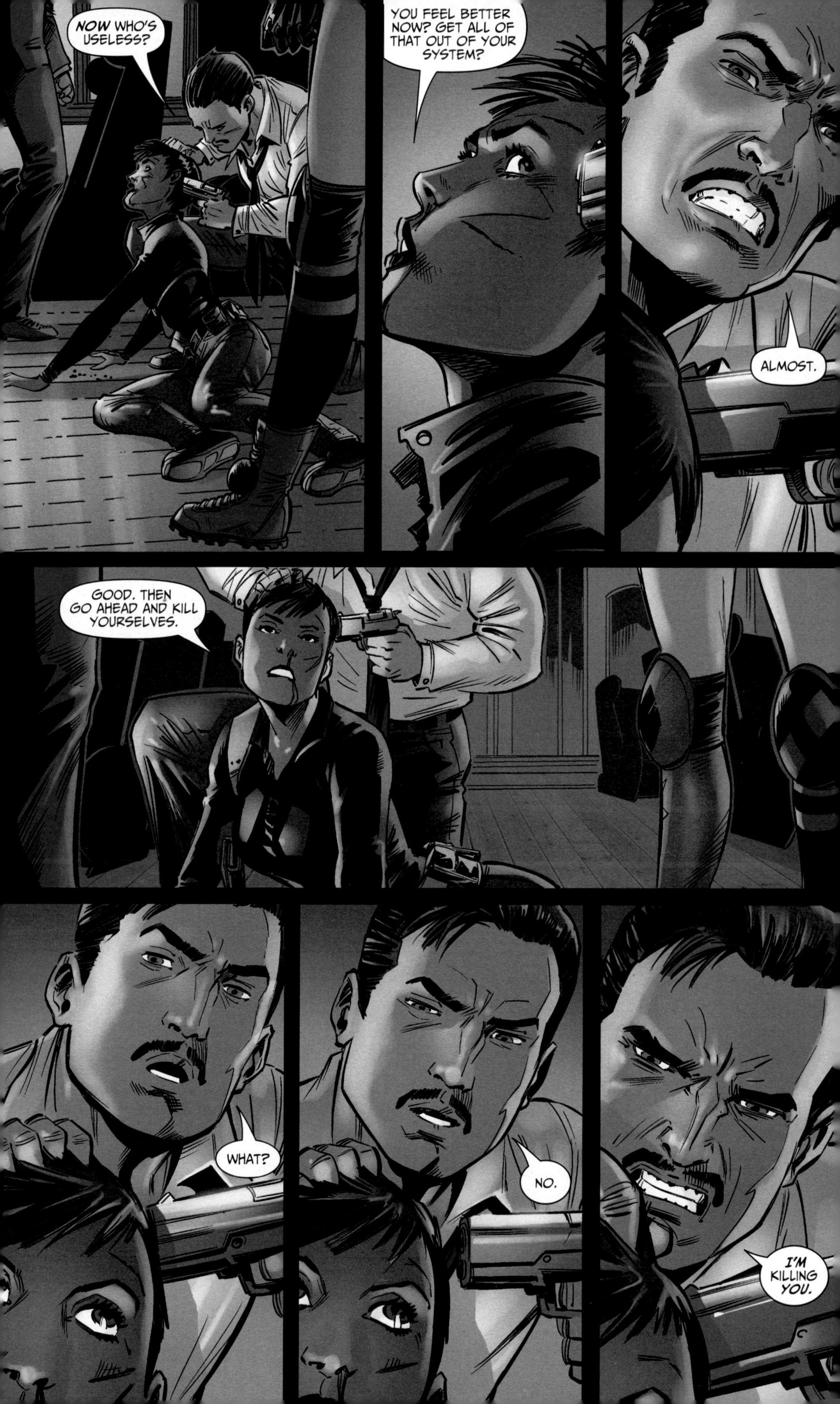
NOW WHO'S USELESS?
YOU FEEL BETTER NOW? GET ALL OF THAT OUT OF YOUR SYSTEM?
ALMOST.
GOOD. THEN GO AHEAD AND KILL YOURSELVES.
WHAT?
NO.
I'M KILLING YOU.

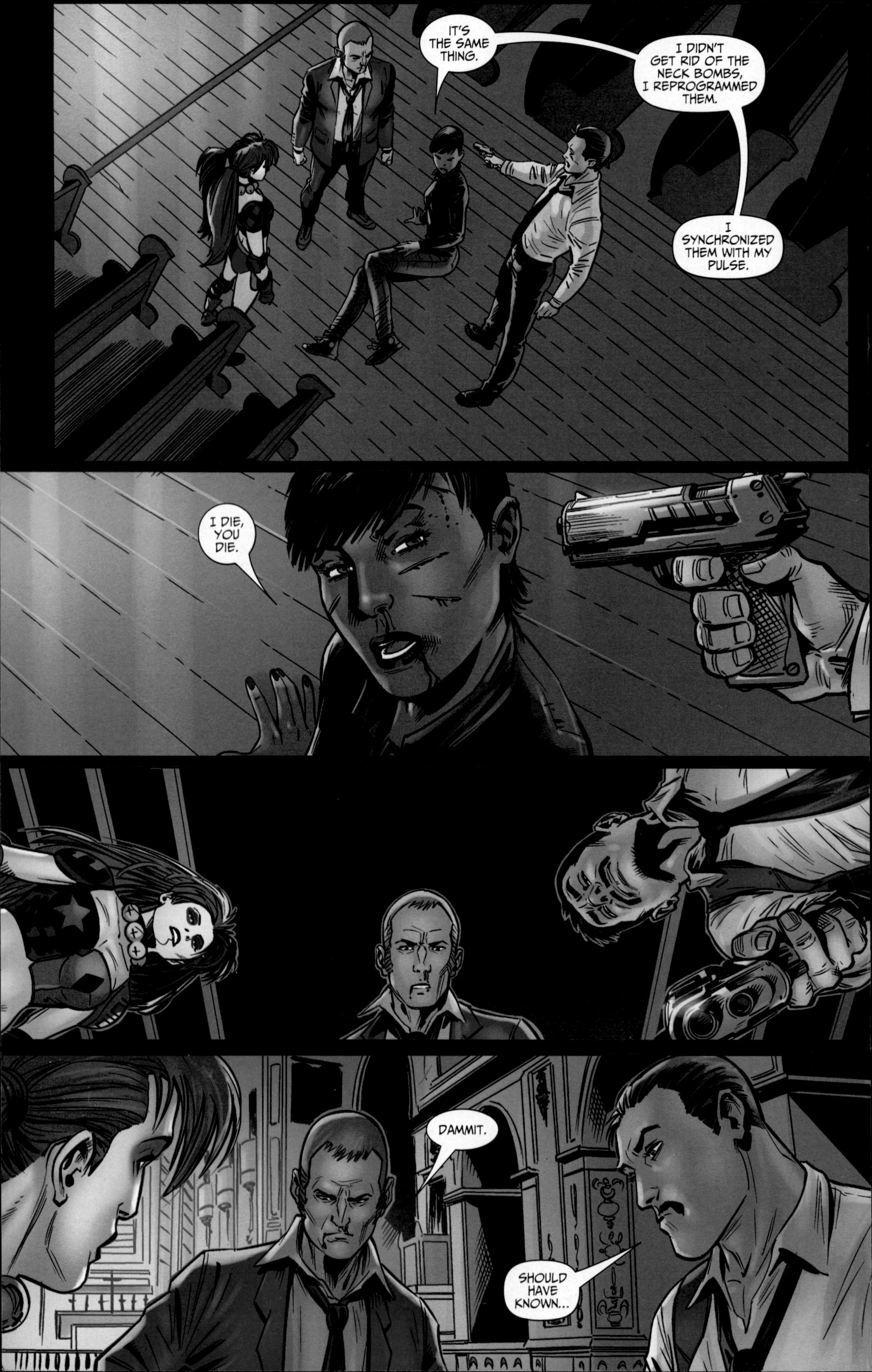
IT'S THE SAME THING.
I DIDN'T GET RID OF THE NECK BOMBS, I REPROGRAMMED THEM.
I SYNCHRONIZED THEM WITH MY PULSE.
I DIE, YOU DIE.
DAMMIT.
SHOULD HAVE KNOWN...

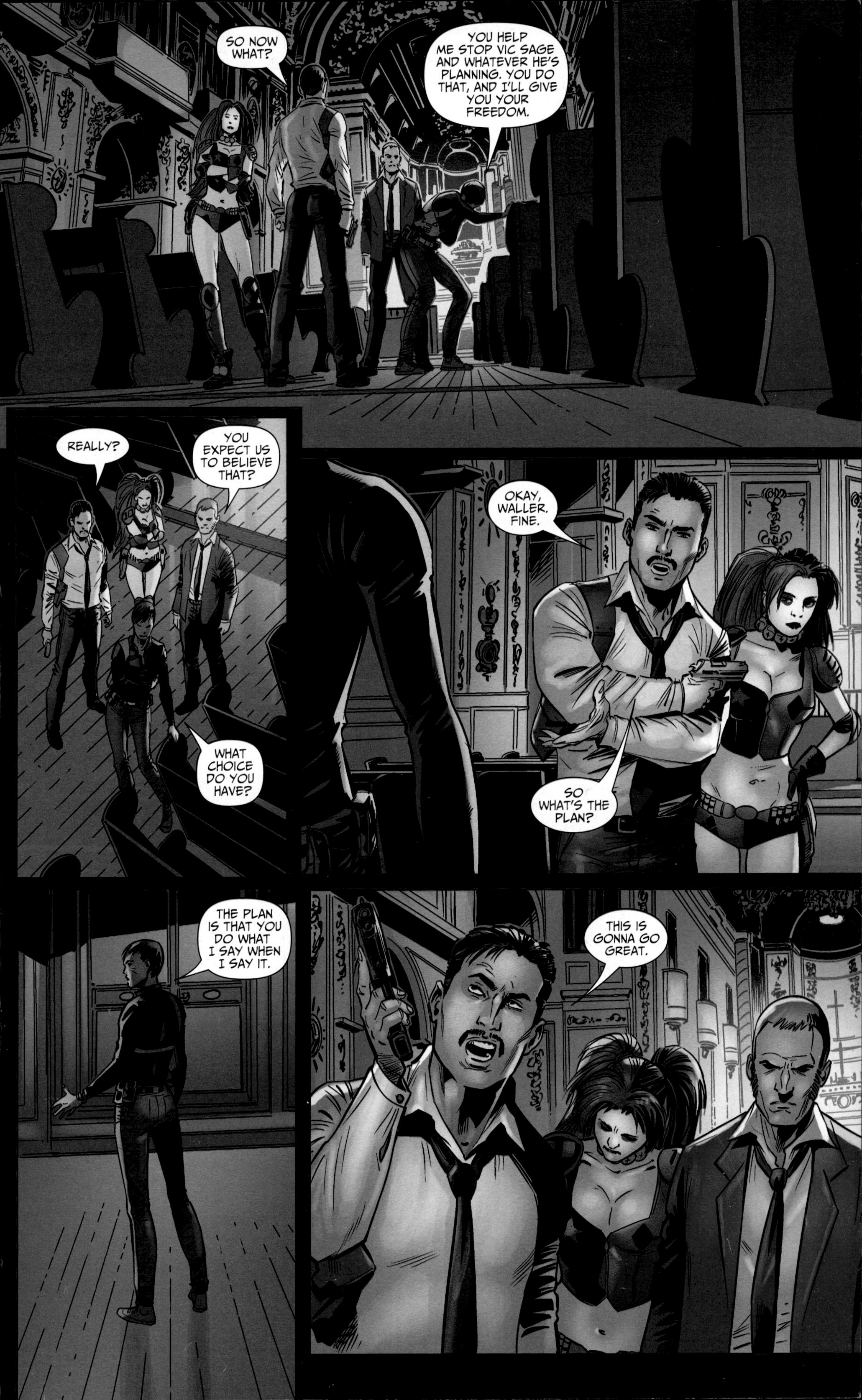
SO NOW WHAT?
YOU HELP ME STOP VIC SAGE AND WHATEVER HE'S PLANNING. YOU DO THAT, AND I'LL GIVE YOU YOUR FREEDOM.
REALLY?
YOU EXPECT US TO BELIEVE THAT?
WHAT CHOICE DO YOU HAVE?
OKAY, WALLER. FINE.
SO WHAT'S THE PLAN?
THE PLAN IS THAT YOU DO WHAT I SAY WHEN I SAY IT.
THIS IS GONNA GO GREAT.

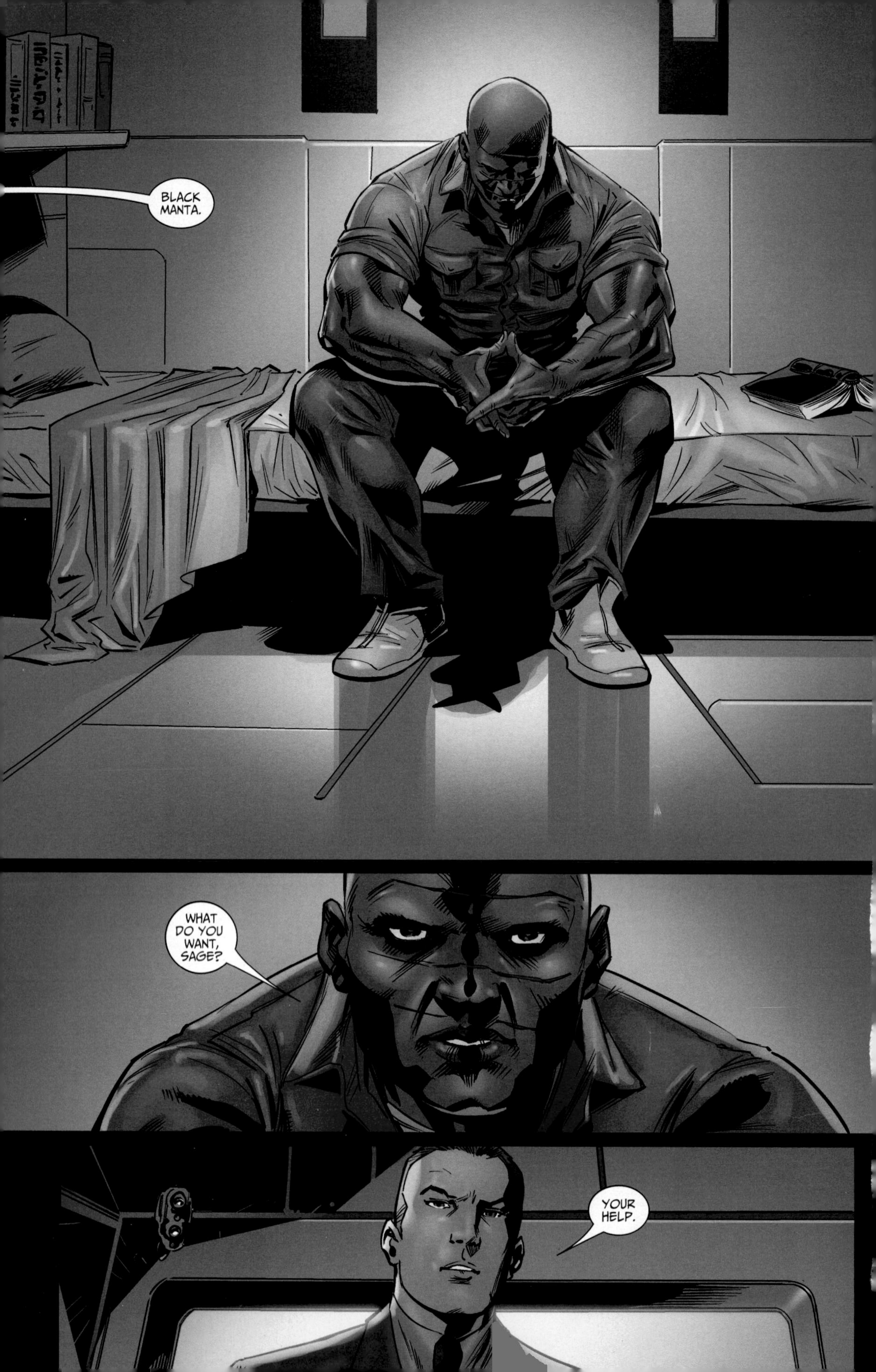
BLACK MANTA.
WHAT DO YOU WANT, SAGE?
YOUR HELP.

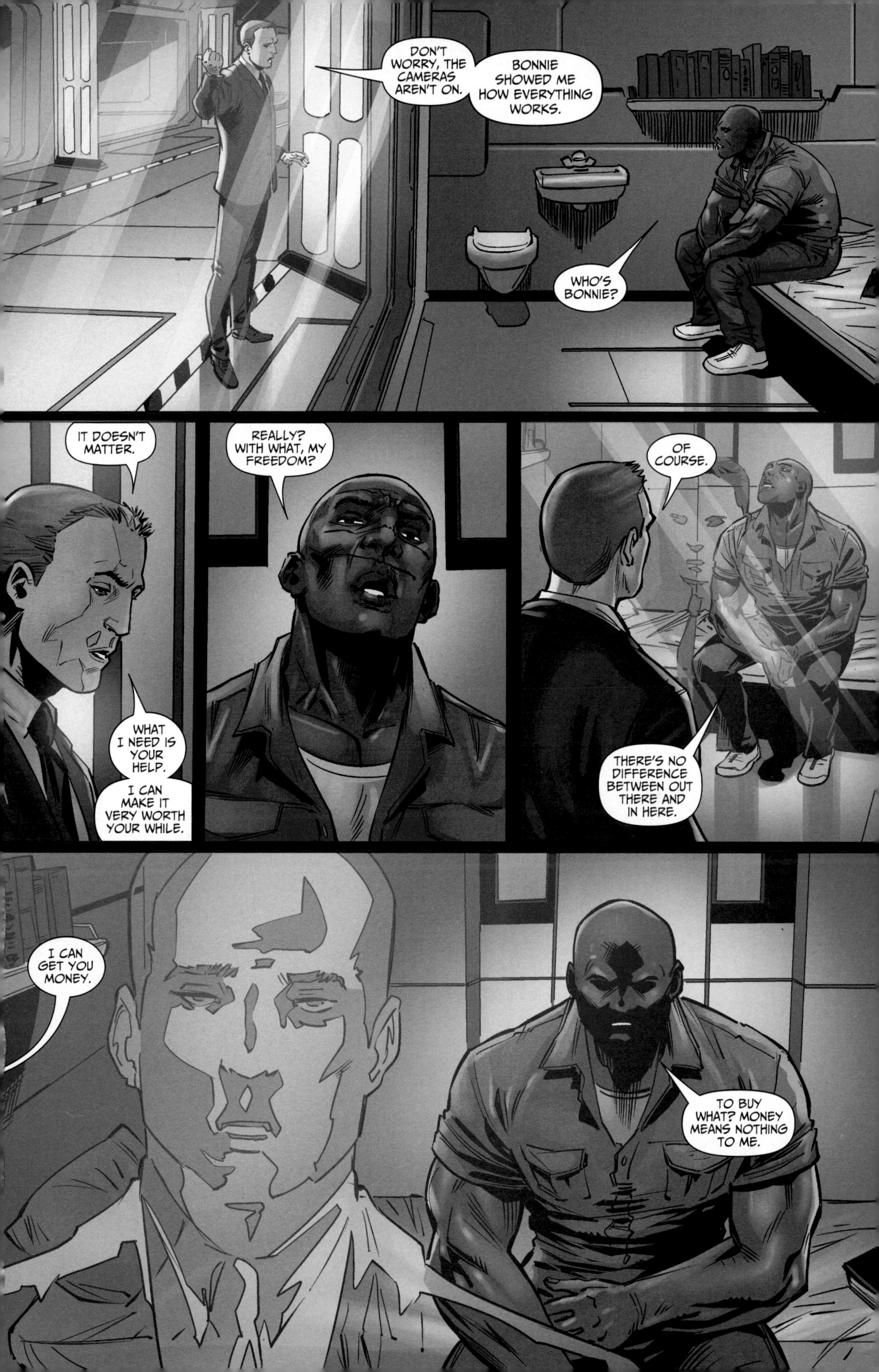
DON'T WORRY, THE CAMERAS AREN'T ON.
BONNIE SHOWED ME HOW EVERYTHING WORKS.
WHO'S BONNIE?
IT DOESN'T MATTER.
WHAT I NEED IS YOUR HELP.
I CAN MAKE IT VERY WORTH YOUR WHILE.
REALLY? WITH WHAT, MY FREEDOM?
OF COURSE.
THERE'S NO DIFFERENCE BETWEEN OUT THERE AND IN HERE.
I CAN GET YOU MONEY.
TO BUY WHAT? MONEY MEANS NOTHING TO ME.

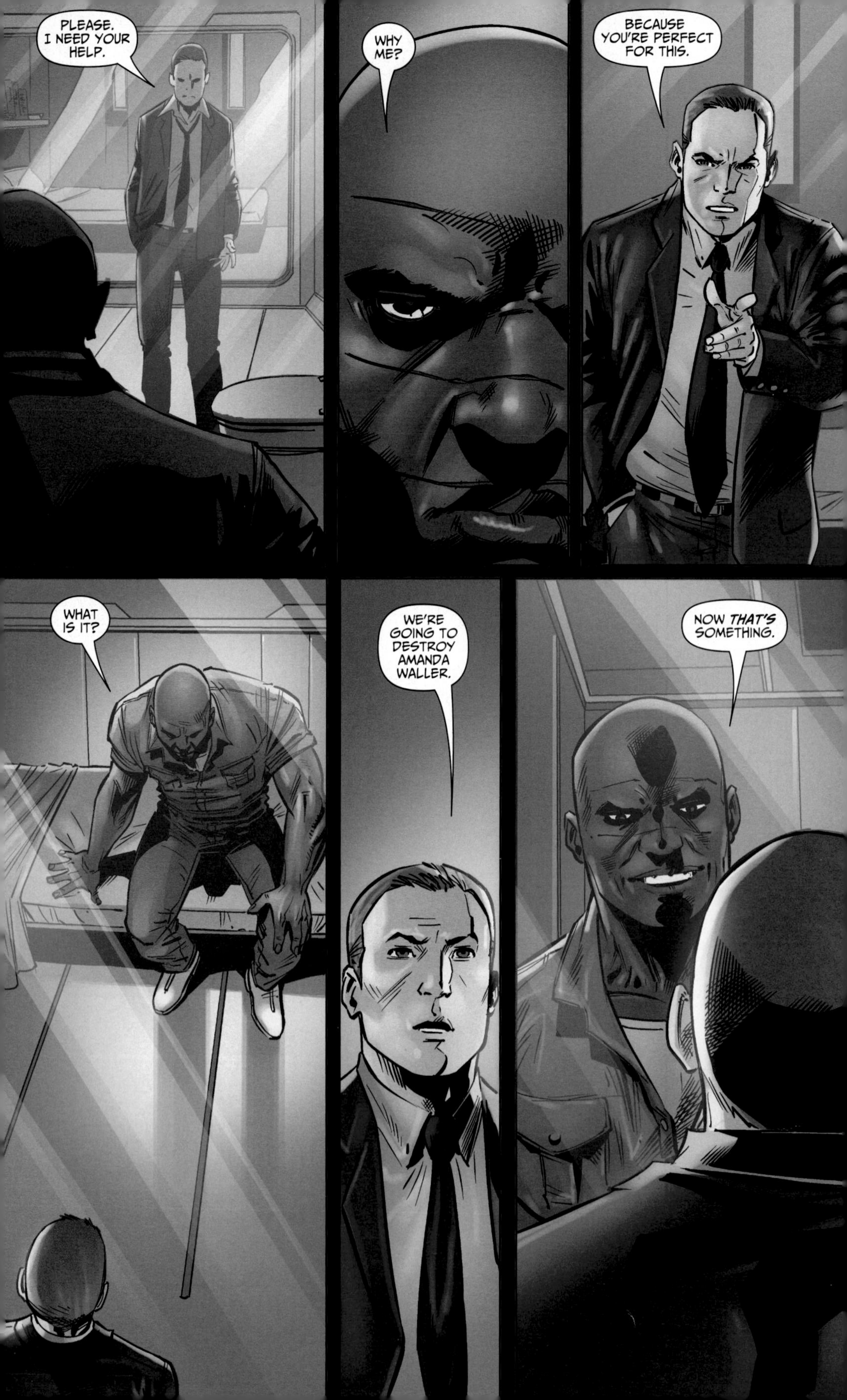
PLEASE. I NEED YOUR HELP.
WHY ME?
BECAUSE YOU'RE PERFECT FOR THIS.
WHAT IS IT?
WE'RE GOING TO DESTROY AMANDA WALLER.
NOW *THAT'S* SOMETHING.

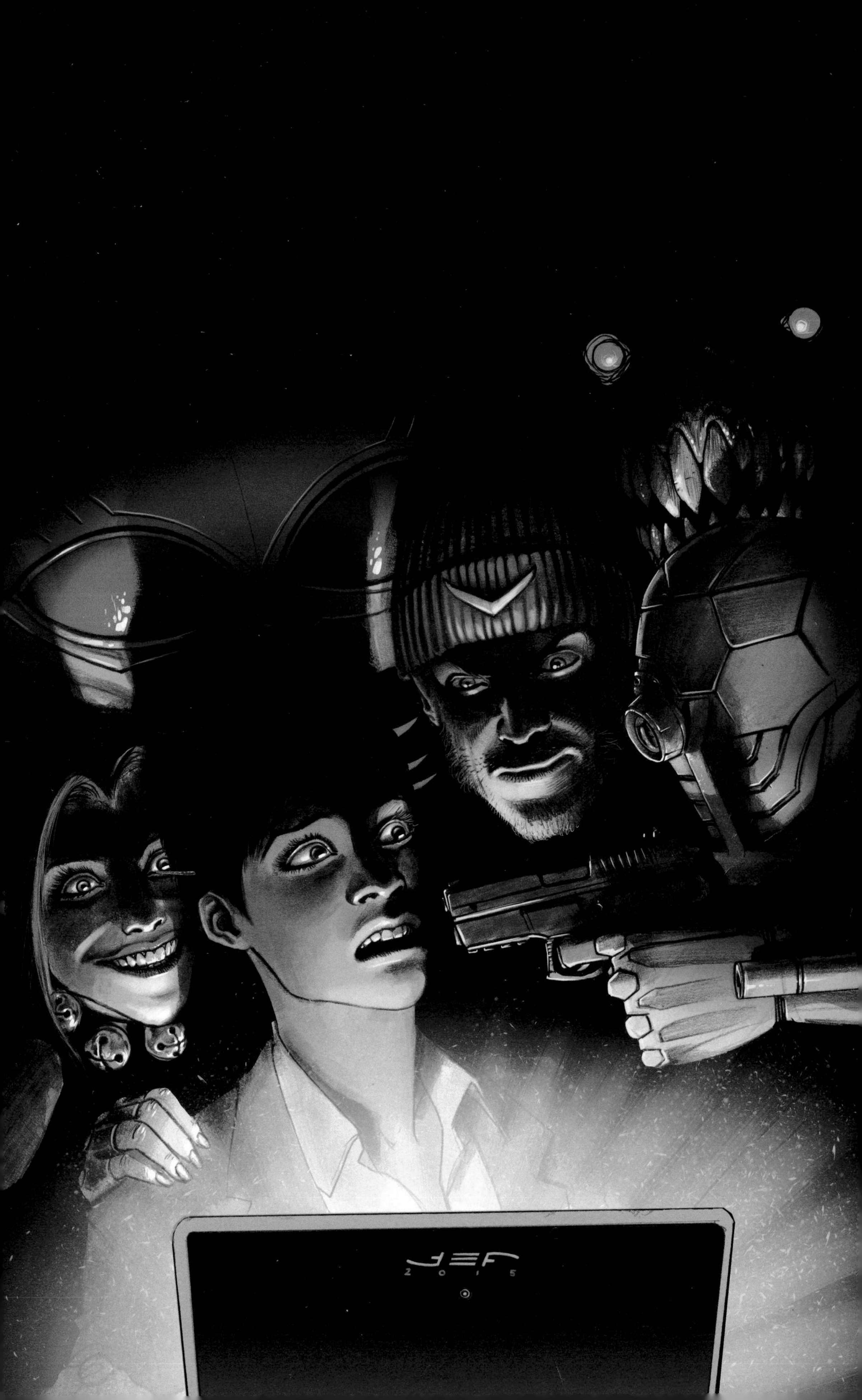

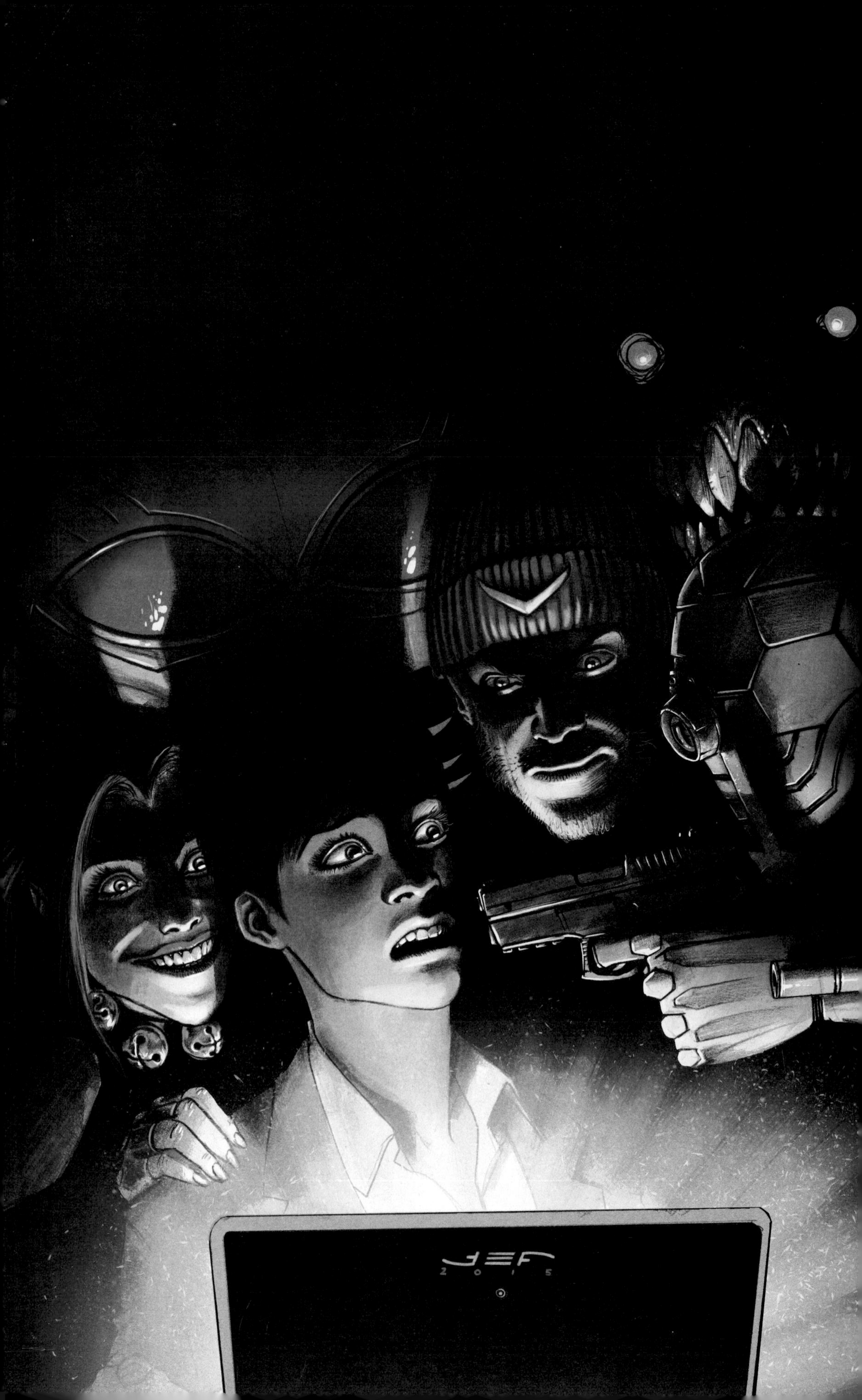

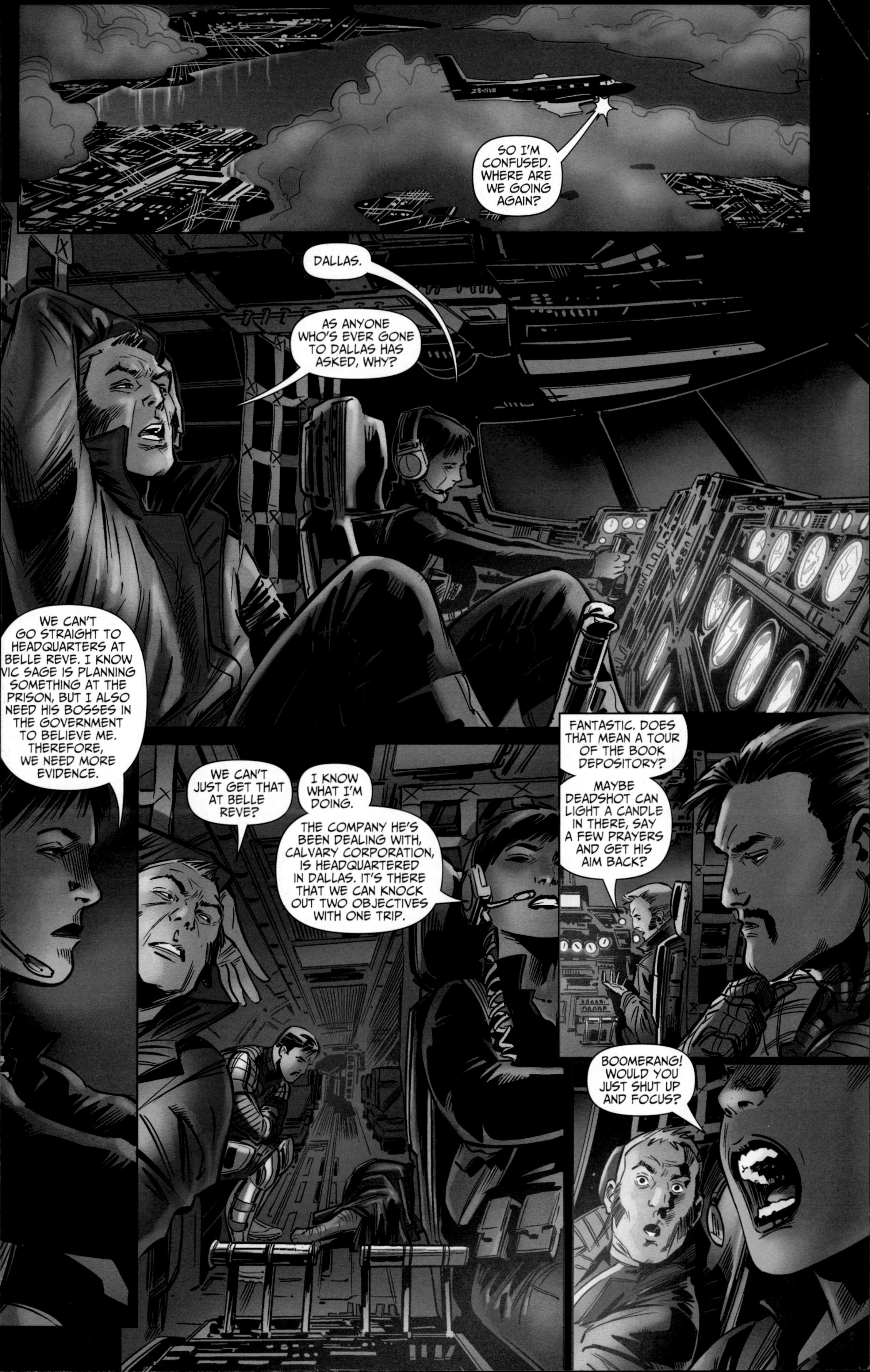
SO I'M CONFUSED. WHERE ARE WE GOING AGAIN?
DALLAS.
AS ANYONE WHO'S EVER GONE TO DALLAS HAS ASKED, WHY?
WE CAN'T GO STRAIGHT TO HEADQUARTERS AT BELLE REVE. I KNOW VIC SAGE IS PLANNING SOMETHING AT THE PRISON, BUT I ALSO NEED HIS BOSSES IN THE GOVERNMENT TO BELIEVE ME. THEREFORE, WE NEED MORE EVIDENCE.
WE CAN'T JUST GET THAT AT BELLE REVE?
I KNOW WHAT I'M DOING.
THE COMPANY HE'S BEEN DEALING WITH, CALVARY CORPORATION, IS HEADQUARTERED IN DALLAS. IT'S THERE THAT WE CAN KNOCK OUT TWO OBJECTIVES WITH ONE TRIP.
FANTASTIC. DOES THAT MEAN A TOUR OF THE BOOK DEPOSITORY?
MAYBE DEADSHOT CAN LIGHT A CANDLE IN THERE, SAY A FEW PRAYERS AND GET HIS AIM BACK?
BOOMERANG! WOULD YOU JUST SHUT UP AND FOCUS?

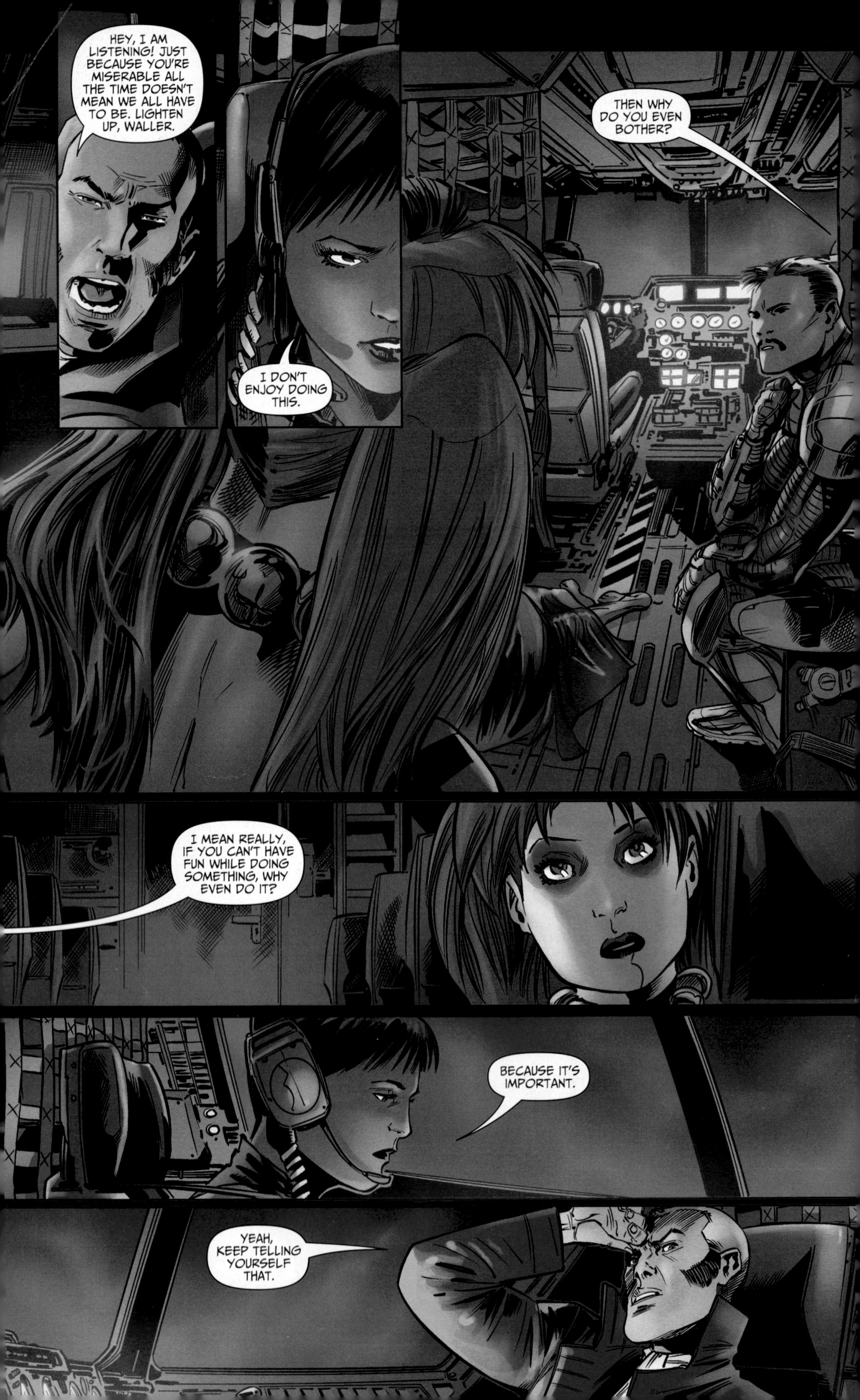
HEY, I AM LISTENING! JUST BECAUSE YOU'RE MISERABLE ALL THE TIME DOESN'T MEAN WE ALL HAVE TO BE. LIGHTEN UP, WALLER.
I DON'T ENJOY DOING THIS.
THEN WHY DO YOU EVEN BOTHER?
I MEAN REALLY, IF YOU CAN'T HAVE FUN WHILE DOING SOMETHING, WHY EVEN DO IT?
BECAUSE IT'S IMPORTANT.
YEAH, KEEP TELLING YOURSELF THAT.

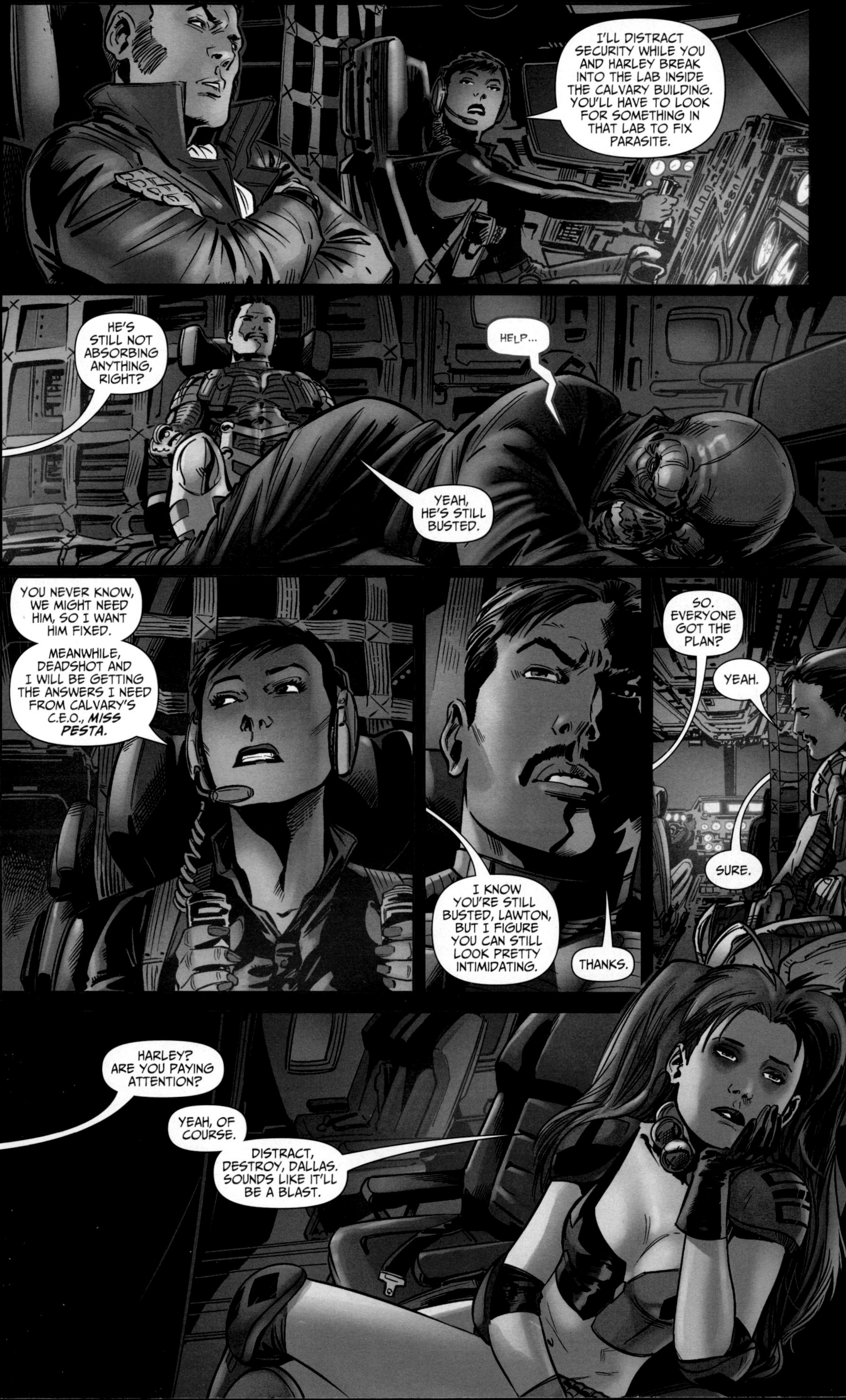
I'LL DISTRACT SECURITY WHILE YOU AND HARLEY BREAK INTO THE LAB INSIDE THE CALVARY BUILDING. YOU'LL HAVE TO LOOK FOR SOMETHING IN THAT LAB TO FIX PARASITE.
HE'S STILL NOT ABSORBING ANYTHING, RIGHT?
HELP...
YEAH, HE'S STILL BUSTED.
YOU NEVER KNOW, WE MIGHT NEED HIM, SO I WANT HIM FIXED.
MEANWHILE, DEADSHOT AND I WILL BE GETTING THE ANSWERS I NEED FROM CALVARY'S C.E.O., *MISS PESTA.*
I KNOW YOU'RE STILL BUSTED, LAWTON, BUT I FIGURE YOU CAN STILL LOOK PRETTY INTIMIDATING.
THANKS.
SO. EVERYONE GOT THE PLAN?
YEAH.
SURE.
HARLEY? ARE YOU PAYING ATTENTION?
YEAH, OF COURSE.
DISTRACT, DESTROY, DALLAS. SOUNDS LIKE IT'LL BE A BLAST.

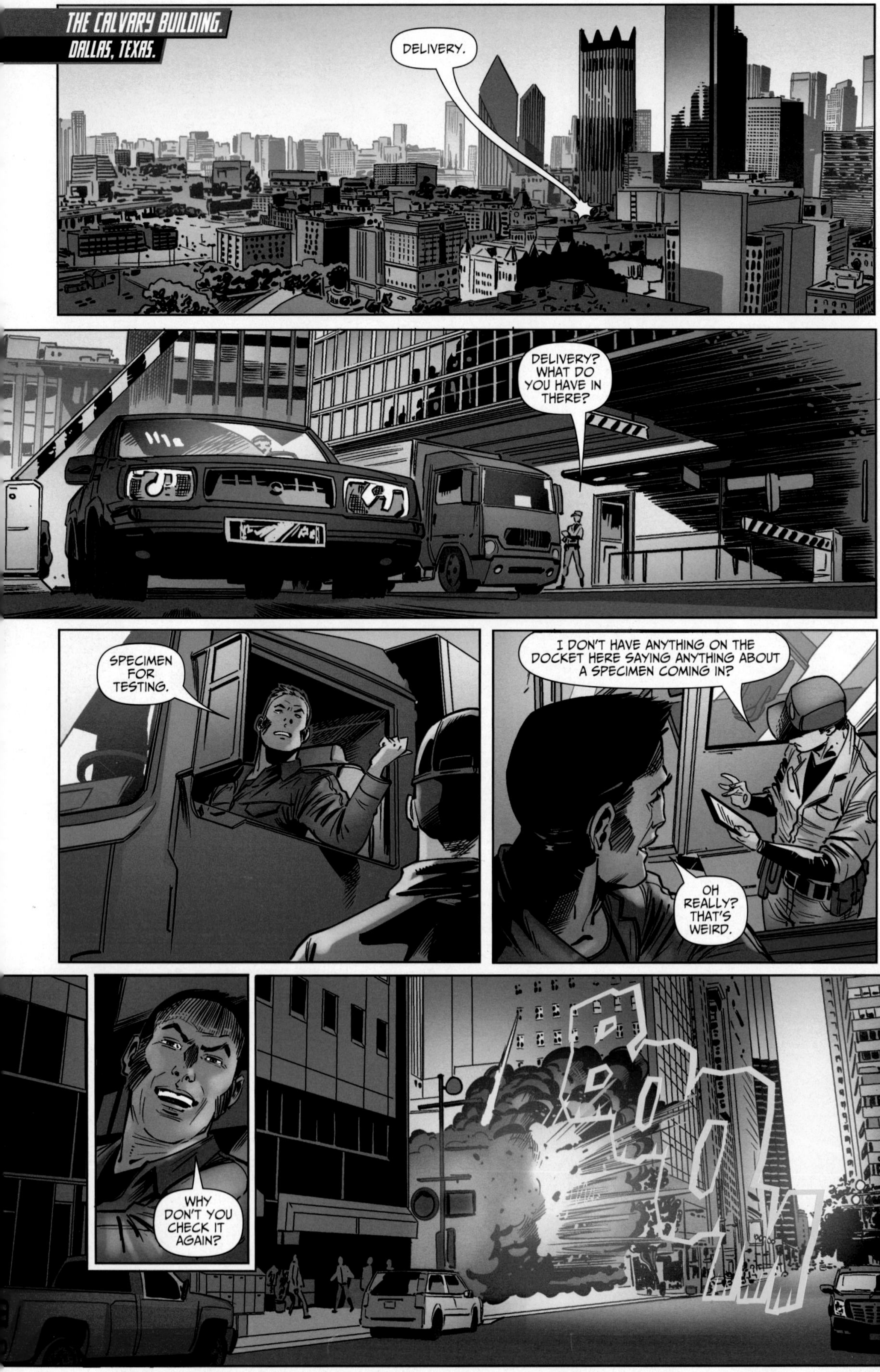
THE CALVARY BUILDING.
DALLAS, TEXAS.
DELIVERY.
DELIVERY? WHAT DO YOU HAVE IN THERE?
SPECIMEN FOR TESTING.
I DON'T HAVE ANYTHING ON THE DOCKET HERE SAYING ANYTHING ABOUT A SPECIMEN COMING IN?
OH REALLY? THAT'S WEIRD.
WHY DON'T YOU CHECK IT AGAIN?

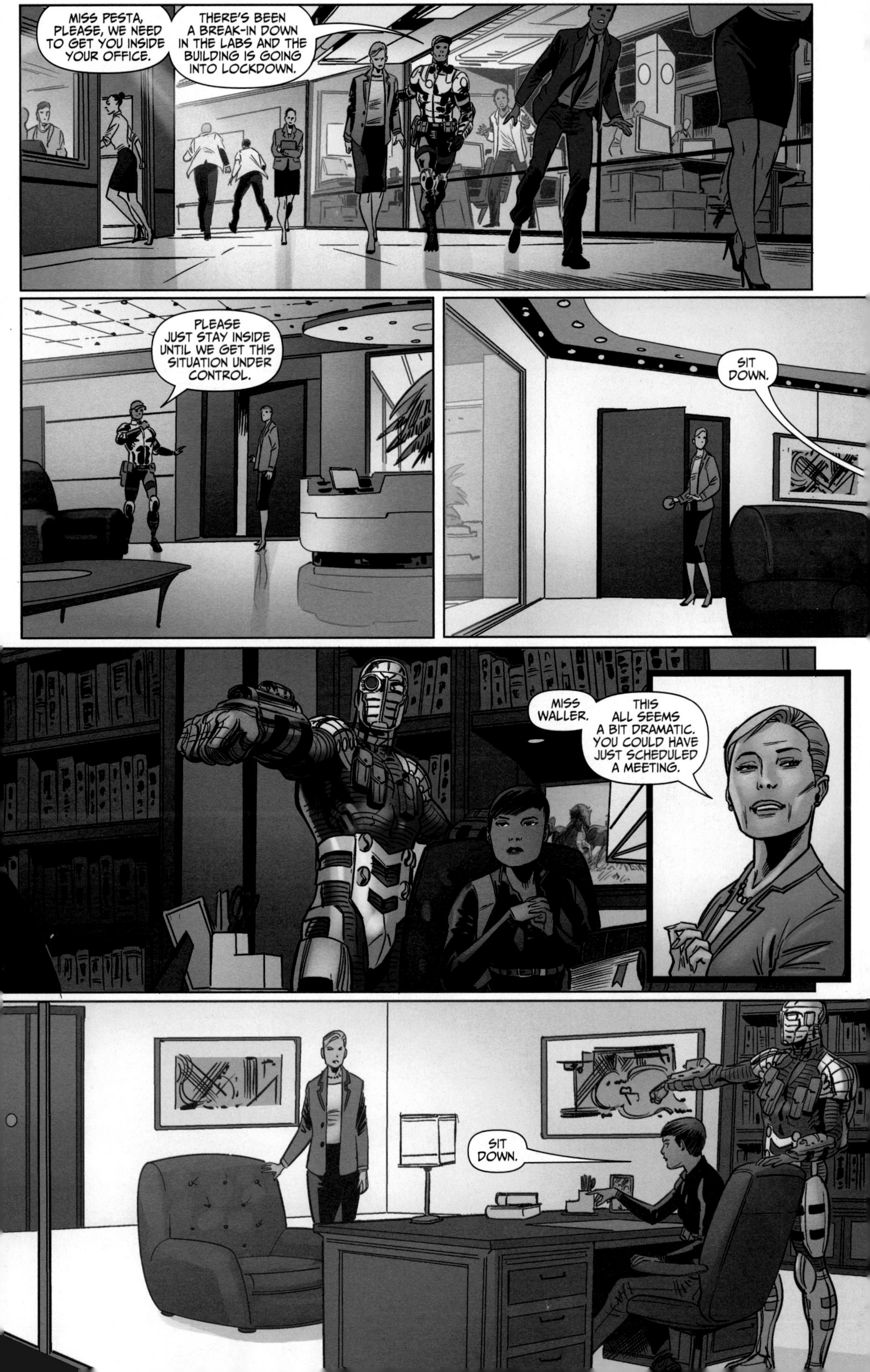
MISS PESTA, PLEASE, WE NEED TO GET YOU INSIDE YOUR OFFICE.
THERE'S BEEN A BREAK-IN DOWN IN THE LABS AND THE BUILDING IS GOING INTO LOCKDOWN.
PLEASE JUST STAY INSIDE UNTIL WE GET THIS SITUATION UNDER CONTROL.
SIT DOWN.
MISS WALLER.
THIS ALL SEEMS A BIT DRAMATIC. YOU COULD HAVE JUST SCHEDULED A MEETING.
SIT DOWN.

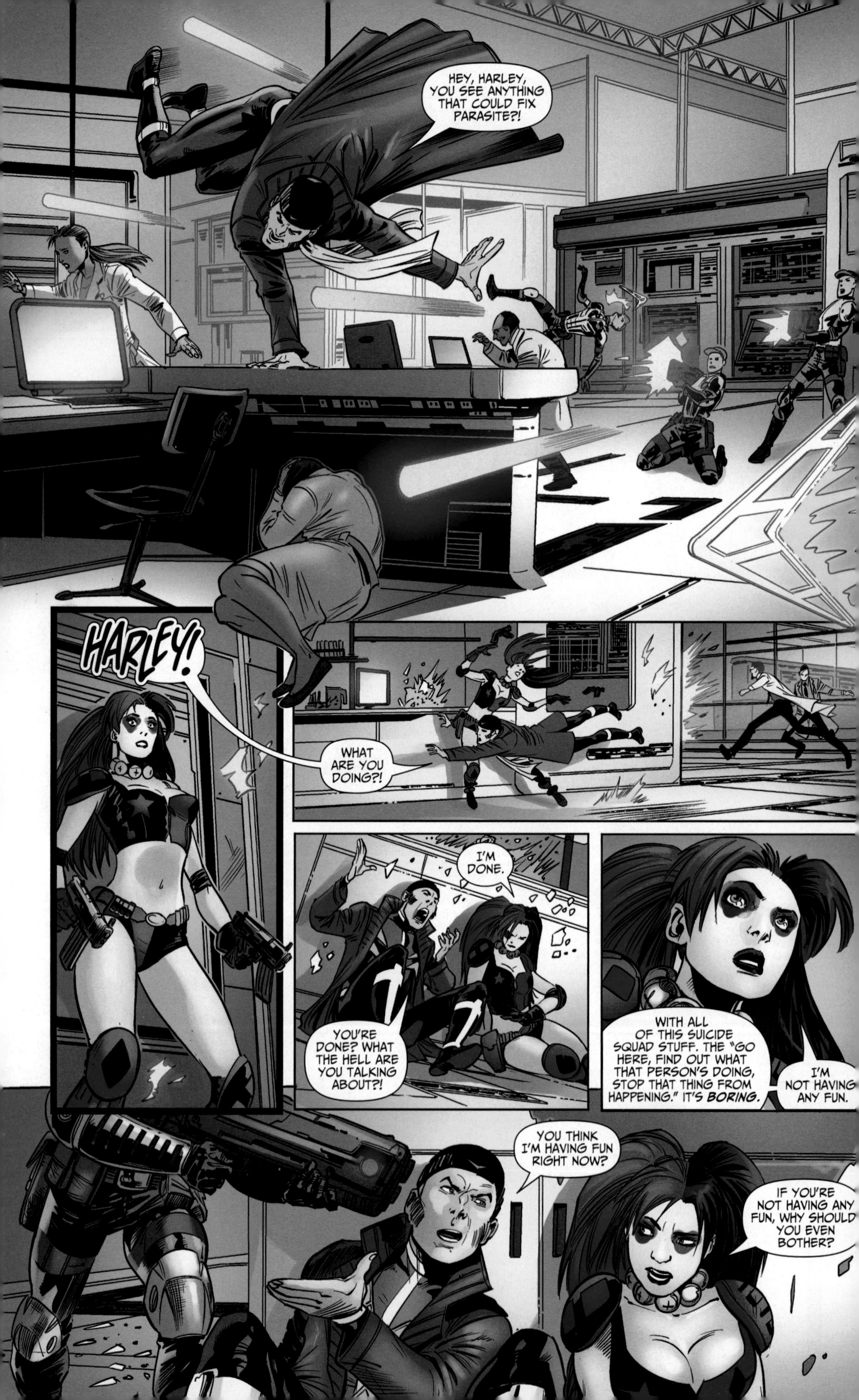

HEY, HARLEY, YOU SEE ANYTHING THAT COULD FIX PARASITE?!
HARLEY!
WHAT ARE YOU DOING?!
I'M DONE.
YOU'RE DONE? WHAT THE HELL ARE YOU TALKING ABOUT?!
WITH ALL OF THIS SUICIDE SQUAD STUFF. THE "GO HERE, FIND OUT WHAT THAT PERSON'S DOING, STOP THAT THING FROM HAPPENING." IT'S BORING.
I'M NOT HAVING ANY FUN.
YOU THINK I'M HAVING FUN RIGHT NOW?
IF YOU'RE NOT HAVING ANY FUN, WHY SHOULD YOU EVEN BOTHER?

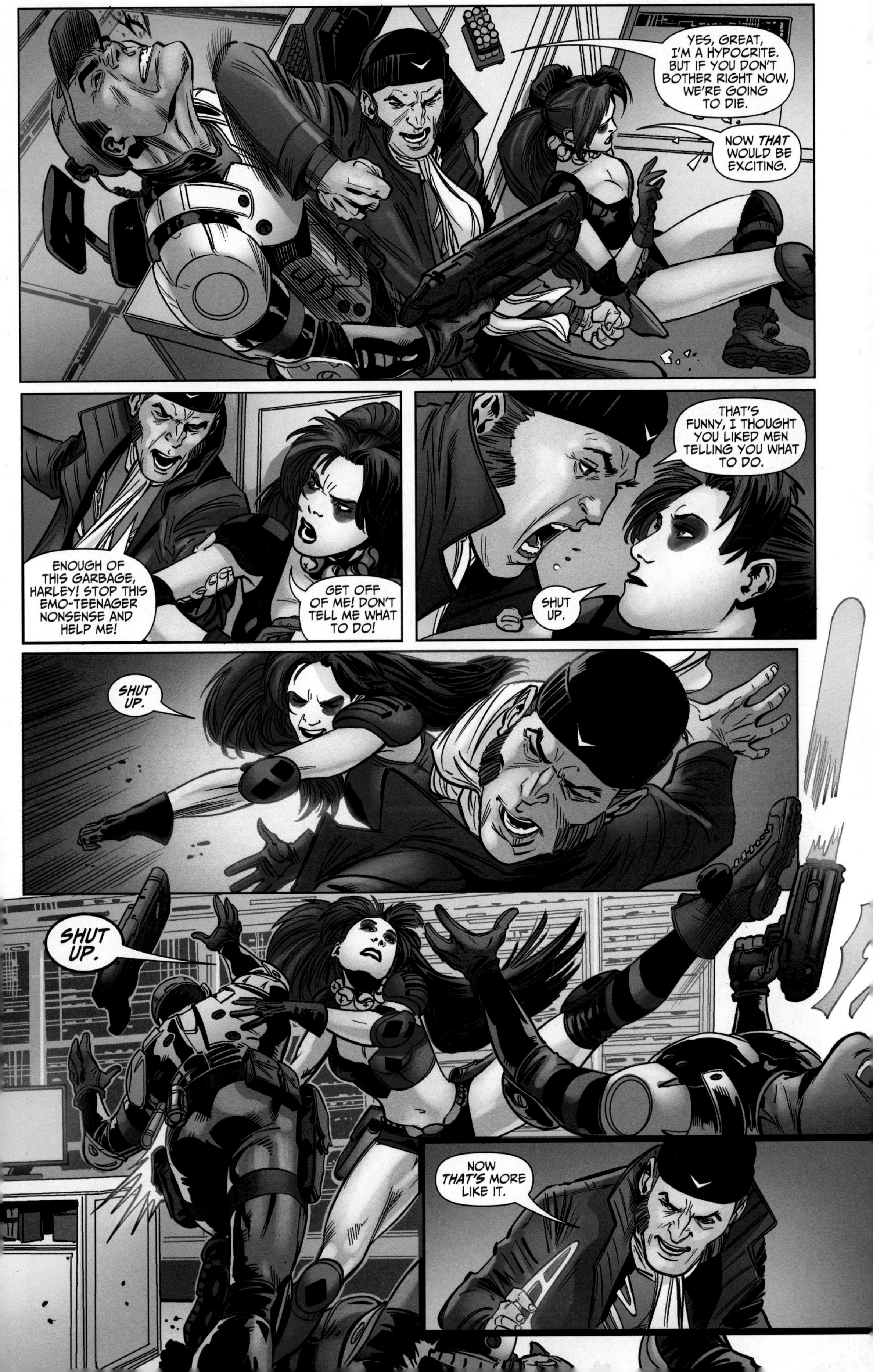
YES, GREAT, I'M A HYPOCRITE. BUT IF YOU DON'T BOTHER RIGHT NOW, WE'RE GOING TO DIE.
NOW *THAT* WOULD BE EXCITING.
ENOUGH OF THIS GARBAGE, HARLEY! STOP THIS EMO-TEENAGER NONSENSE AND HELP ME!
GET OFF OF ME! DON'T TELL ME WHAT TO DO!
THAT'S FUNNY, I THOUGHT YOU LIKED MEN TELLING YOU WHAT TO DO.
SHUT UP.
SHUT UP.
SHUT UP.
NOW *THAT'S* MORE LIKE IT.

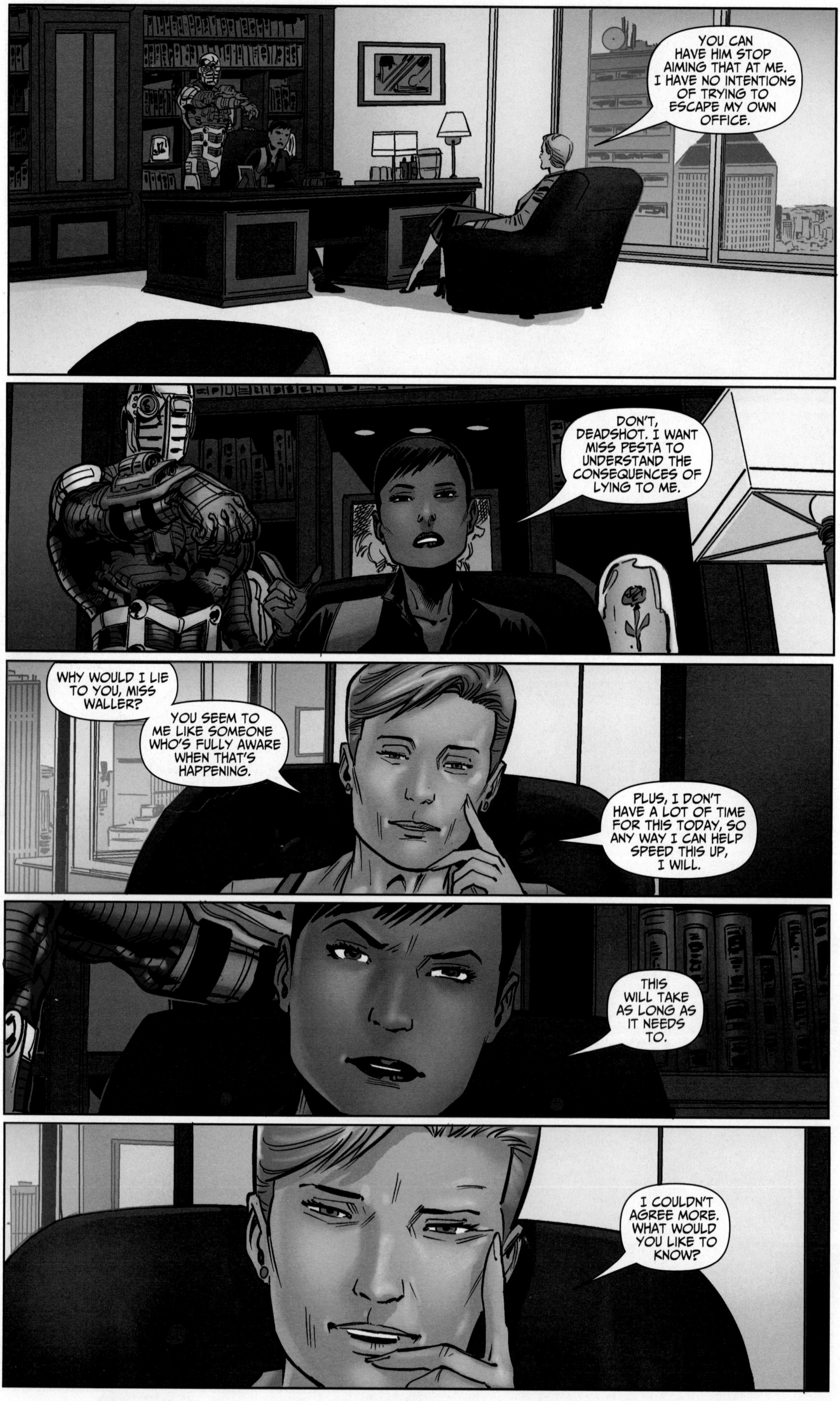
YOU CAN HAVE HIM STOP AIMING THAT AT ME. I HAVE NO INTENTIONS OF TRYING TO ESCAPE MY OWN OFFICE.
DON'T, DEADSHOT. I WANT MISS PESTA TO UNDERSTAND THE CONSEQUENCES OF LYING TO ME.
WHY WOULD I LIE TO YOU, MISS WALLER?
YOU SEEM TO ME LIKE SOMEONE WHO'S FULLY AWARE WHEN THAT'S HAPPENING.
PLUS, I DON'T HAVE A LOT OF TIME FOR THIS TODAY, SO ANY WAY I CAN HELP SPEED THIS UP, I WILL.
THIS WILL TAKE AS LONG AS IT NEEDS TO.
I COULDN'T AGREE MORE. WHAT WOULD YOU LIKE TO KNOW?

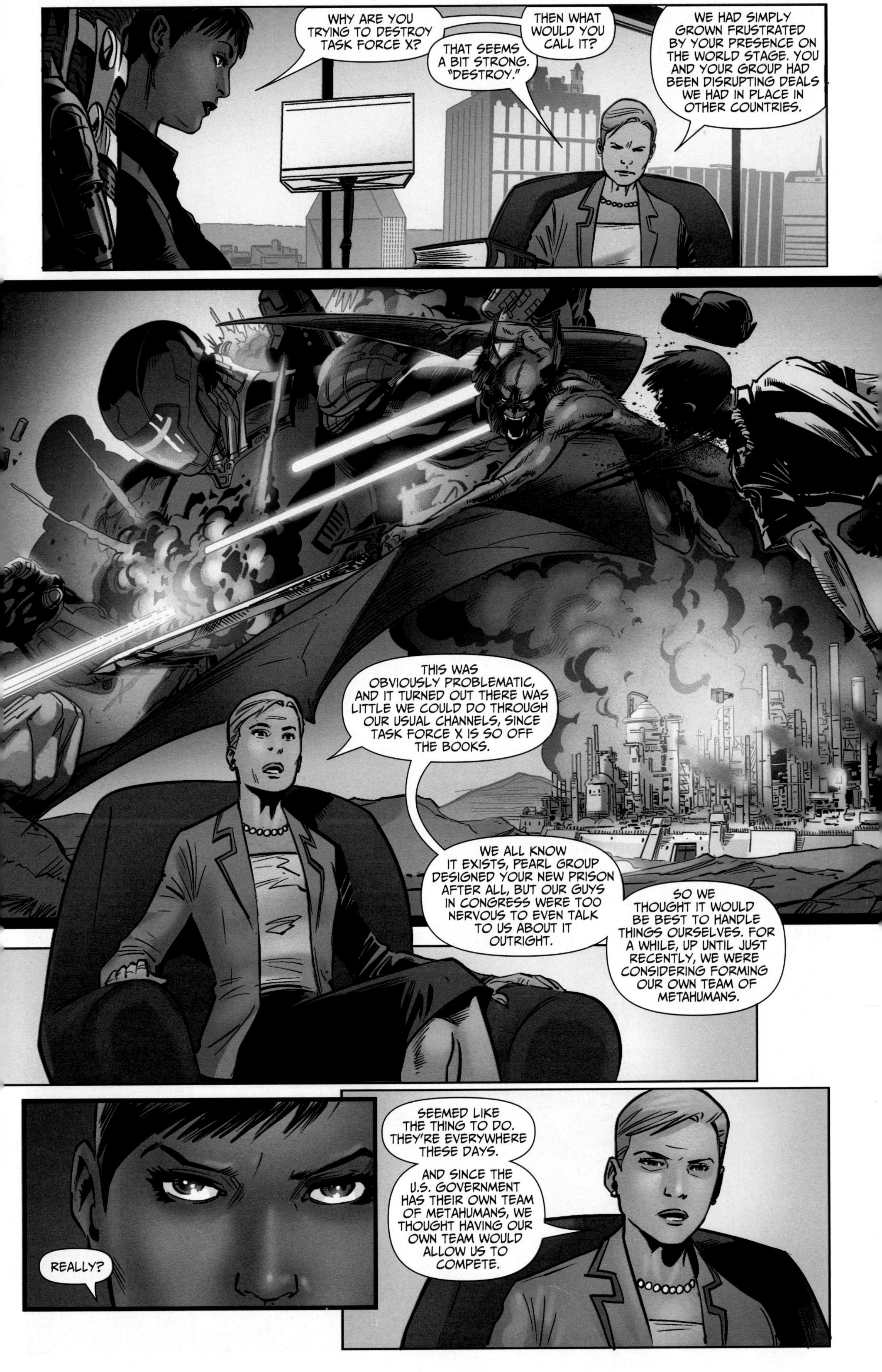
WHY ARE YOU TRYING TO DESTROY TASK FORCE X?
THAT SEEMS A BIT STRONG. "DESTROY."
THEN WHAT WOULD YOU CALL IT?
WE HAD SIMPLY GROWN FRUSTRATED BY YOUR PRESENCE ON THE WORLD STAGE. YOU AND YOUR GROUP HAD BEEN DISRUPTING DEALS WE HAD IN PLACE IN OTHER COUNTRIES.
THIS WAS OBVIOUSLY PROBLEMATIC, AND IT TURNED OUT THERE WAS LITTLE WE COULD DO THROUGH OUR USUAL CHANNELS, SINCE TASK FORCE X IS SO OFF THE BOOKS.
WE ALL KNOW IT EXISTS, PEARL GROUP DESIGNED YOUR NEW PRISON AFTER ALL, BUT OUR GUYS IN CONGRESS WERE TOO NERVOUS TO EVEN TALK TO US ABOUT IT OUTRIGHT.
SO WE THOUGHT IT WOULD BE BEST TO HANDLE THINGS OURSELVES. FOR A WHILE, UP UNTIL JUST RECENTLY, WE WERE CONSIDERING FORMING OUR OWN TEAM OF METAHUMANS.
REALLY?
SEEMED LIKE THE THING TO DO. THEY'RE EVERYWHERE THESE DAYS.
AND SINCE THE U.S. GOVERNMENT HAS THEIR OWN TEAM OF METAHUMANS, WE THOUGHT HAVING OUR OWN TEAM WOULD ALLOW US TO COMPETE.

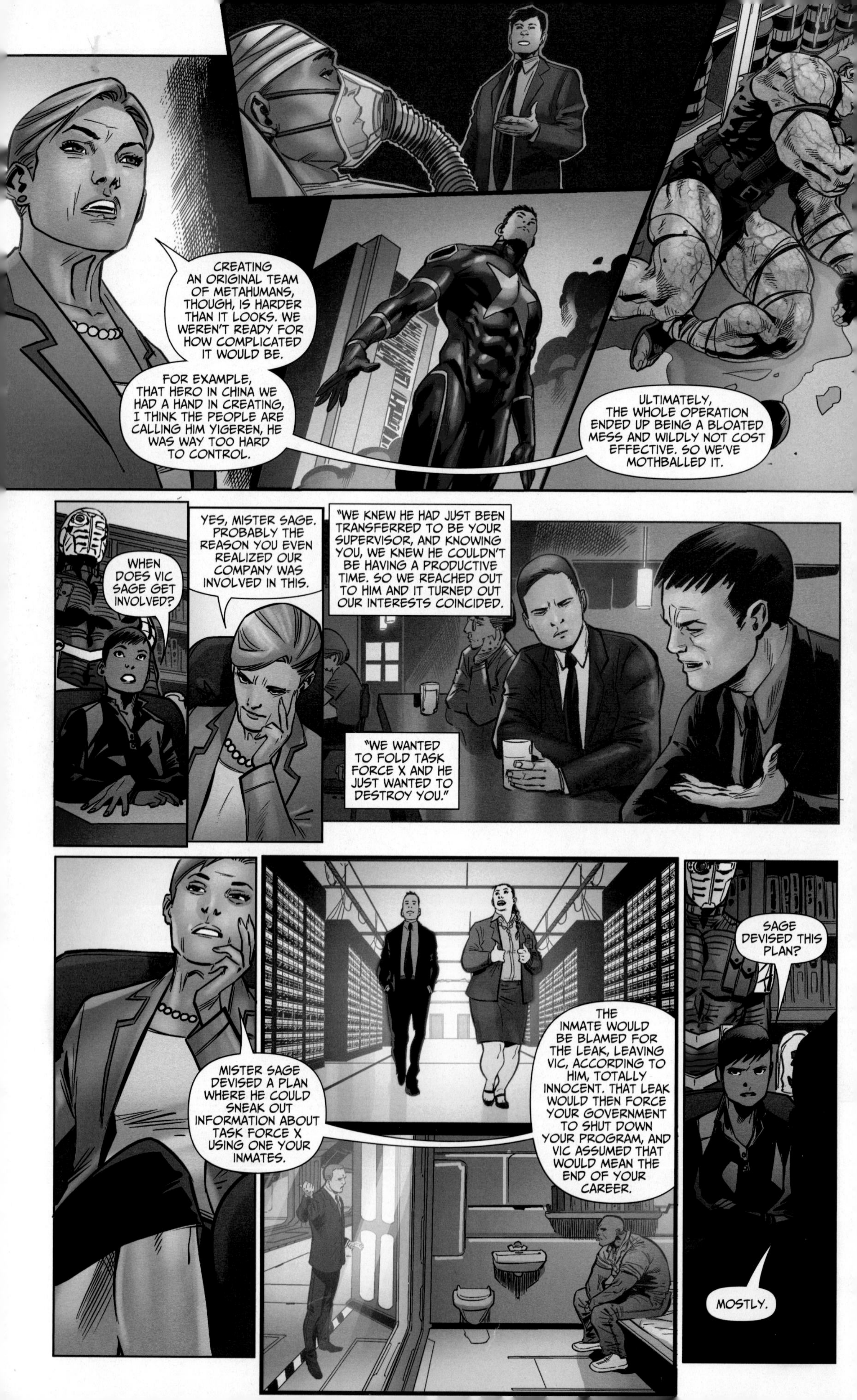
CREATING AN ORIGINAL TEAM OF METAHUMANS, THOUGH, IS HARDER THAN IT LOOKS. WE WEREN'T READY FOR HOW COMPLICATED IT WOULD BE.
FOR EXAMPLE, THAT HERO IN CHINA WE HAD A HAND IN CREATING, I THINK THE PEOPLE ARE CALLING HIM YIGEREN, HE WAS WAY TOO HARD TO CONTROL.
ULTIMATELY, THE WHOLE OPERATION ENDED UP BEING A BLOATED MESS AND WILDLY NOT COST EFFECTIVE. SO WE'VE MOTHBALLED IT.
WHEN DOES VIC SAGE GET INVOLVED?
YES, MISTER SAGE. PROBABLY THE REASON YOU EVEN REALIZED OUR COMPANY WAS INVOLVED IN THIS.
"WE KNEW HE HAD JUST BEEN TRANSFERRED TO BE YOUR SUPERVISOR, AND KNOWING YOU, WE KNEW HE COULDN'T BE HAVING A PRODUCTIVE TIME. SO WE REACHED OUT TO HIM AND IT TURNED OUT OUR INTERESTS COINCIDED.
"WE WANTED TO FOLD TASK FORCE X AND HE JUST WANTED TO DESTROY YOU."
MISTER SAGE DEVISED A PLAN WHERE HE COULD SNEAK OUT INFORMATION ABOUT TASK FORCE X USING ONE YOUR INMATES.
THE INMATE WOULD BE BLAMED FOR THE LEAK, LEAVING VIC, ACCORDING TO HIM, TOTALLY INNOCENT. THAT LEAK WOULD THEN FORCE YOUR GOVERNMENT TO SHUT DOWN YOUR PROGRAM, AND VIC ASSUMED THAT WOULD MEAN THE END OF YOUR CAREER.
SAGE DEVISED THIS PLAN?
MOSTLY.

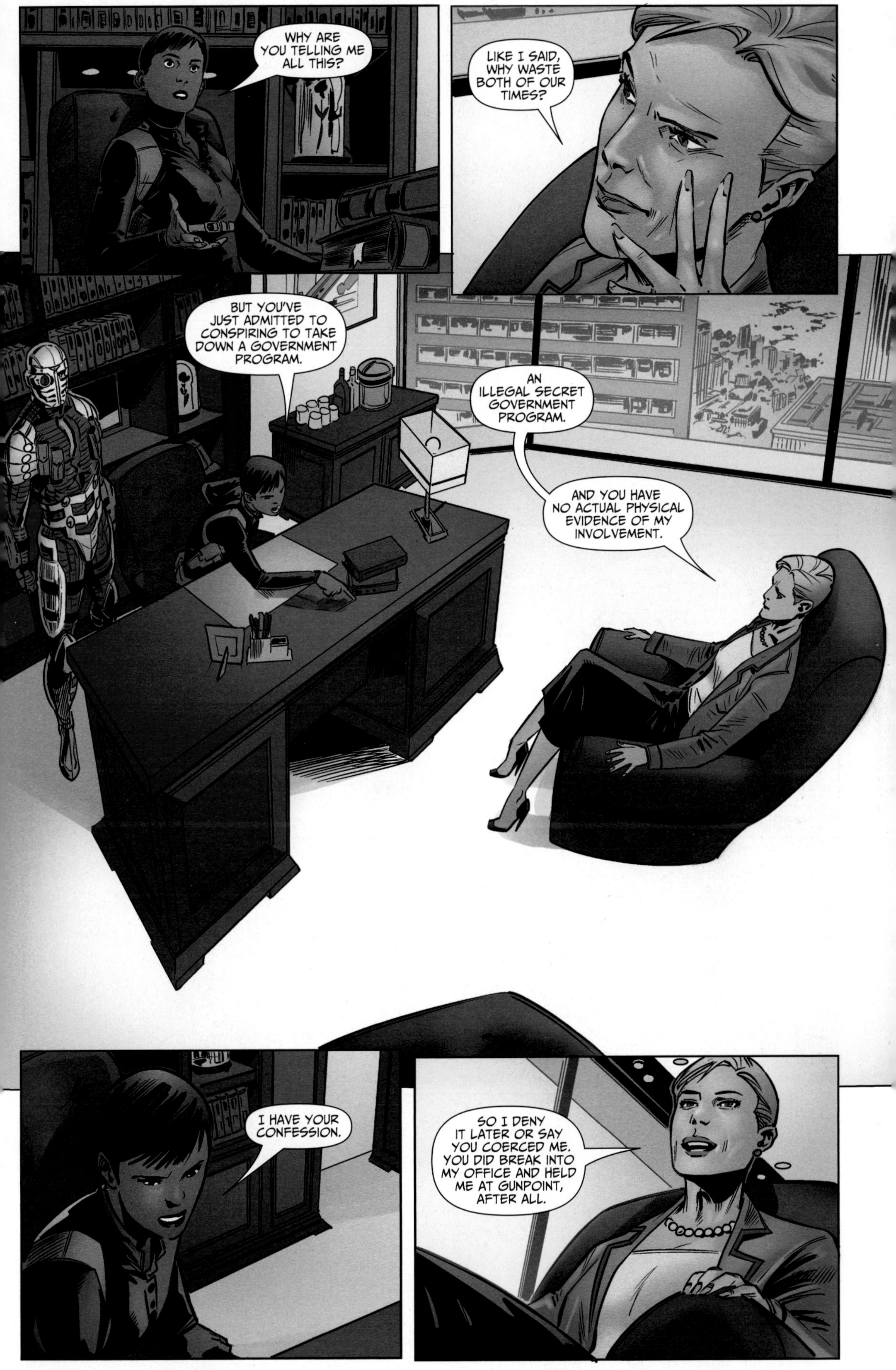
WHY ARE YOU TELLING ME ALL THIS?
LIKE I SAID, WHY WASTE BOTH OF OUR TIMES?
BUT YOU'VE JUST ADMITTED TO CONSPIRING TO TAKE DOWN A GOVERNMENT PROGRAM.
AN ILLEGAL SECRET GOVERNMENT PROGRAM.
AND YOU HAVE NO ACTUAL PHYSICAL EVIDENCE OF MY INVOLVEMENT.
I HAVE YOUR CONFESSION.
SO I DENY IT LATER OR SAY YOU COERCED ME. YOU DID BREAK INTO MY OFFICE AND HELD ME AT GUNPOINT, AFTER ALL.

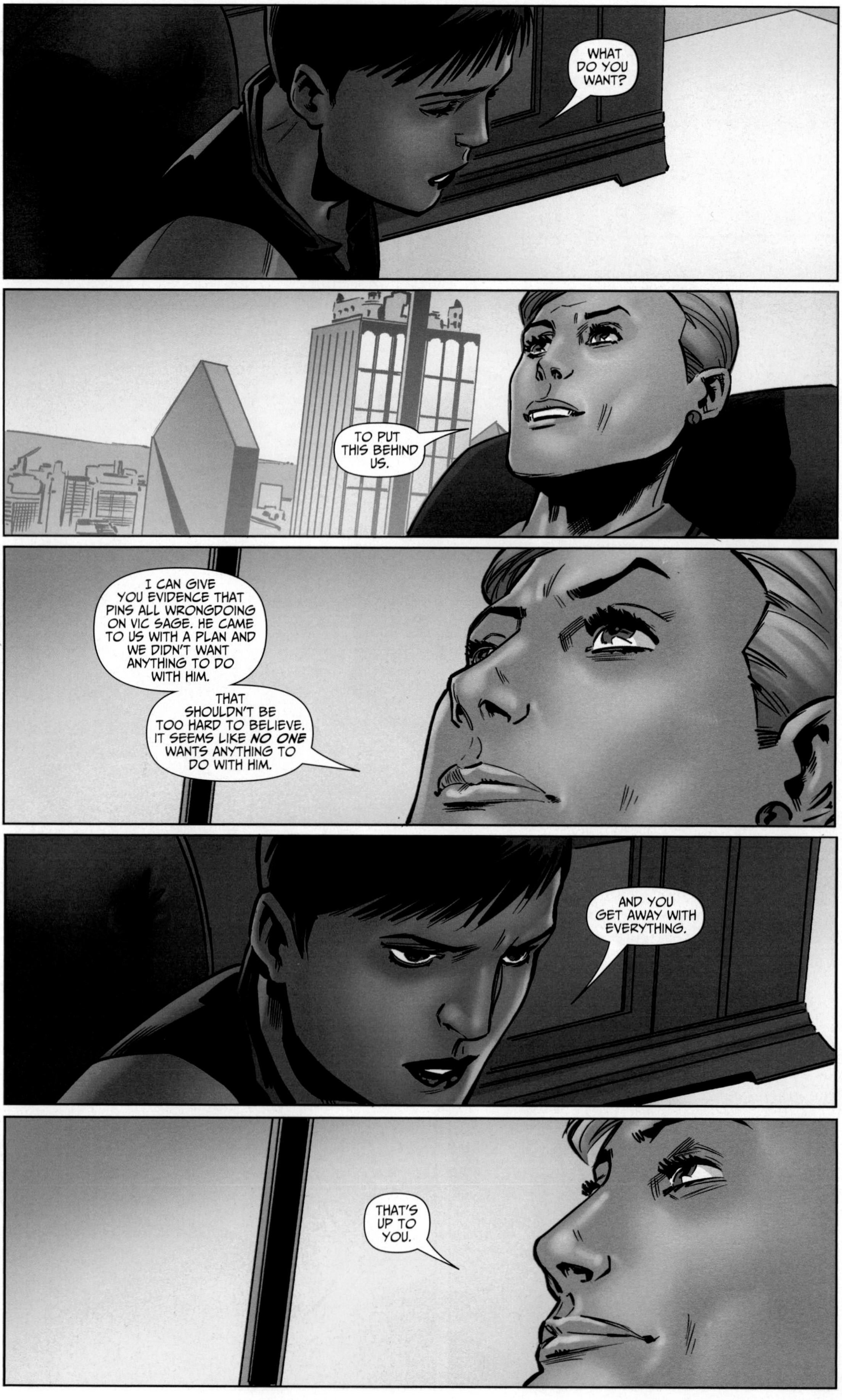
WHAT DO YOU WANT?
TO PUT THIS BEHIND US.
I CAN GIVE YOU EVIDENCE THAT PINS ALL WRONGDOING ON VIC SAGE. HE CAME TO US WITH A PLAN AND WE DIDN'T WANT ANYTHING TO DO WITH HIM.
THAT SHOULDN'T BE TOO HARD TO BELIEVE. IT SEEMS LIKE *NO ONE* WANTS ANYTHING TO DO WITH HIM.
AND YOU GET AWAY WITH EVERYTHING.
THAT'S UP TO YOU.

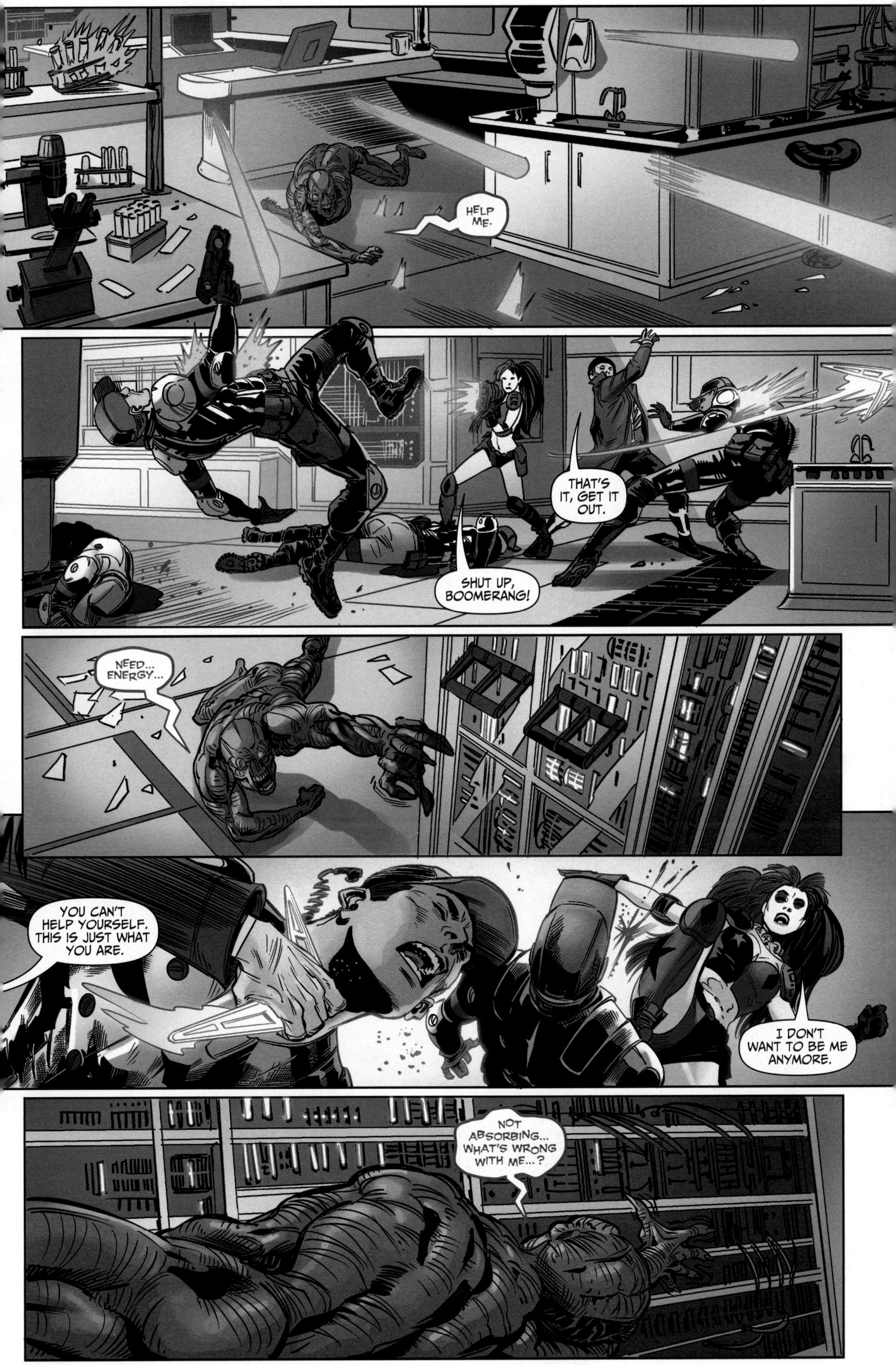
HELP ME.
THAT'S IT, GET IT OUT.
SHUT UP, BOOMERANG!
NEED... ENERGY...
YOU CAN'T HELP YOURSELF. THIS IS JUST WHAT YOU ARE.
I DON'T WANT TO BE ME ANYMORE.
NOT ABSORBING... WHAT'S WRONG WITH ME...?

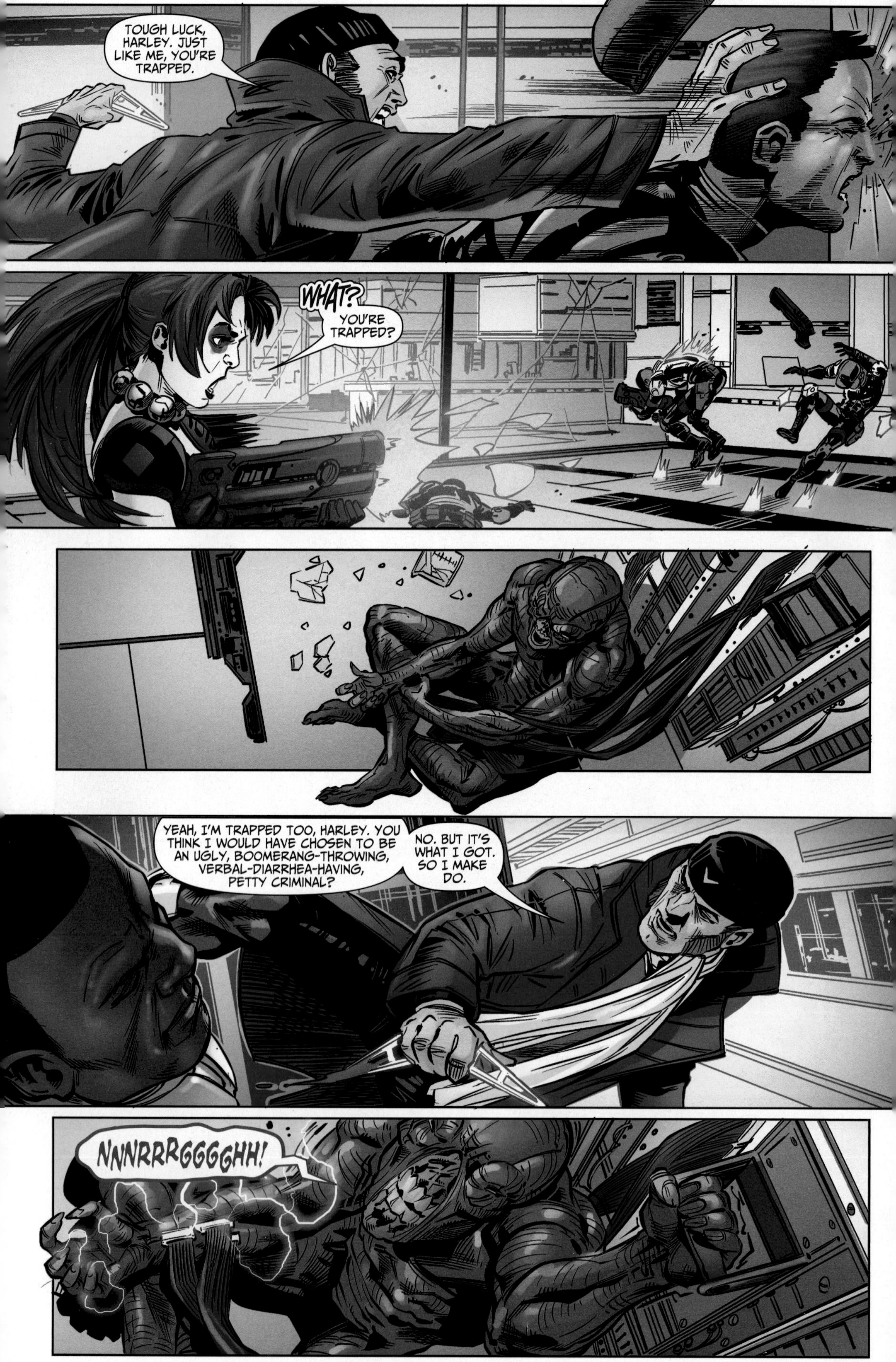
TOUGH LUCK, HARLEY. JUST LIKE ME, YOU'RE TRAPPED.
WHAT?
YOU'RE TRAPPED?
YEAH, I'M TRAPPED TOO, HARLEY. YOU THINK I WOULD HAVE CHOSEN TO BE AN UGLY, BOOMERANG-THROWING, VERBAL-DIARRHEA-HAVING, PETTY CRIMINAL?
NO. BUT IT'S WHAT I GOT. SO I MAKE DO.
NNNRRRGGGGHH!

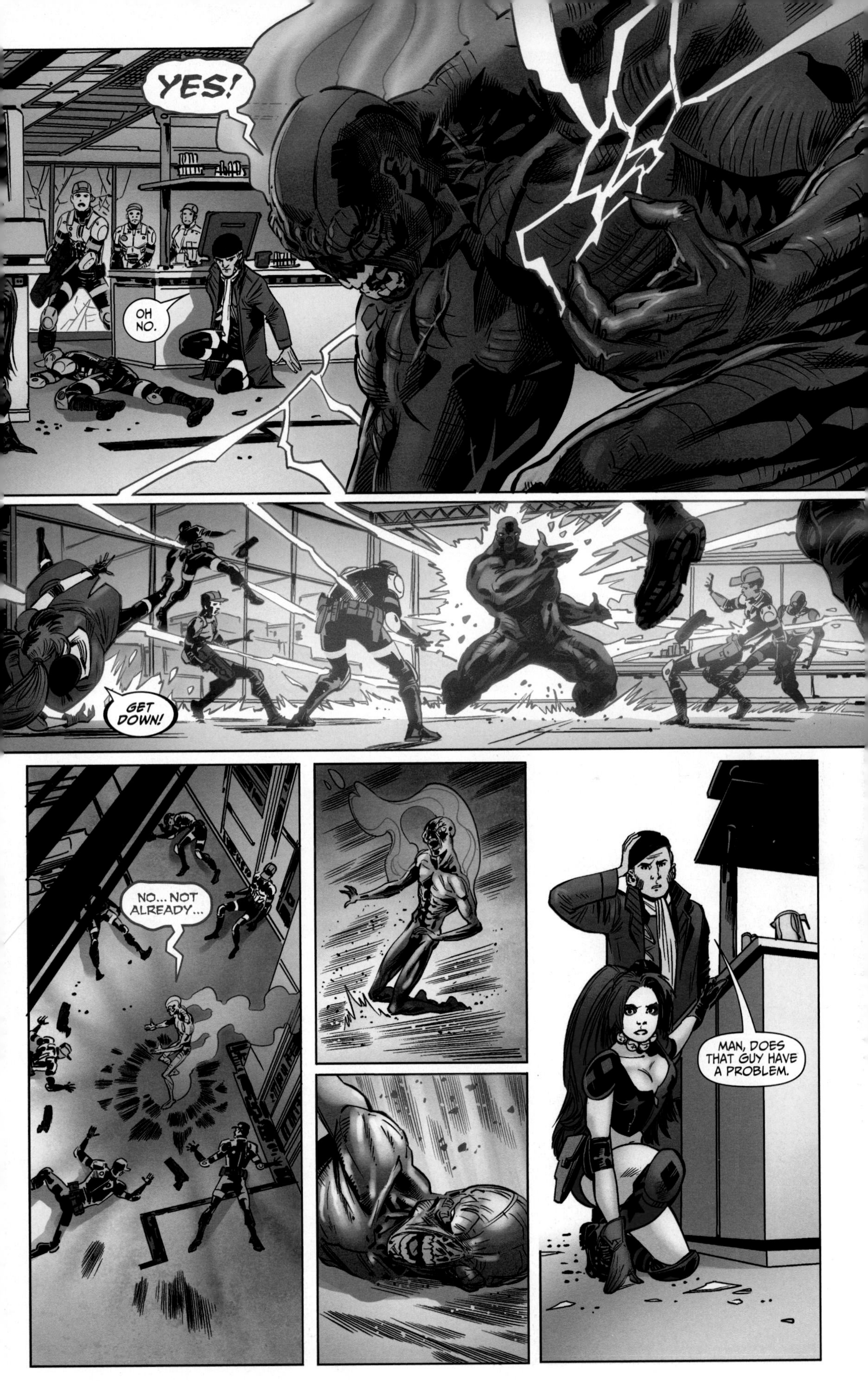
YES!
OH NO.
GET DOWN!
NO... NOT ALREADY...
MAN, DOES THAT GUY HAVE A PROBLEM.

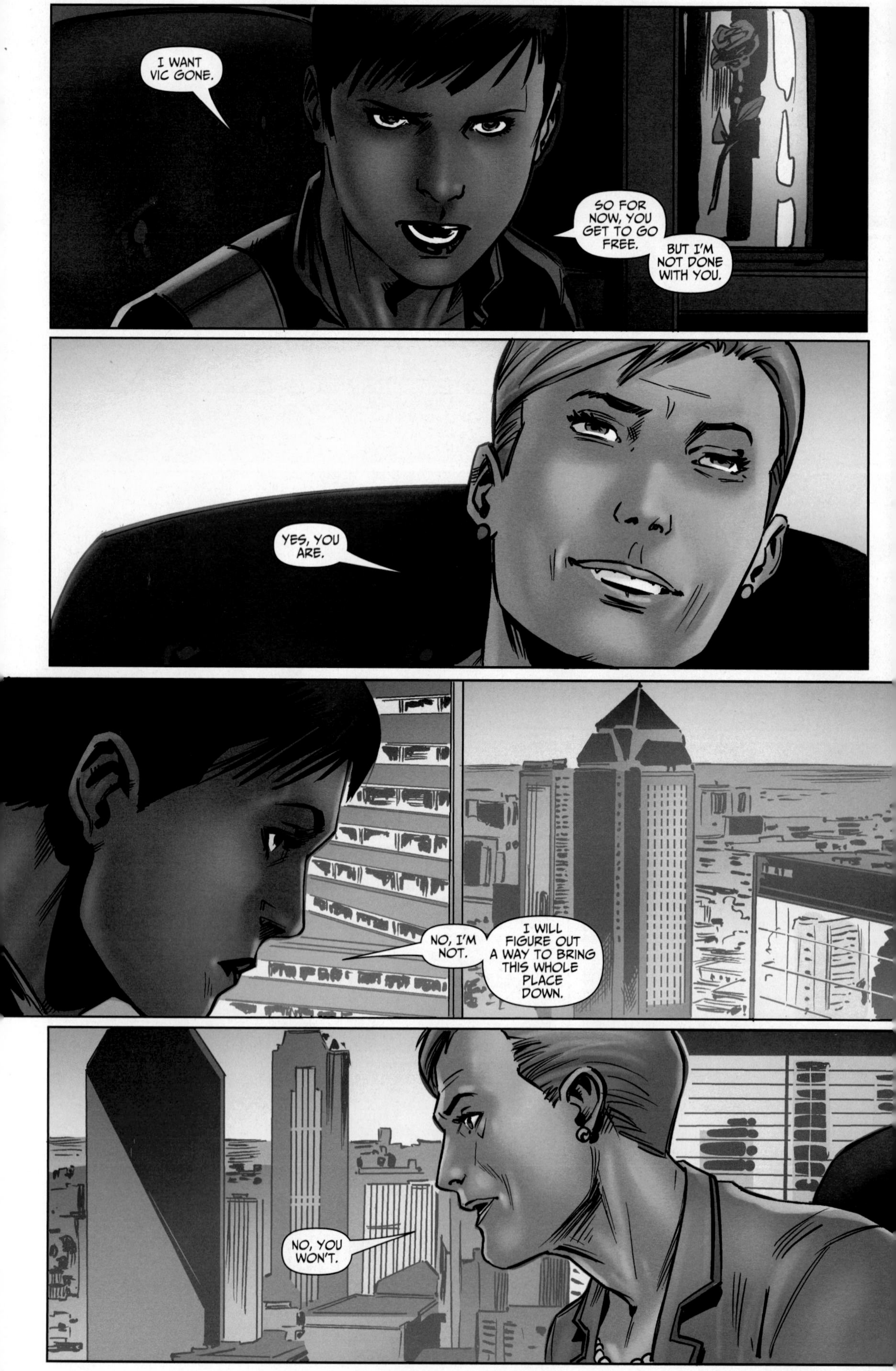
I WANT VIC GONE.
SO FOR NOW, YOU GET TO GO FREE.
BUT I'M NOT DONE WITH YOU.
YES, YOU ARE.
NO, I'M NOT.
I WILL FIGURE OUT A WAY TO BRING THIS WHOLE PLACE DOWN.
NO, YOU WON'T.

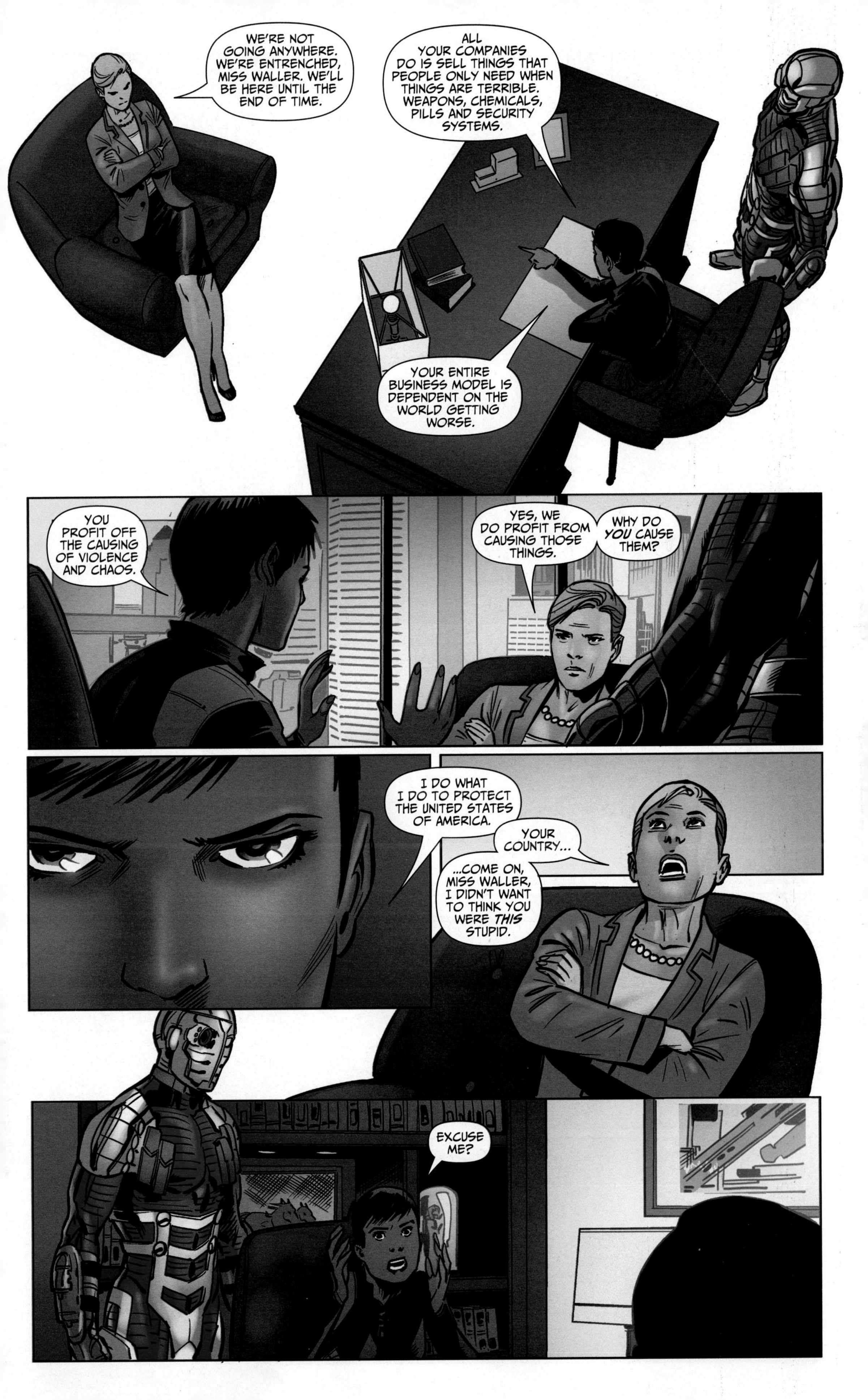
WE'RE NOT GOING ANYWHERE. WE'RE ENTRENCHED, MISS WALLER. WE'LL BE HERE UNTIL THE END OF TIME.
ALL YOUR COMPANIES DO IS SELL THINGS THAT PEOPLE ONLY NEED WHEN THINGS ARE TERRIBLE. WEAPONS, CHEMICALS, PILLS AND SECURITY SYSTEMS.
YOUR ENTIRE BUSINESS MODEL IS DEPENDENT ON THE WORLD GETTING WORSE.
YOU PROFIT OFF THE CAUSING OF VIOLENCE AND CHAOS.
YES, WE DO PROFIT FROM CAUSING THOSE THINGS.
WHY DO *YOU* CAUSE THEM?
I DO WHAT I DO TO PROTECT THE UNITED STATES OF AMERICA.
YOUR COUNTRY...
...COME ON, MISS WALLER, I DIDN'T WANT TO THINK YOU WERE *THIS* STUPID.
EXCUSE ME?

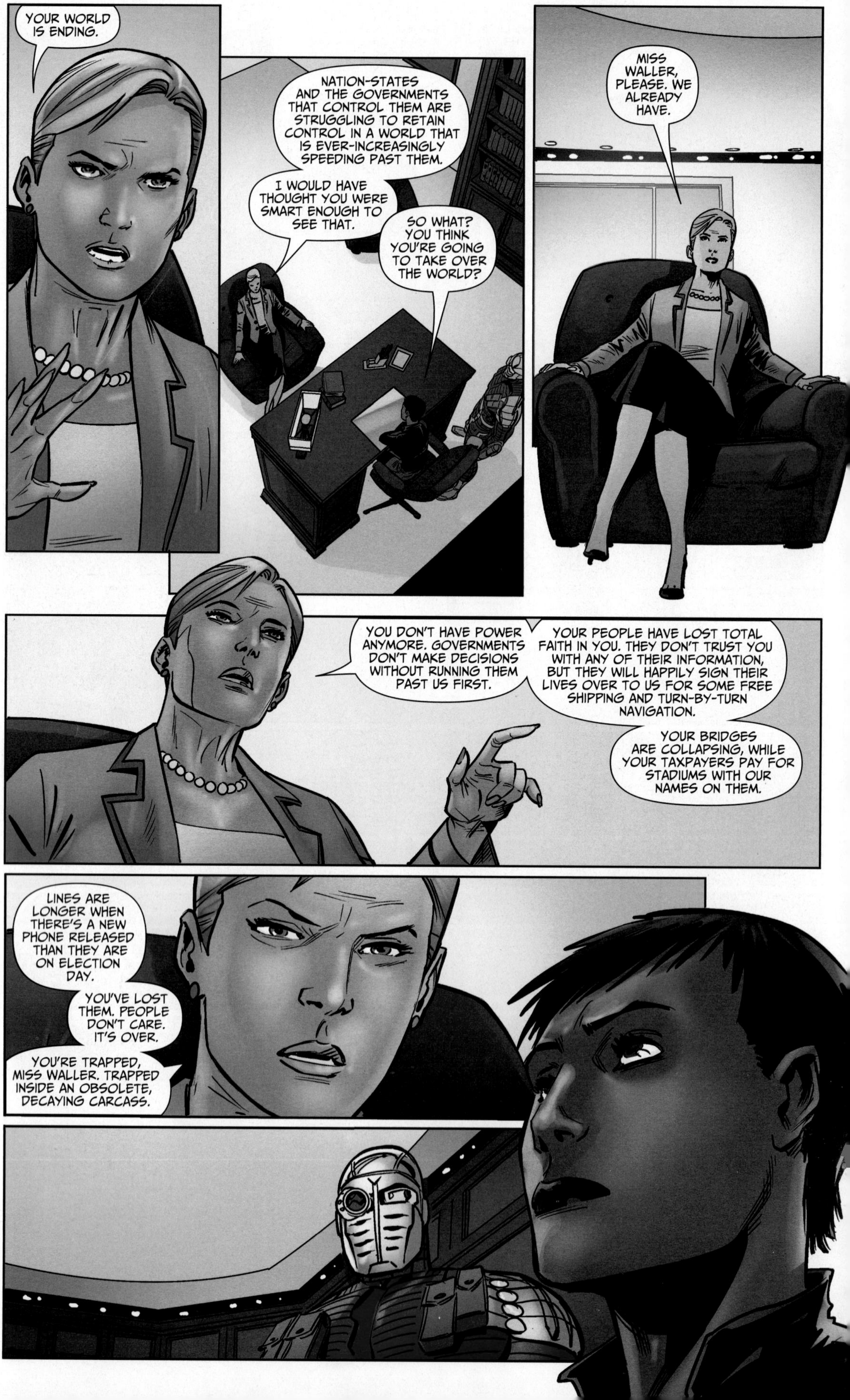
YOUR WORLD IS ENDING.
NATION-STATES AND THE GOVERNMENTS THAT CONTROL THEM ARE STRUGGLING TO RETAIN CONTROL IN A WORLD THAT IS EVER-INCREASINGLY SPEEDING PAST THEM.
I WOULD HAVE THOUGHT YOU WERE SMART ENOUGH TO SEE THAT.
SO WHAT? YOU THINK YOU'RE GOING TO TAKE OVER THE WORLD?
MISS WALLER, PLEASE. WE ALREADY HAVE.
YOU DON'T HAVE POWER ANYMORE. GOVERNMENTS DON'T MAKE DECISIONS WITHOUT RUNNING THEM PAST US FIRST.
YOUR PEOPLE HAVE LOST TOTAL FAITH IN YOU. THEY DON'T TRUST YOU WITH ANY OF THEIR INFORMATION, BUT THEY WILL HAPPILY SIGN THEIR LIVES OVER TO US FOR SOME FREE SHIPPING AND TURN-BY-TURN NAVIGATION.
YOUR BRIDGES ARE COLLAPSING, WHILE YOUR TAXPAYERS PAY FOR STADIUMS WITH OUR NAMES ON THEM.
LINES ARE LONGER WHEN THERE'S A NEW PHONE RELEASED THAN THEY ARE ON ELECTION DAY.
YOU'VE LOST THEM. PEOPLE DON'T CARE. IT'S OVER.
YOU'RE TRAPPED, MISS WALLER. TRAPPED INSIDE AN OBSOLETE, DECAYING CARCASS.

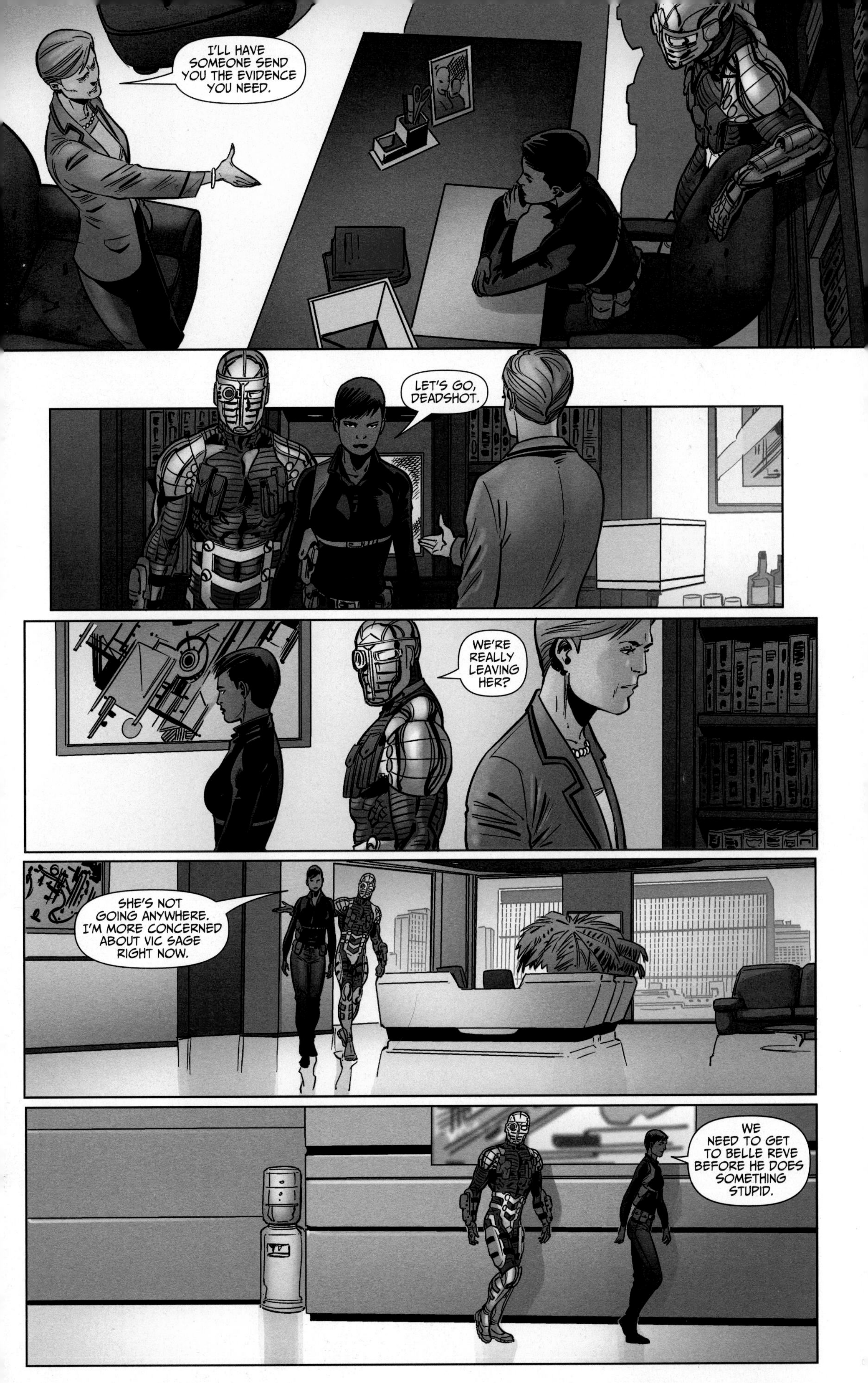
I'LL HAVE SOMEONE SEND YOU THE EVIDENCE YOU NEED.
LET'S GO, DEADSHOT.
WE'RE REALLY LEAVING HER?
SHE'S NOT GOING ANYWHERE. I'M MORE CONCERNED ABOUT VIC SAGE RIGHT NOW.
WE NEED TO GET TO BELLE REVE BEFORE HE DOES SOMETHING STUPID.

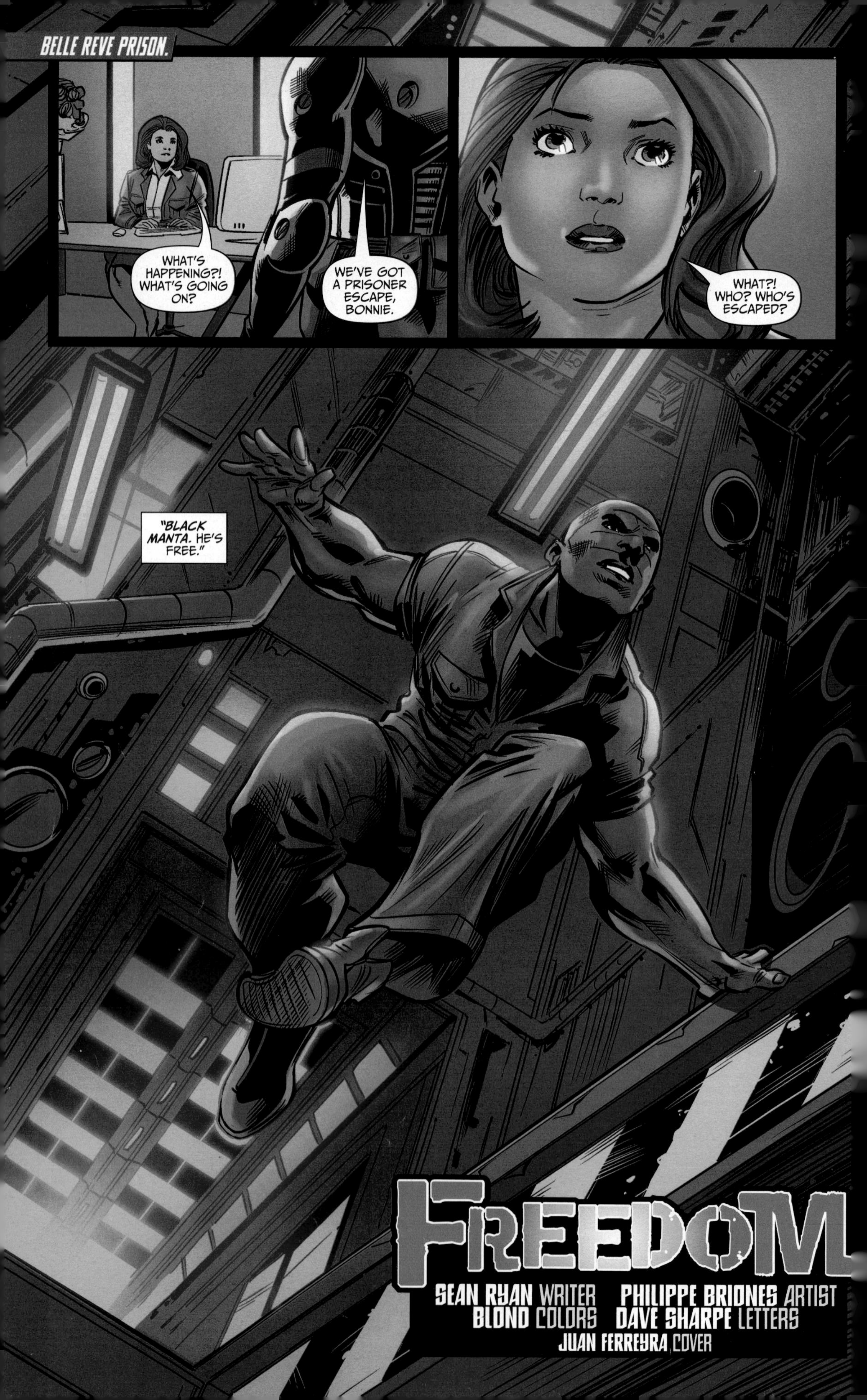
BELLE REVE PRISON.
WHAT'S HAPPENING?! WHAT'S GOING ON?
WE'VE GOT A PRISONER ESCAPE, BONNIE.
WHAT?! WHO? WHO'S ESCAPED?
"BLACK MANTA. HE'S FREE."
FREEDOM
SEAN RYAN WRITER PHILIPPE BRIONES ARTIST
BLOND COLORS DAVE SHARPE LETTERS
JUAN FERREYRA COVER

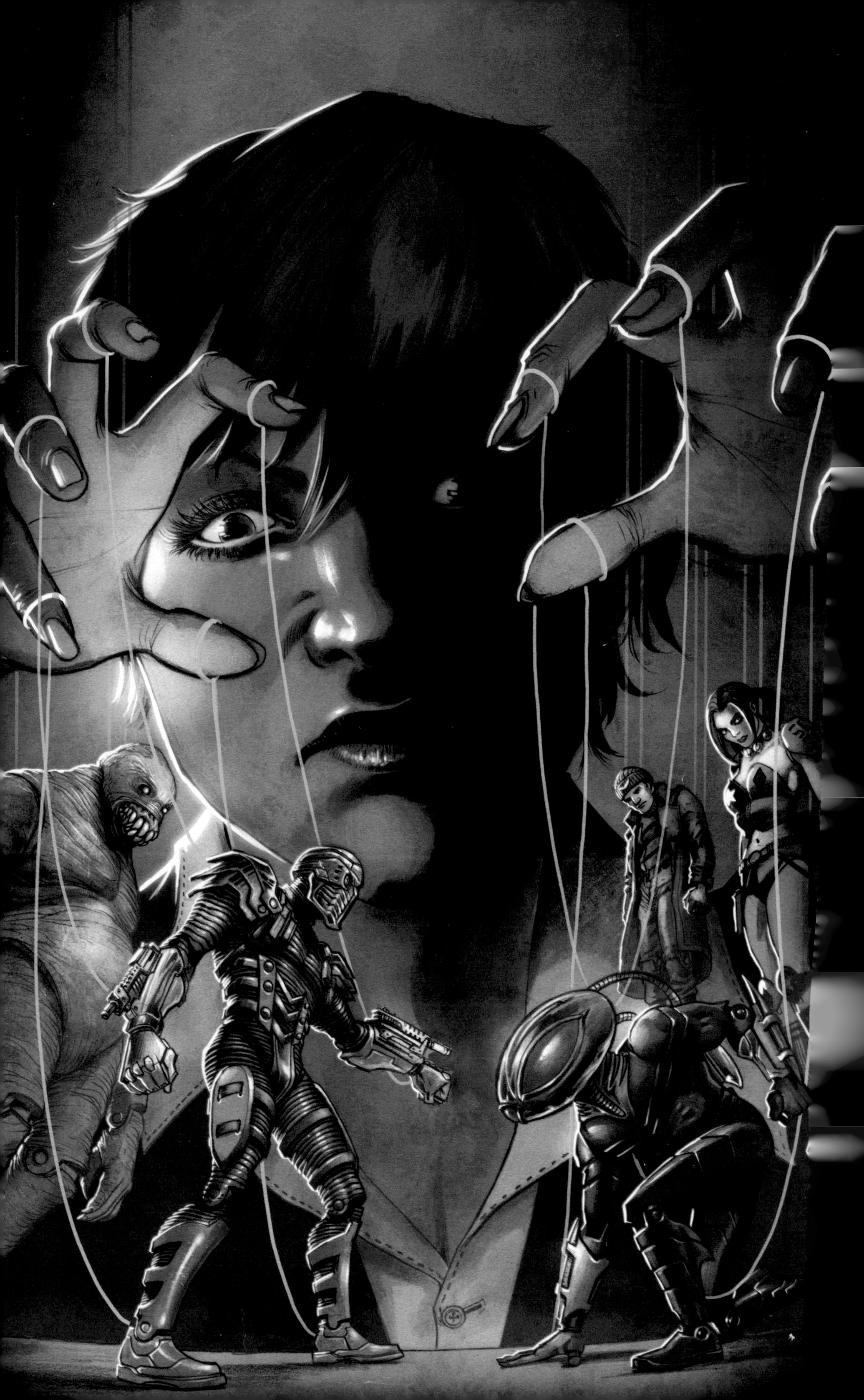

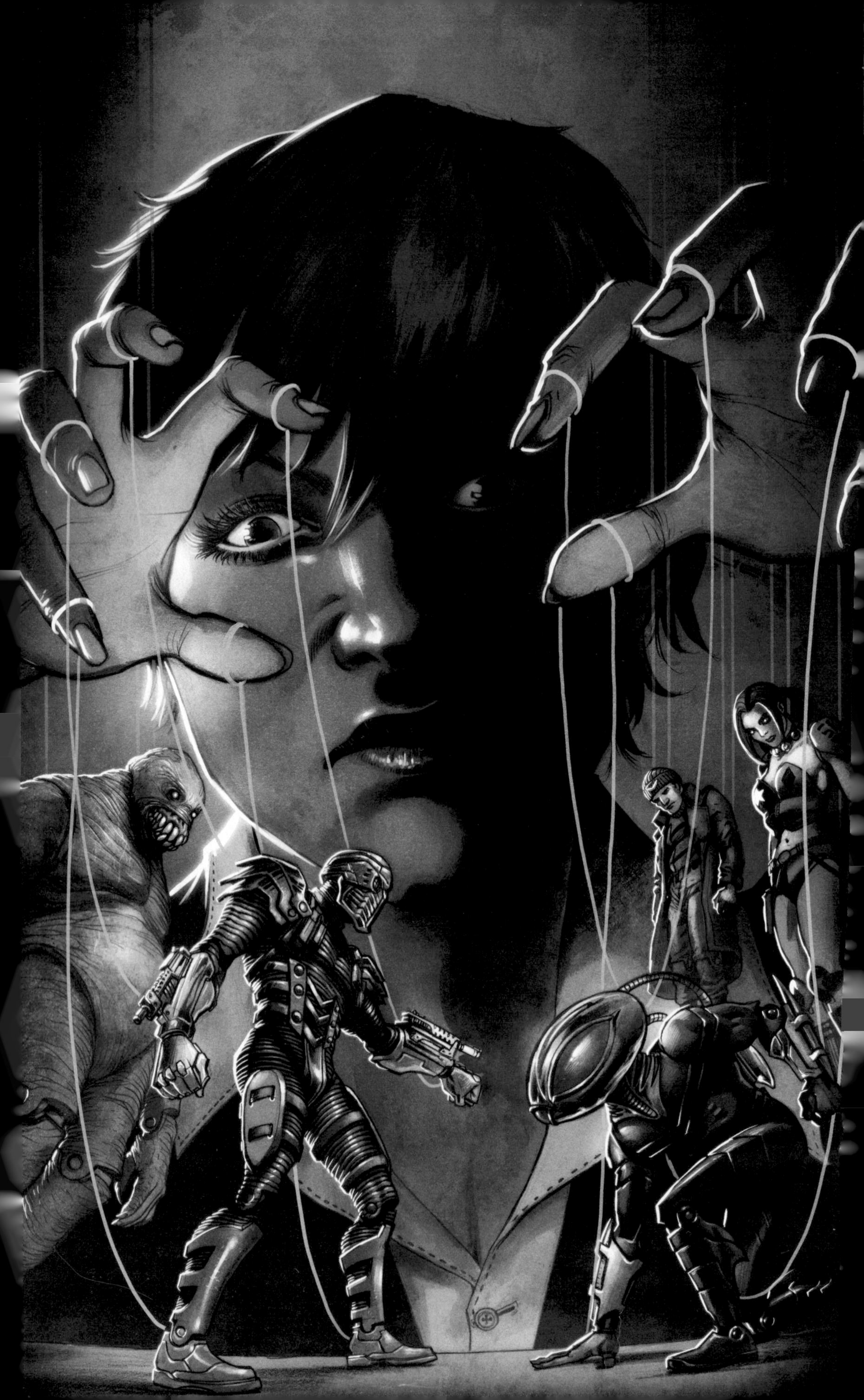

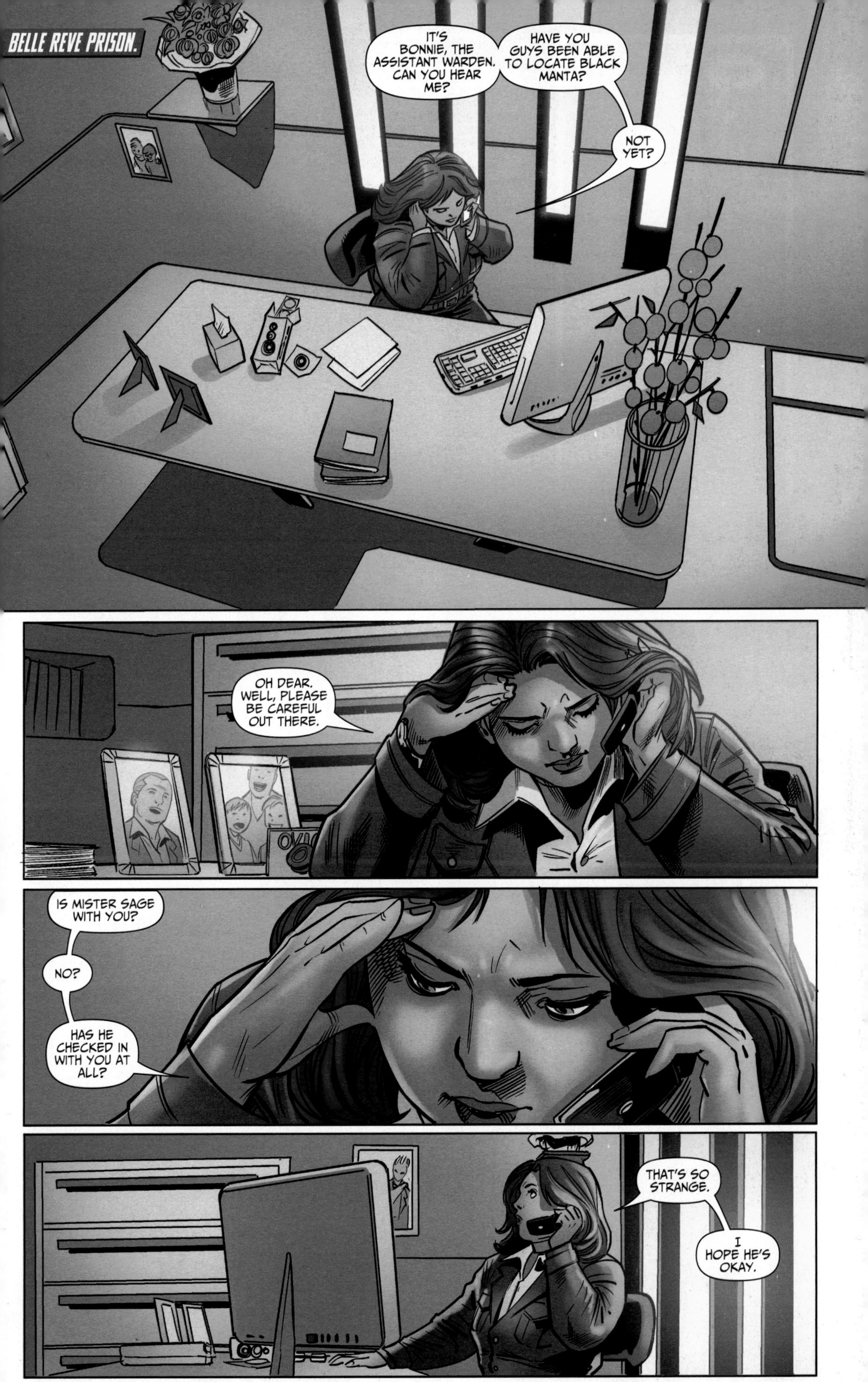
BELLE REVE PRISON.
IT'S BONNIE, THE ASSISTANT WARDEN. CAN YOU HEAR ME?
HAVE YOU GUYS BEEN ABLE TO LOCATE BLACK MANTA?
NOT YET?
OH DEAR. WELL, PLEASE BE CAREFUL OUT THERE.
IS MISTER SAGE WITH YOU?
NO?
HAS HE CHECKED IN WITH YOU AT ALL?
THAT'S SO STRANGE.
I HOPE HE'S OKAY.

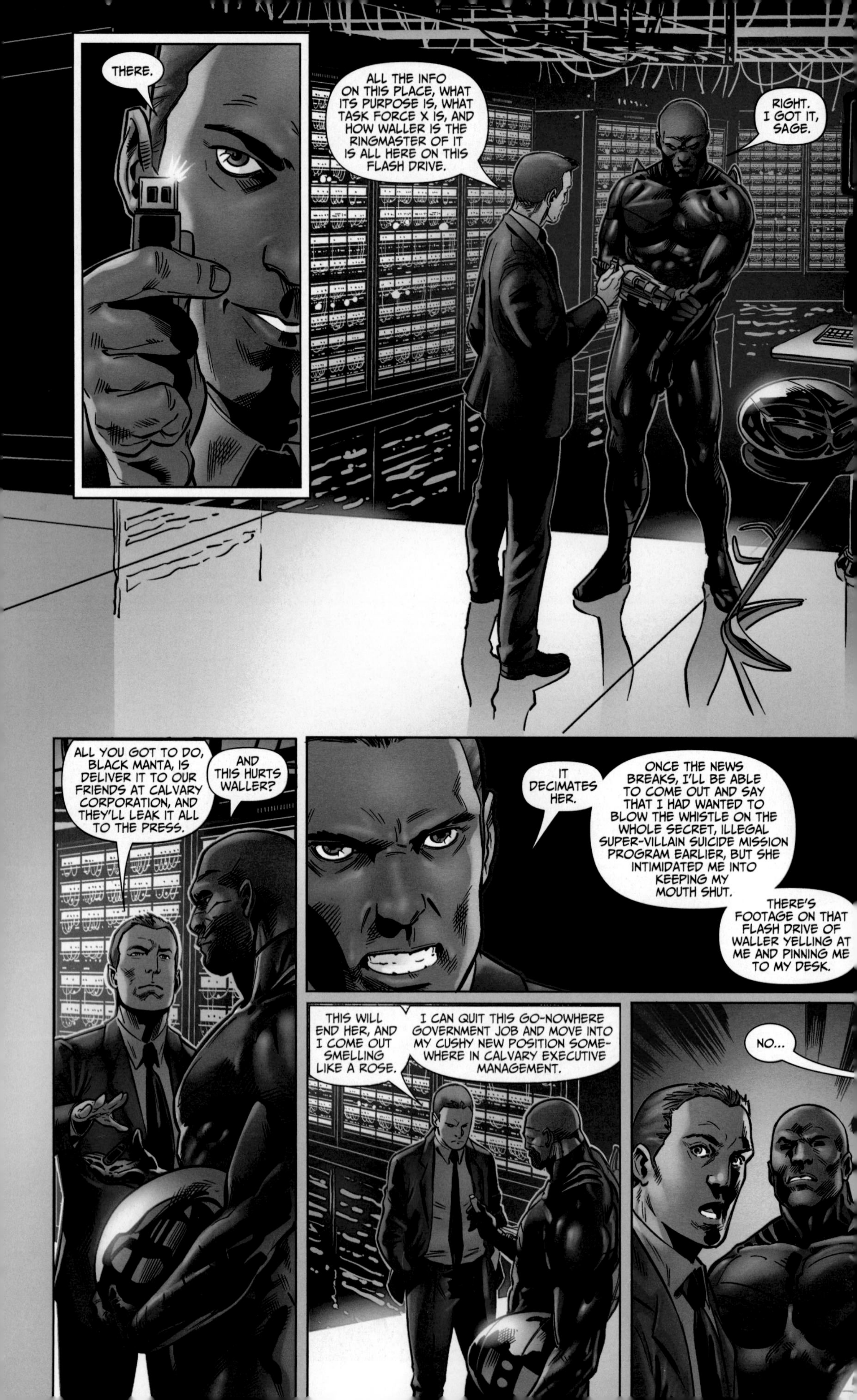
THERE.
ALL THE INFO ON THIS PLACE, WHAT ITS PURPOSE IS, WHAT TASK FORCE X IS, AND HOW WALLER IS THE RINGMASTER OF IT IS ALL HERE ON THIS FLASH DRIVE.
RIGHT. I GOT IT, SAGE.
ALL YOU GOT TO DO, BLACK MANTA, IS DELIVER IT TO OUR FRIENDS AT CALVARY CORPORATION, AND THEY'LL LEAK IT ALL TO THE PRESS.
AND THIS HURTS WALLER?
IT DECIMATES HER.
ONCE THE NEWS BREAKS, I'LL BE ABLE TO COME OUT AND SAY THAT I HAD WANTED TO BLOW THE WHISTLE ON THE WHOLE SECRET, ILLEGAL SUPER-VILLAIN SUICIDE MISSION PROGRAM EARLIER, BUT SHE INTIMIDATED ME INTO KEEPING MY MOUTH SHUT.
THERE'S FOOTAGE ON THAT FLASH DRIVE OF WALLER YELLING AT ME AND PINNING ME TO MY DESK.
THIS WILL END HER, AND I COME OUT SMELLING LIKE A ROSE.
I CAN QUIT THIS GO-NOWHERE GOVERNMENT JOB AND MOVE INTO MY CUSHY NEW POSITION SOME-WHERE IN CALVARY EXECUTIVE MANAGEMENT.
NO...

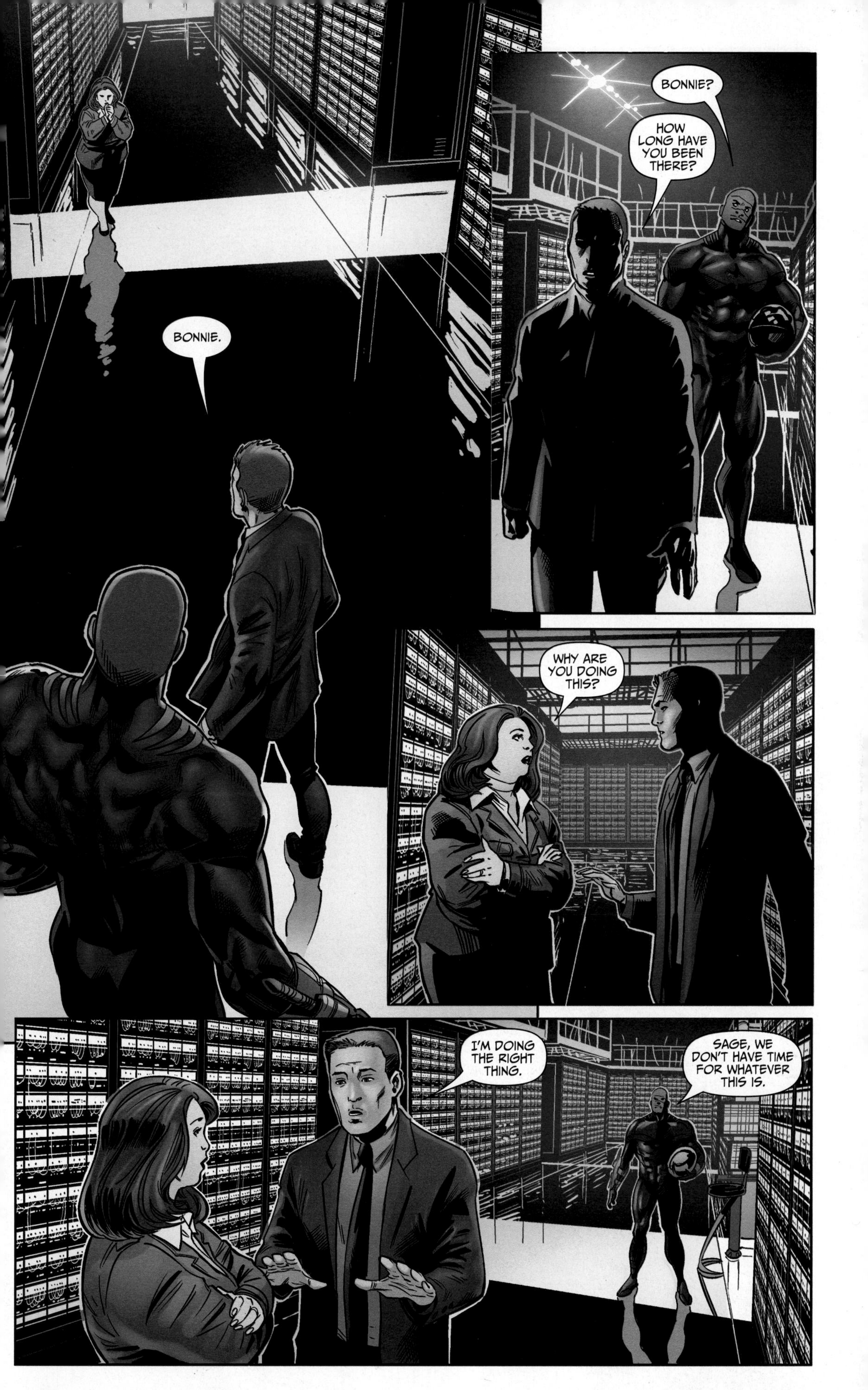
BONNIE.
BONNIE?
HOW LONG HAVE YOU BEEN THERE?
WHY ARE YOU DOING THIS?
I'M DOING THE RIGHT THING.
SAGE, WE DON'T HAVE TIME FOR WHATEVER THIS IS.

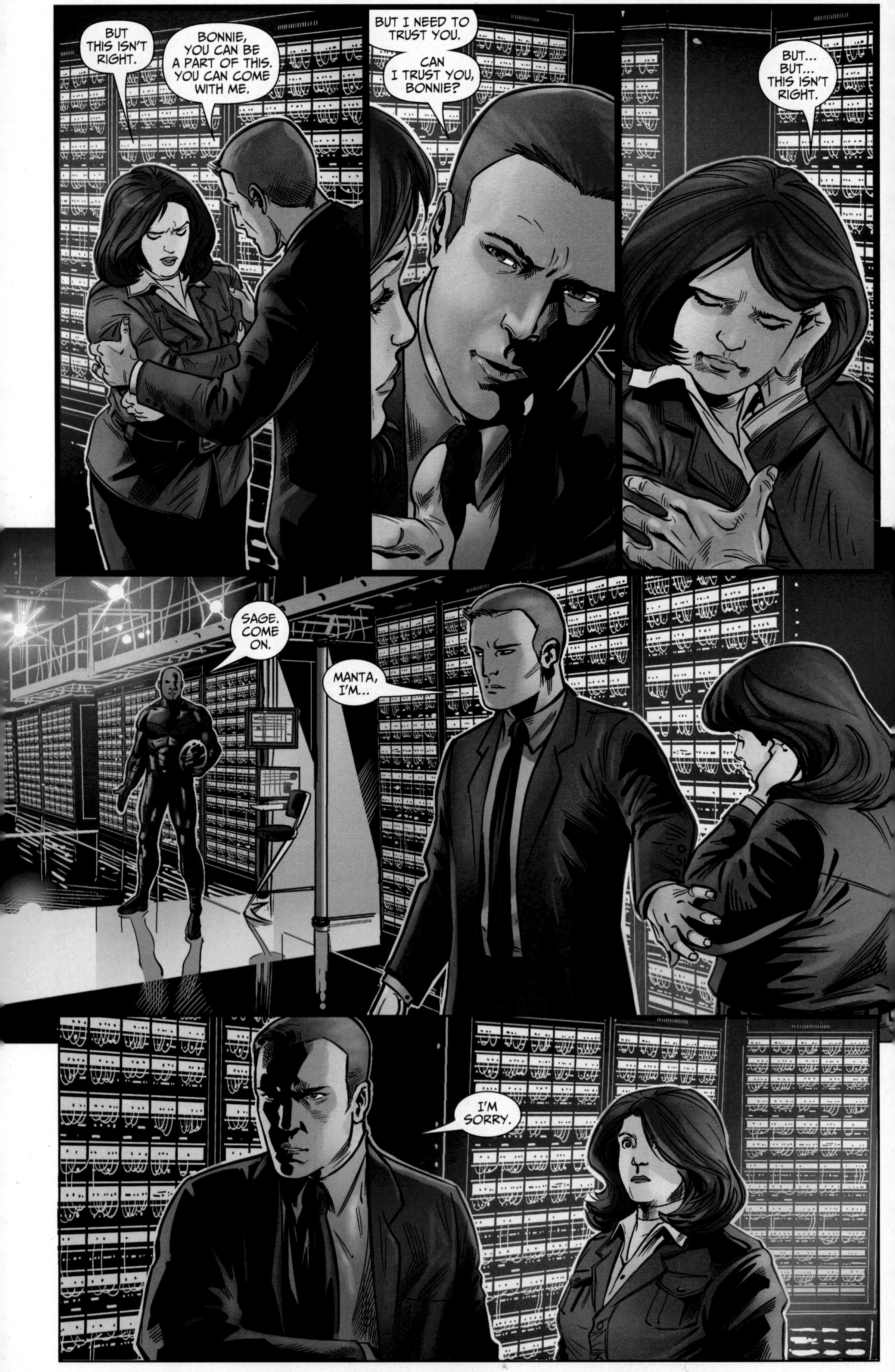
BUT THIS ISN'T RIGHT.
BONNIE, YOU CAN BE A PART OF THIS. YOU CAN COME WITH ME.
BUT I NEED TO TRUST YOU.
CAN I TRUST YOU, BONNIE?
BUT... BUT... THIS ISN'T RIGHT.
SAGE. COME ON.
MANTA, I'M...
I'M SORRY.

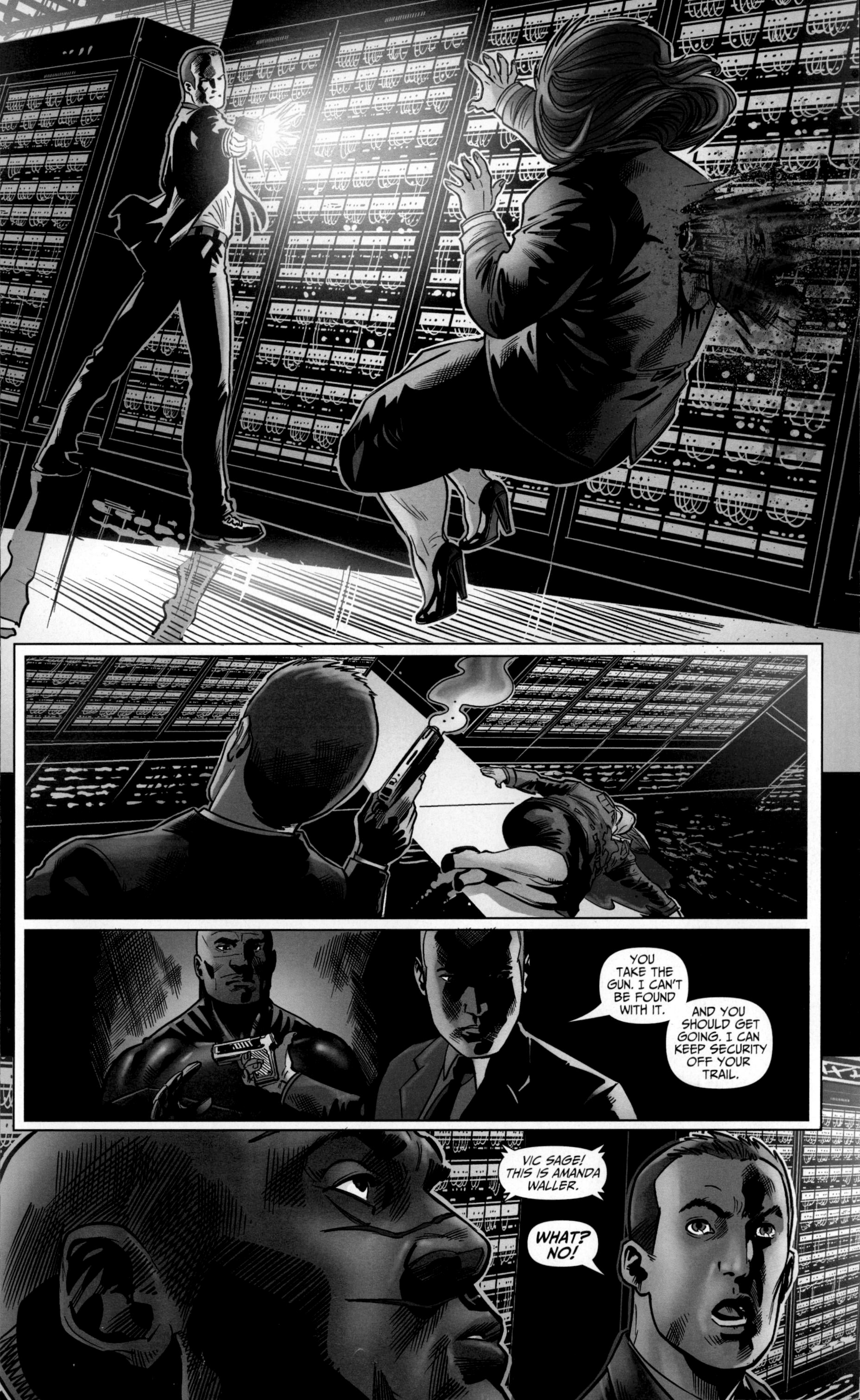
YOU TAKE THE GUN. I CAN'T BE FOUND WITH IT.
AND YOU SHOULD GET GOING. I CAN KEEP SECURITY OFF YOUR TRAIL.
VIC SAGE! THIS IS AMANDA WALLER.
WHAT? NO!

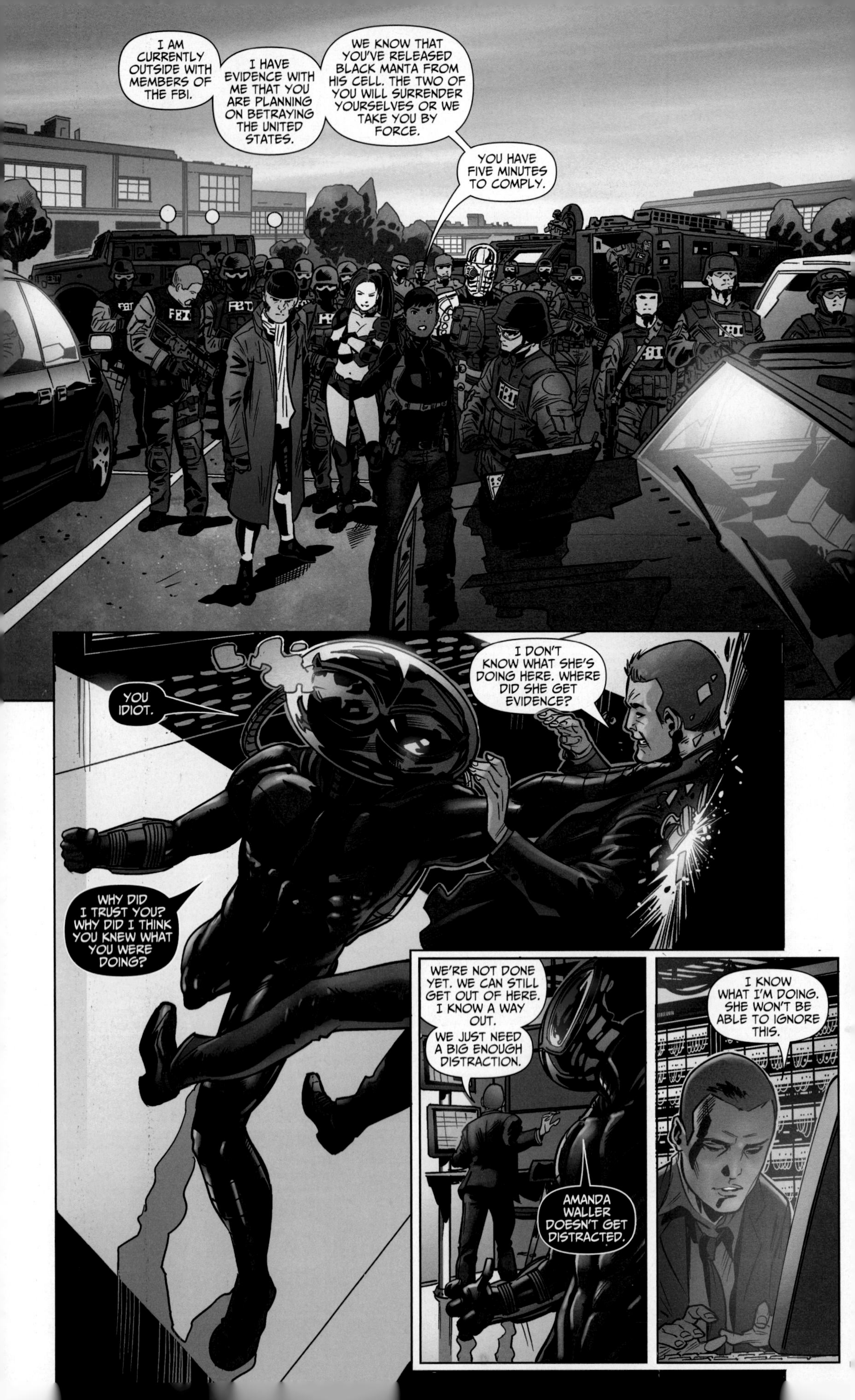

I AM CURRENTLY OUTSIDE WITH MEMBERS OF THE FBI.
I HAVE EVIDENCE WITH ME THAT YOU ARE PLANNING ON BETRAYING THE UNITED STATES.
WE KNOW THAT YOU'VE RELEASED BLACK MANTA FROM HIS CELL. THE TWO OF YOU WILL SURRENDER YOURSELVES OR WE TAKE YOU BY FORCE.
YOU HAVE FIVE MINUTES TO COMPLY.
I DON'T KNOW WHAT SHE'S DOING HERE. WHERE DID SHE GET EVIDENCE?
YOU IDIOT.
WHY DID I TRUST YOU? WHY DID I THINK YOU KNEW WHAT YOU WERE DOING?
WE'RE NOT DONE YET. WE CAN STILL GET OUT OF HERE. I KNOW A WAY OUT.
WE JUST NEED A BIG ENOUGH DISTRACTION.
AMANDA WALLER DOESN'T GET DISTRACTED.
I KNOW WHAT I'M DOING. SHE WON'T BE ABLE TO IGNORE THIS.

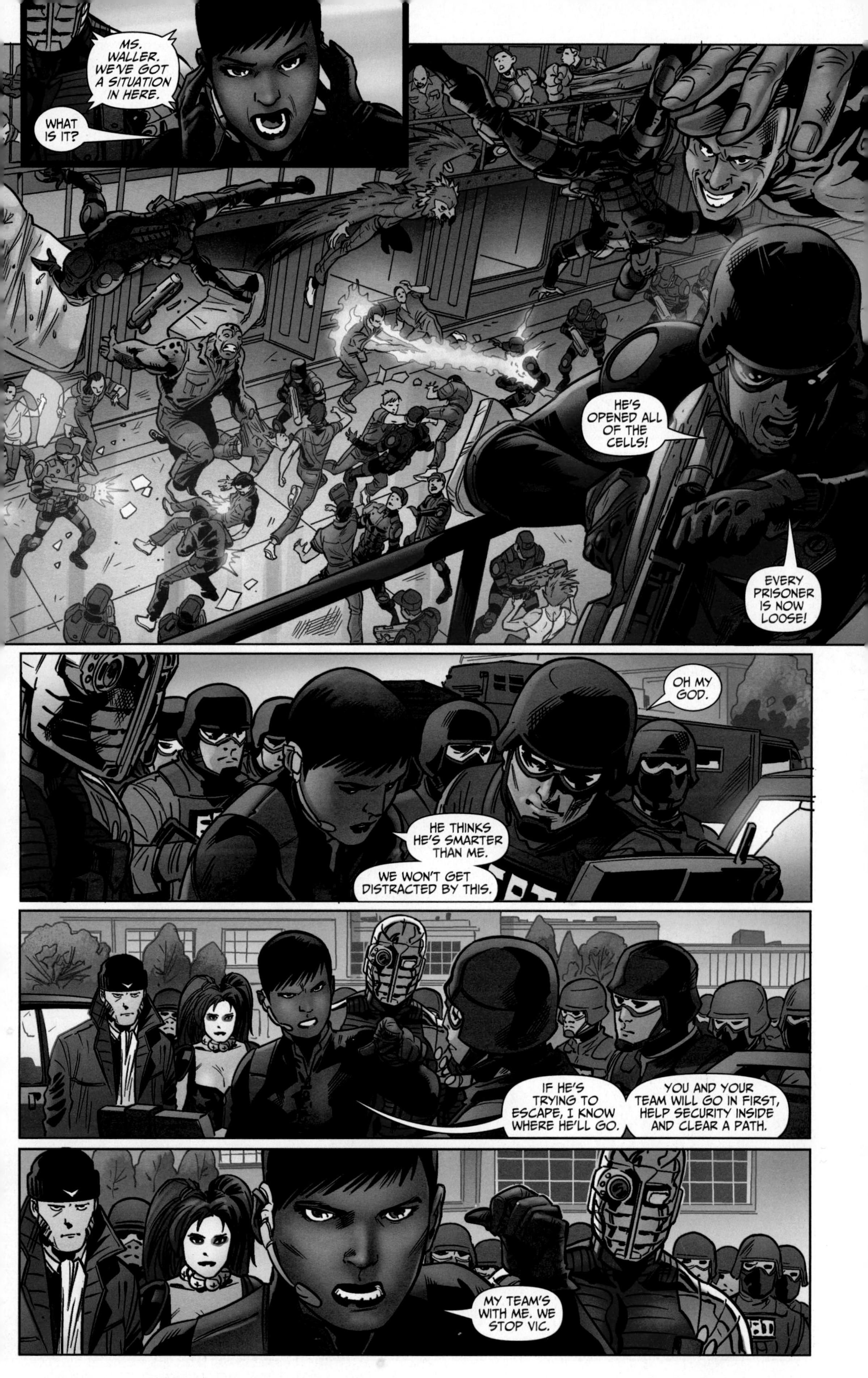
MS. WALLER. WE'VE GOT A SITUATION IN HERE.
WHAT IS IT?
HE'S OPENED ALL OF THE CELLS!
EVERY PRISONER IS NOW LOOSE!
OH MY GOD.
HE THINKS HE'S SMARTER THAN ME.
WE WON'T GET DISTRACTED BY THIS.
IF HE'S TRYING TO ESCAPE, I KNOW WHERE HE'LL GO.
YOU AND YOUR TEAM WILL GO IN FIRST, HELP SECURITY INSIDE AND CLEAR A PATH.
MY TEAM'S WITH ME. WE STOP VIC.

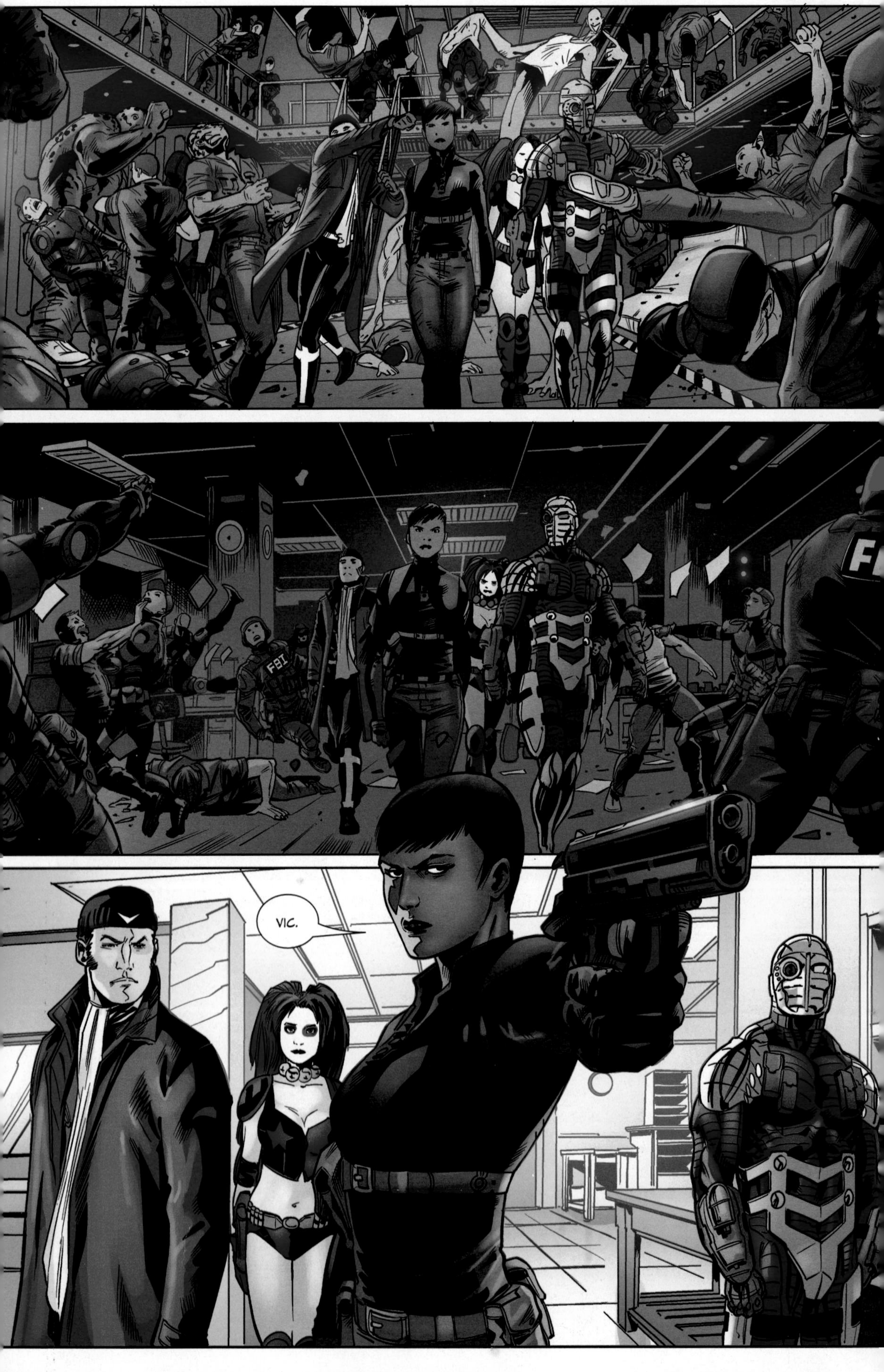
FBI
FBI
VIC.

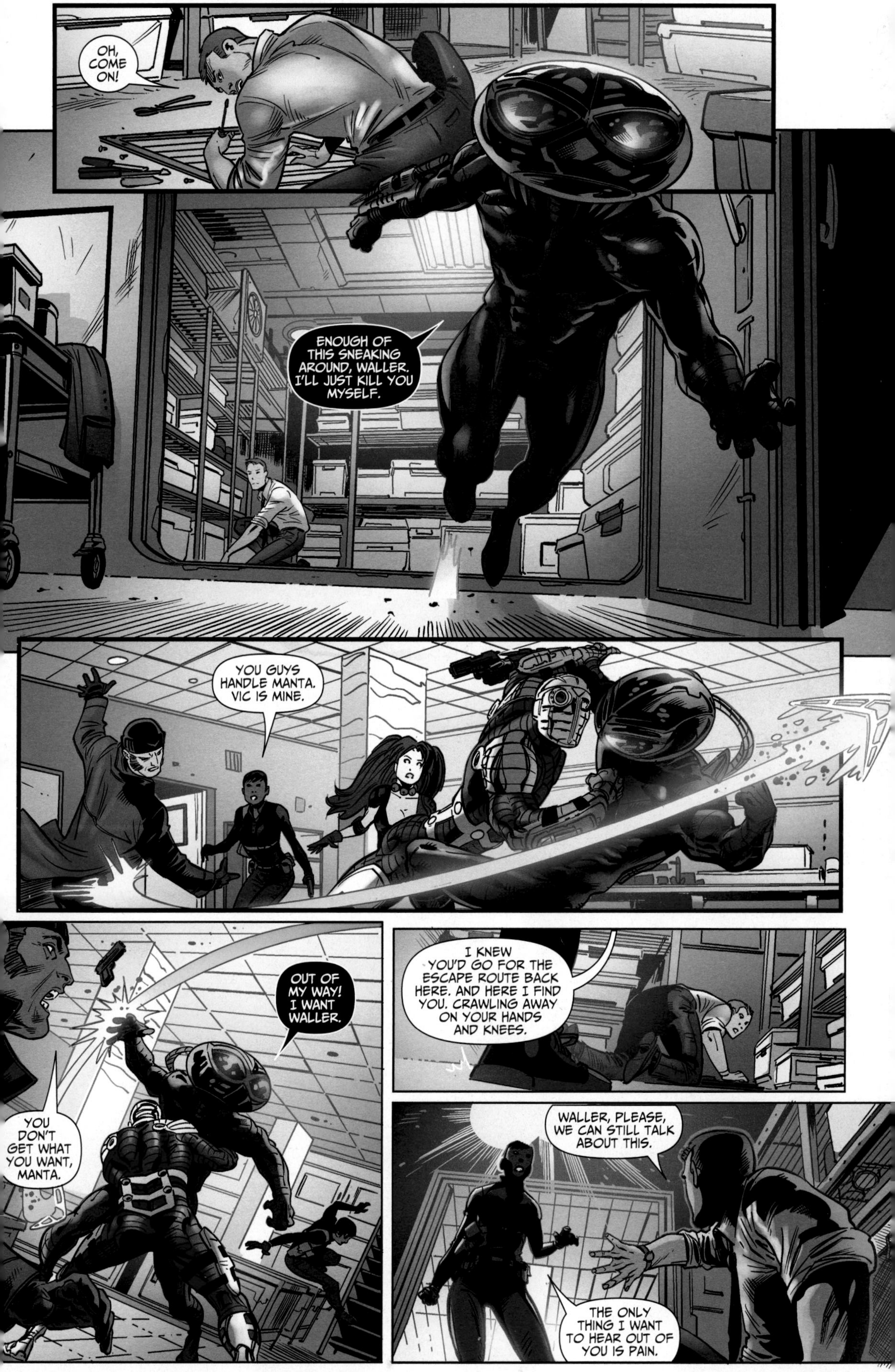
OH, COME ON!
ENOUGH OF THIS SNEAKING AROUND, WALLER. I'LL JUST KILL YOU MYSELF.
YOU GUYS HANDLE MANTA. VIC IS MINE.
OUT OF MY WAY! I WANT WALLER.
YOU DON'T GET WHAT YOU WANT, MANTA.
I KNEW YOU'D GO FOR THE ESCAPE ROUTE BACK HERE. AND HERE I FIND YOU. CRAWLING AWAY ON YOUR HANDS AND KNEES.
WALLER, PLEASE, WE CAN STILL TALK ABOUT THIS.
THE ONLY THING I WANT TO HEAR OUT OF YOU IS PAIN.

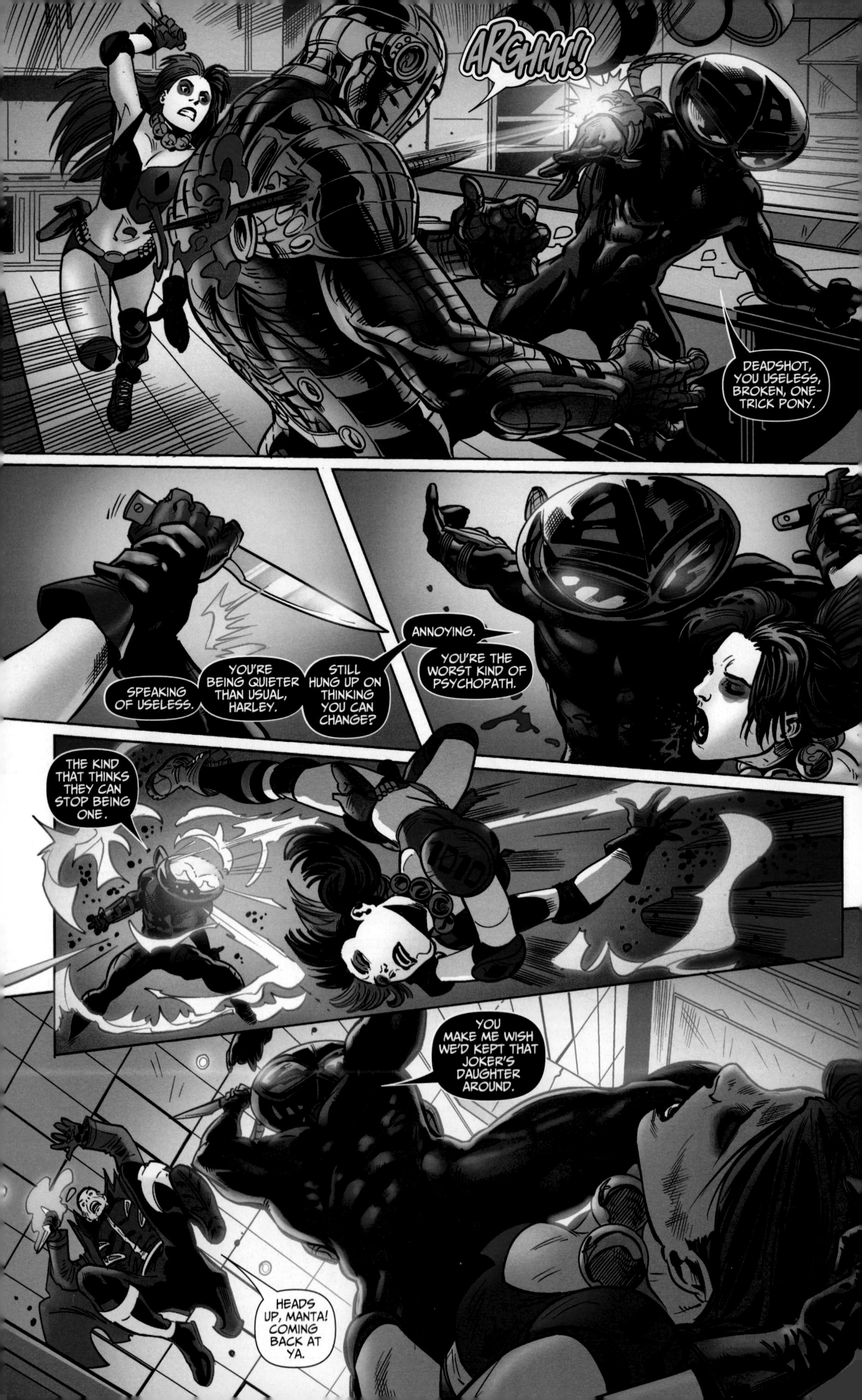
ARGHHH!!
DEADSHOT, YOU USELESS, BROKEN, ONE-TRICK PONY.
SPEAKING OF USELESS.
YOU'RE BEING QUIETER THAN USUAL, HARLEY.
STILL HUNG UP ON THINKING YOU CAN CHANGE?
ANNOYING.
YOU'RE THE WORST KIND OF PSYCHOPATH.
THE KIND THAT THINKS THEY CAN STOP BEING ONE.
YOU MAKE ME WISH WE'D KEPT THAT JOKER'S DAUGHTER AROUND.
HEADS UP, MANTA! COMING BACK AT YA.

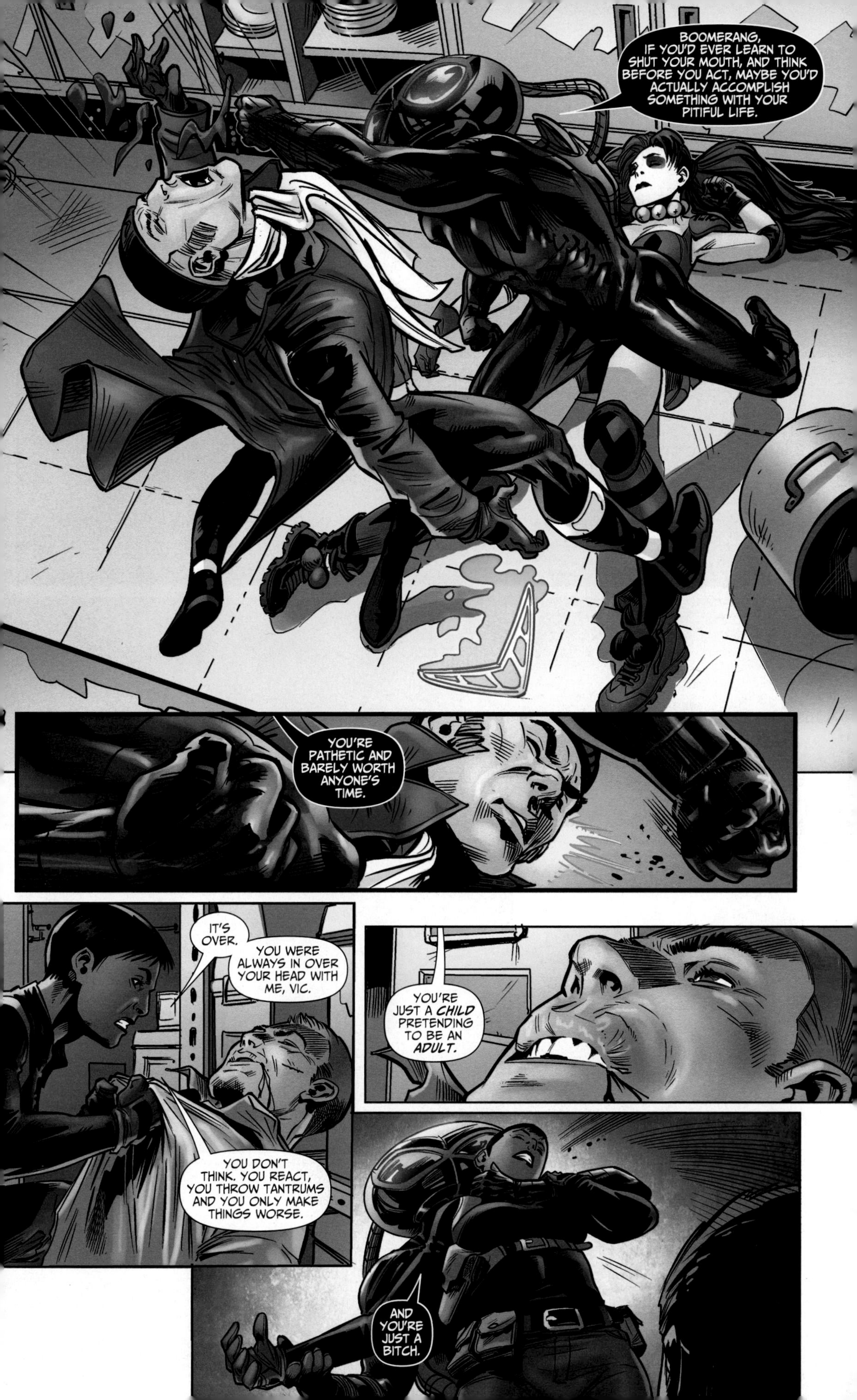
BOOMERANG, IF YOU'D EVER LEARN TO SHUT YOUR MOUTH, AND THINK BEFORE YOU ACT, MAYBE YOU'D ACTUALLY ACCOMPLISH SOMETHING WITH YOUR PITIFUL LIFE.
YOU'RE PATHETIC AND BARELY WORTH ANYONE'S TIME.
IT'S OVER.
YOU WERE ALWAYS IN OVER YOUR HEAD WITH ME, VIC.
YOU DON'T THINK. YOU REACT, YOU THROW TANTRUMS AND YOU ONLY MAKE THINGS WORSE.
YOU'RE JUST A *CHILD* PRETENDING TO BE AN *ADULT.*
AND YOU'RE JUST A BITCH.

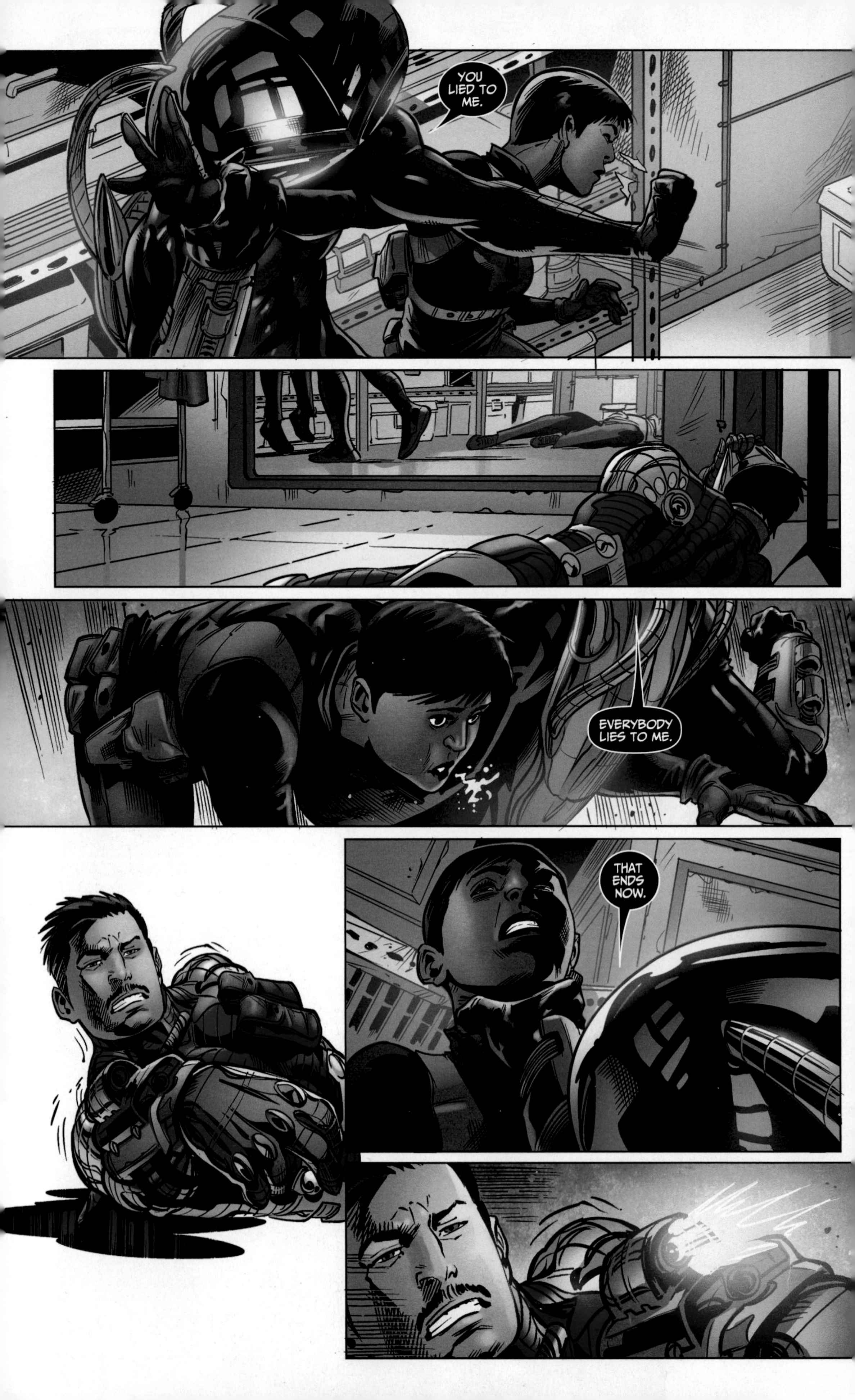
YOU LIED TO ME.
EVERYBODY LIES TO ME.
THAT ENDS NOW.

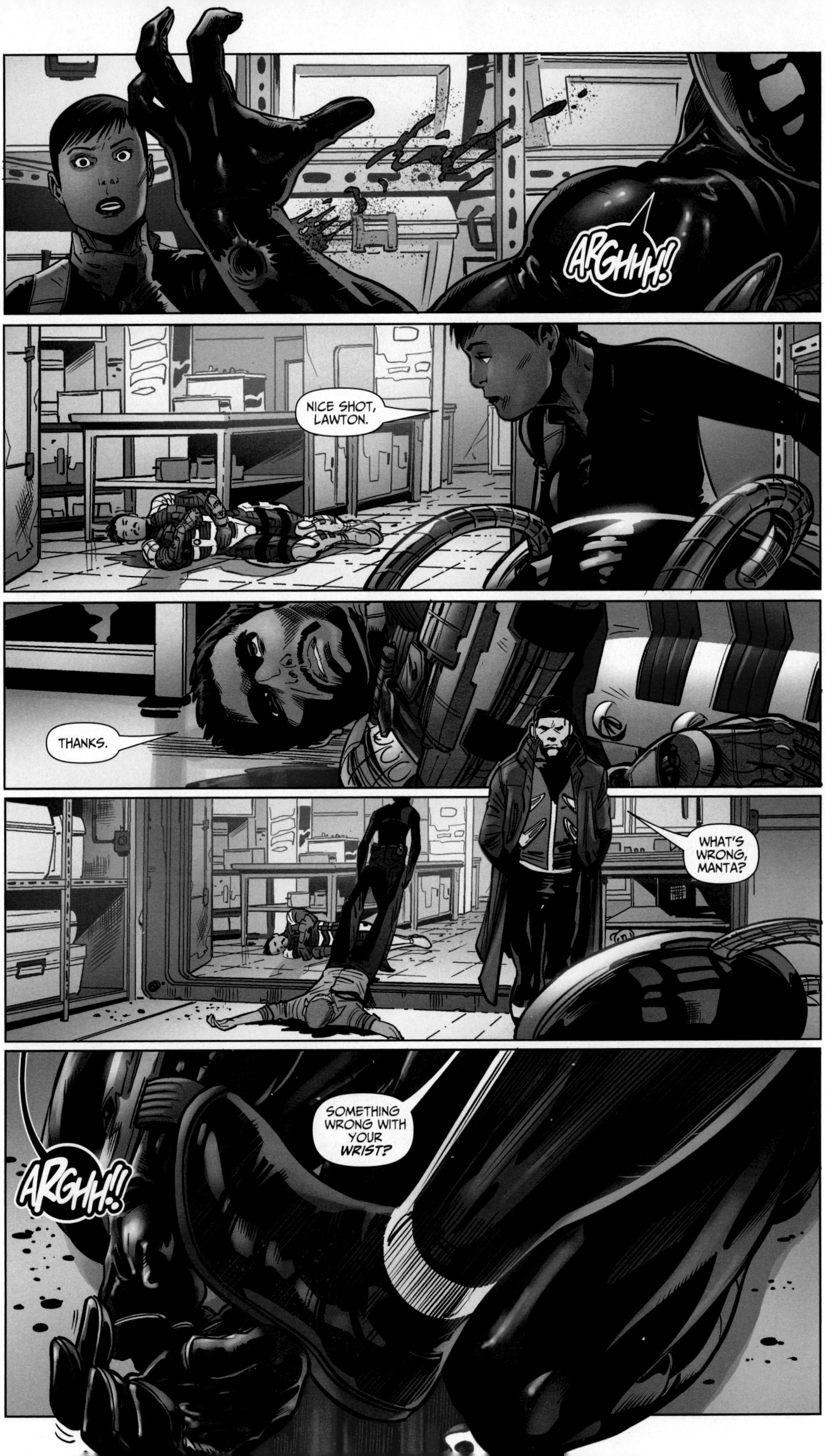
ARGHHH!
NICE SHOT, LAWTON.
THANKS.
WHAT'S WRONG, MANTA?
SOMETHING WRONG WITH YOUR *WRIST*?
ARGHH!!

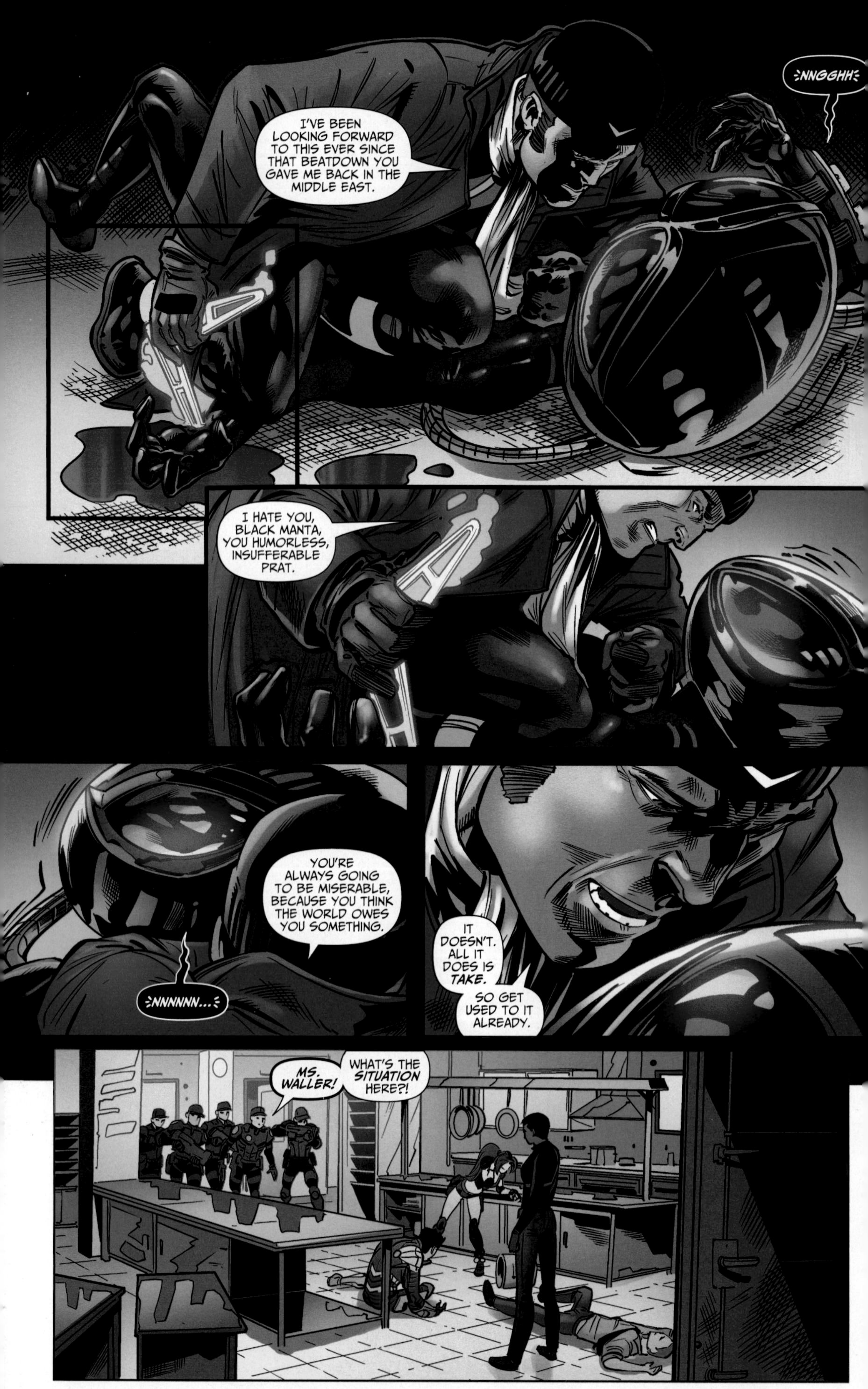
NNGGHH
I'VE BEEN LOOKING FORWARD TO THIS EVER SINCE THAT BEATDOWN YOU GAVE ME BACK IN THE MIDDLE EAST.
I HATE YOU, BLACK MANTA, YOU HUMORLESS, INSUFFERABLE PRAT.
YOU'RE ALWAYS GOING TO BE MISERABLE, BECAUSE YOU THINK THE WORLD OWES YOU SOMETHING.
NNNNNN...
IT DOESN'T. ALL IT DOES IS TAKE.
SO GET USED TO IT ALREADY.
MS. WALLER!
WHAT'S THE SITUATION HERE?!

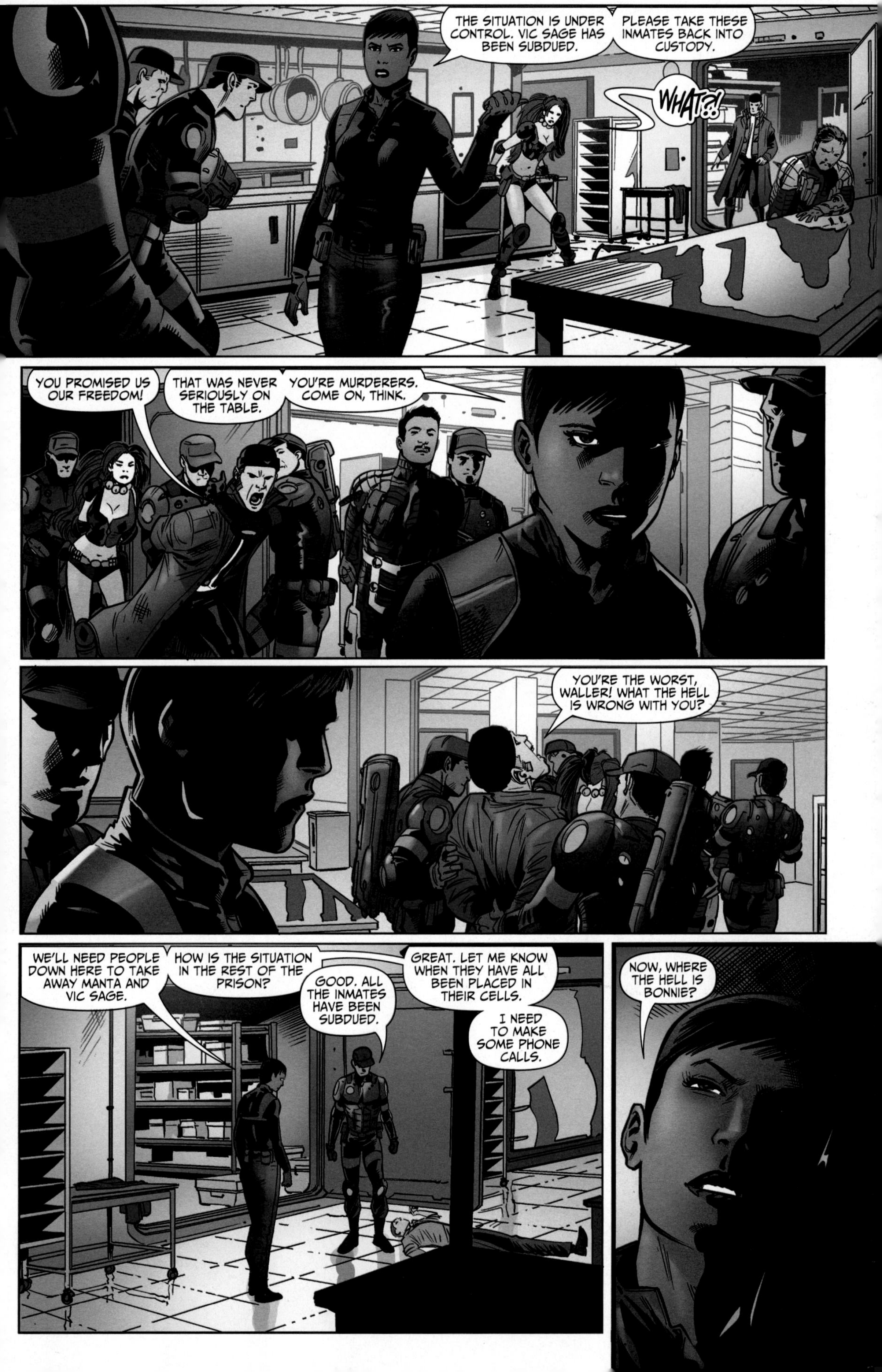
THE SITUATION IS UNDER CONTROL. VIC SAGE HAS BEEN SUBDUED.
PLEASE TAKE THESE INMATES BACK INTO CUSTODY.
WHAT?!
YOU PROMISED US OUR FREEDOM!
THAT WAS NEVER SERIOUSLY ON THE TABLE.
YOU'RE MURDERERS. COME ON, THINK.
YOU'RE THE WORST, WALLER! WHAT THE HELL IS WRONG WITH YOU?
WE'LL NEED PEOPLE DOWN HERE TO TAKE AWAY MANTA AND VIC SAGE.
HOW IS THE SITUATION IN THE REST OF THE PRISON?
GOOD. ALL THE INMATES HAVE BEEN SUBDUED.
GREAT. LET ME KNOW WHEN THEY HAVE ALL BEEN PLACED IN THEIR CELLS.
I NEED TO MAKE SOME PHONE CALLS.
NOW, WHERE THE HELL IS BONNIE?

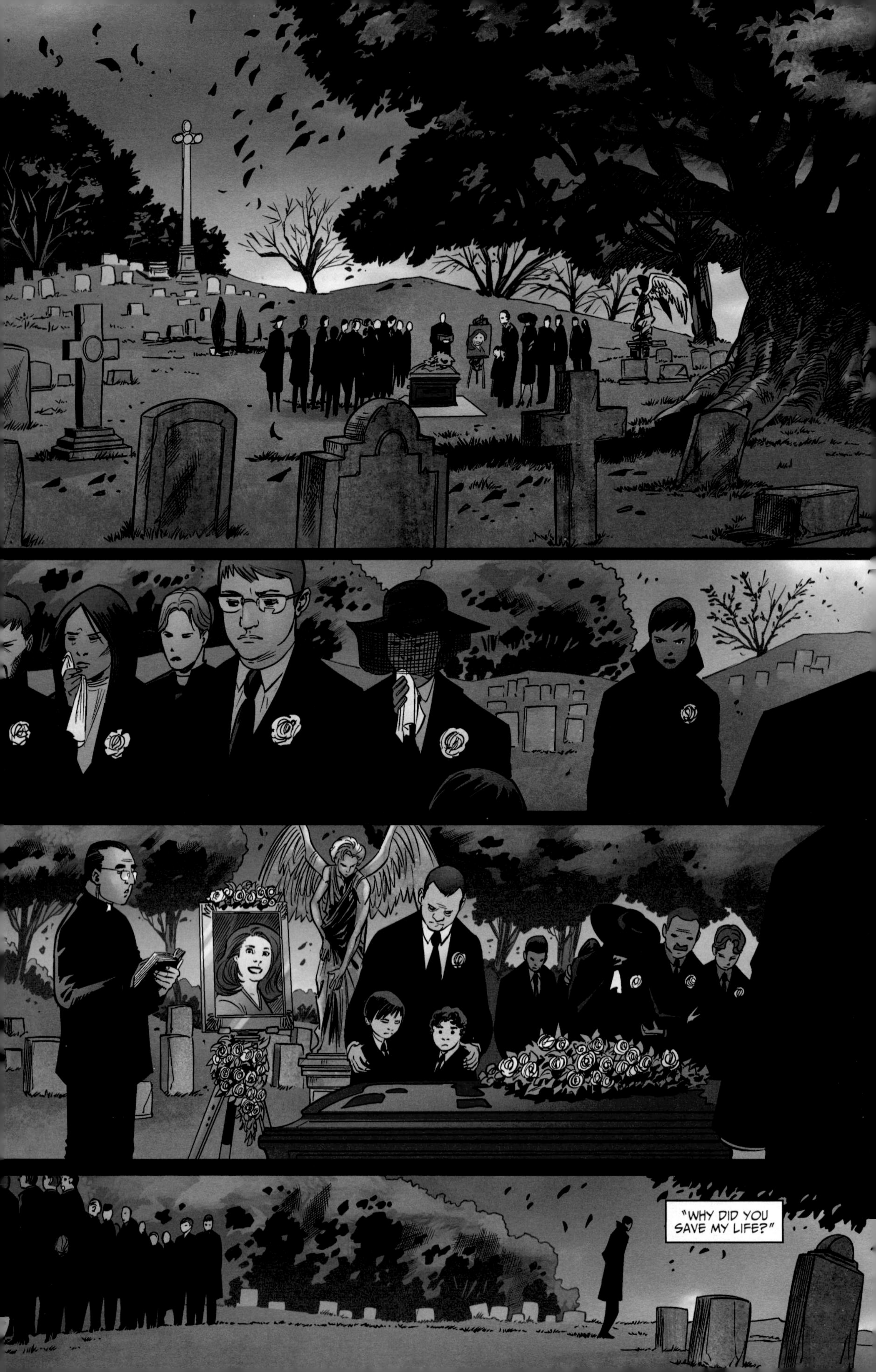
"WHY DID YOU SAVE MY LIFE?"

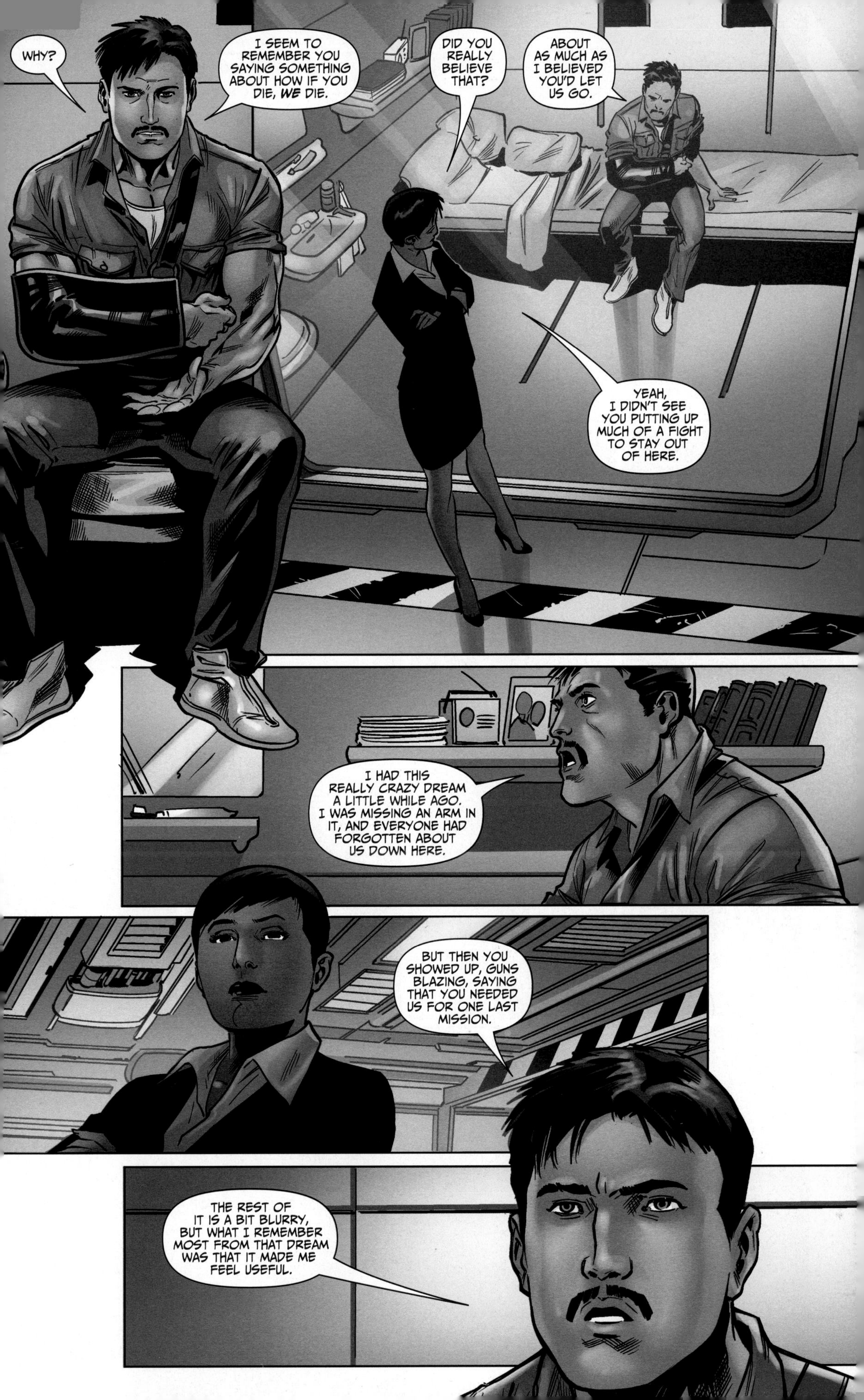
WHY?
I SEEM TO REMEMBER YOU SAYING SOMETHING ABOUT HOW IF YOU DIE, *WE* DIE.
DID YOU REALLY BELIEVE THAT?
ABOUT AS MUCH AS I BELIEVED YOU'D LET US GO.
YEAH, I DIDN'T SEE YOU PUTTING UP MUCH OF A FIGHT TO STAY OUT OF HERE.
I HAD THIS REALLY CRAZY DREAM A LITTLE WHILE AGO. I WAS MISSING AN ARM IN IT, AND EVERYONE HAD FORGOTTEN ABOUT US DOWN HERE.
BUT THEN YOU SHOWED UP, GUNS BLAZING, SAYING THAT YOU NEEDED US FOR ONE LAST MISSION.
THE REST OF IT IS A BIT BLURRY, BUT WHAT I REMEMBER MOST FROM THAT DREAM WAS THAT IT MADE ME FEEL USEFUL.

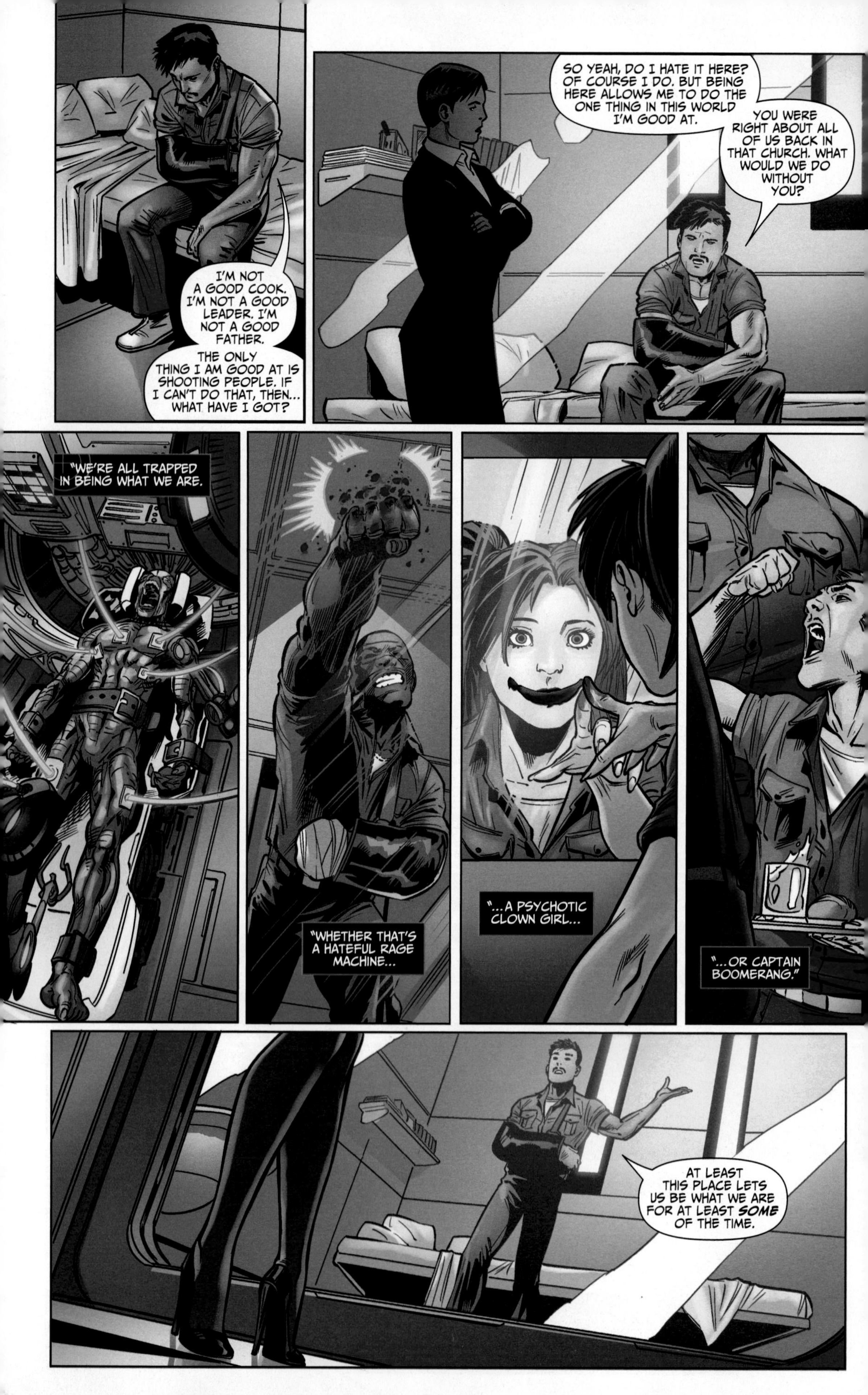
I'M NOT A GOOD COOK. I'M NOT A GOOD LEADER. I'M NOT A GOOD FATHER.
THE ONLY THING I AM GOOD AT IS SHOOTING PEOPLE. IF I CAN'T DO THAT, THEN... WHAT HAVE I GOT?
SO YEAH, DO I HATE IT HERE? OF COURSE I DO. BUT BEING HERE ALLOWS ME TO DO THE ONE THING IN THIS WORLD I'M GOOD AT.
YOU WERE RIGHT ABOUT ALL OF US BACK IN THAT CHURCH. WHAT WOULD WE DO WITHOUT YOU?
"WE'RE ALL TRAPPED IN BEING WHAT WE ARE.
"WHETHER THAT'S A HATEFUL RAGE MACHINE...
"...A PSYCHOTIC CLOWN GIRL...
"...OR CAPTAIN BOOMERANG."
AT LEAST THIS PLACE LETS US BE WHAT WE ARE FOR AT LEAST *SOME* OF THE TIME.

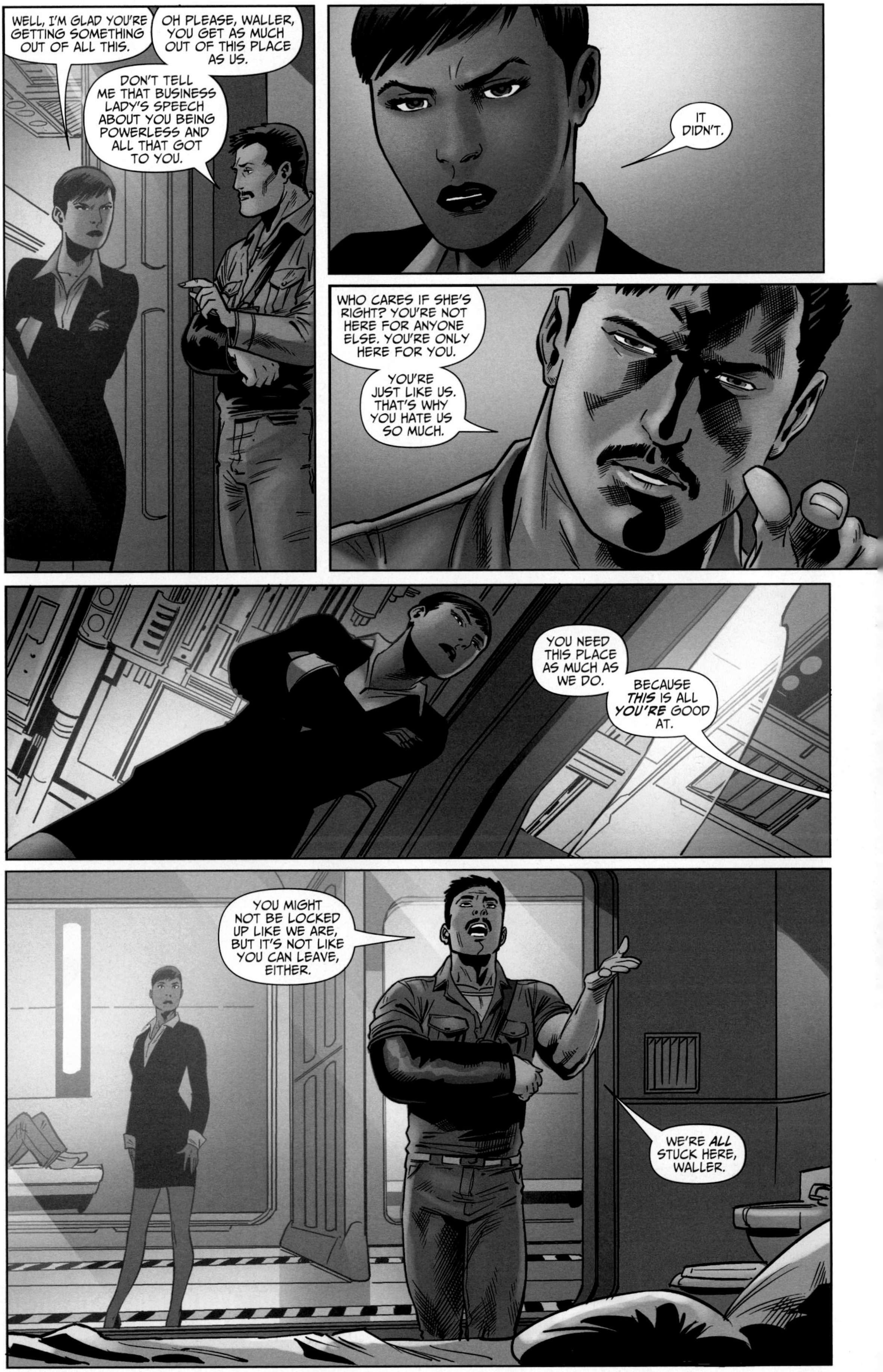
WELL, I'M GLAD YOU'RE GETTING SOMETHING OUT OF ALL THIS.
OH PLEASE, WALLER, YOU GET AS MUCH OUT OF THIS PLACE AS US.
DON'T TELL ME THAT BUSINESS LADY'S SPEECH ABOUT YOU BEING POWERLESS AND ALL THAT GOT TO YOU.
IT DIDN'T.
WHO CARES IF SHE'S RIGHT? YOU'RE NOT HERE FOR ANYONE ELSE. YOU'RE ONLY HERE FOR YOU.
YOU'RE JUST LIKE US. THAT'S WHY YOU HATE US SO MUCH.
YOU NEED THIS PLACE AS MUCH AS WE DO.
BECAUSE *THIS* IS ALL *YOU'RE* GOOD AT.
YOU MIGHT NOT BE LOCKED UP LIKE WE ARE, BUT IT'S NOT LIKE YOU CAN LEAVE, EITHER.
WE'RE *ALL* STUCK HERE, WALLER.

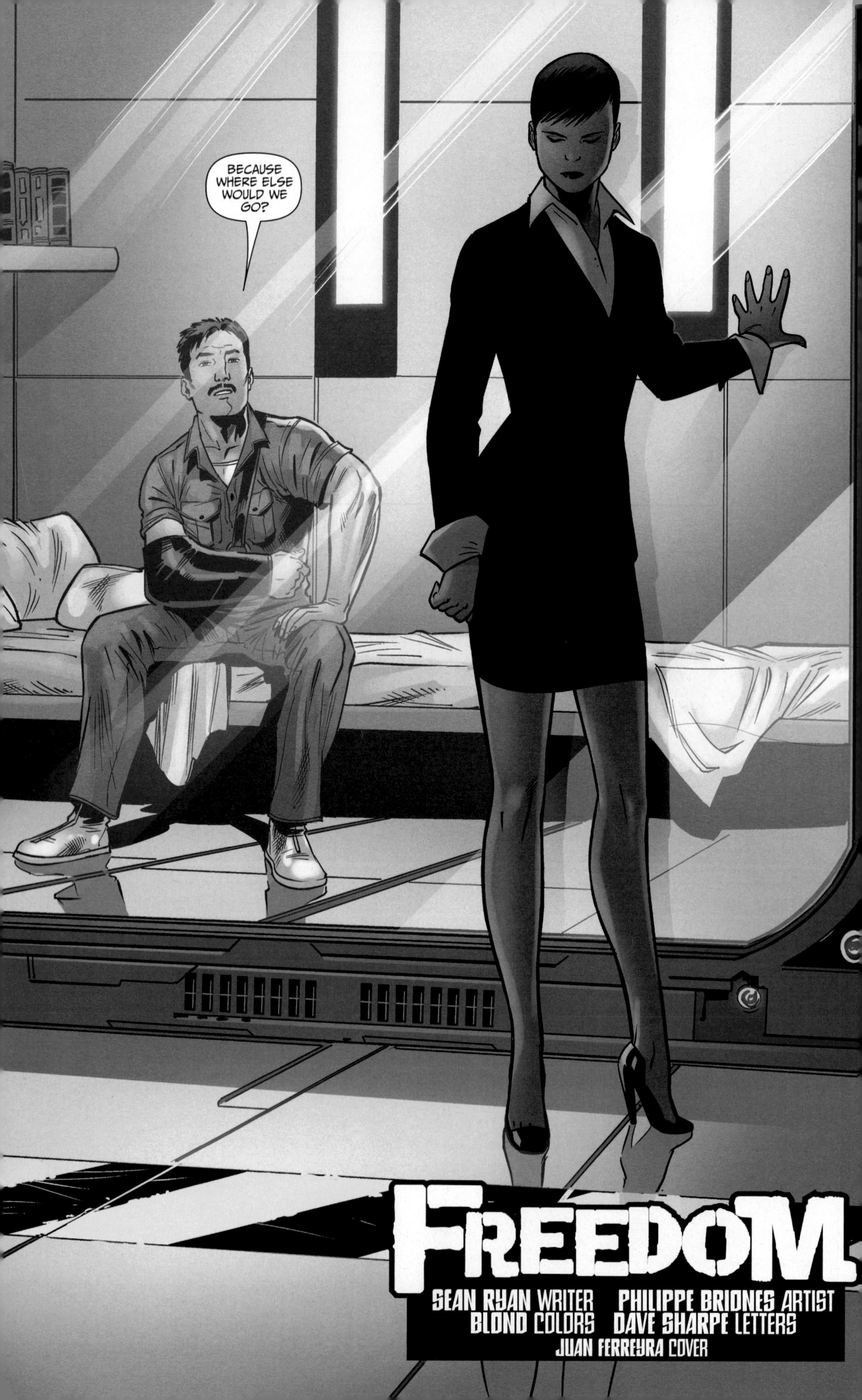
BECAUSE WHERE ELSE WOULD WE GO?
FREEDOM
SEAN RYAN WRITER PHILIPPE BRIONES ARTIST
BLOND COLORS DAVE SHARPE LETTERS
JUAN FERREYRA COVER

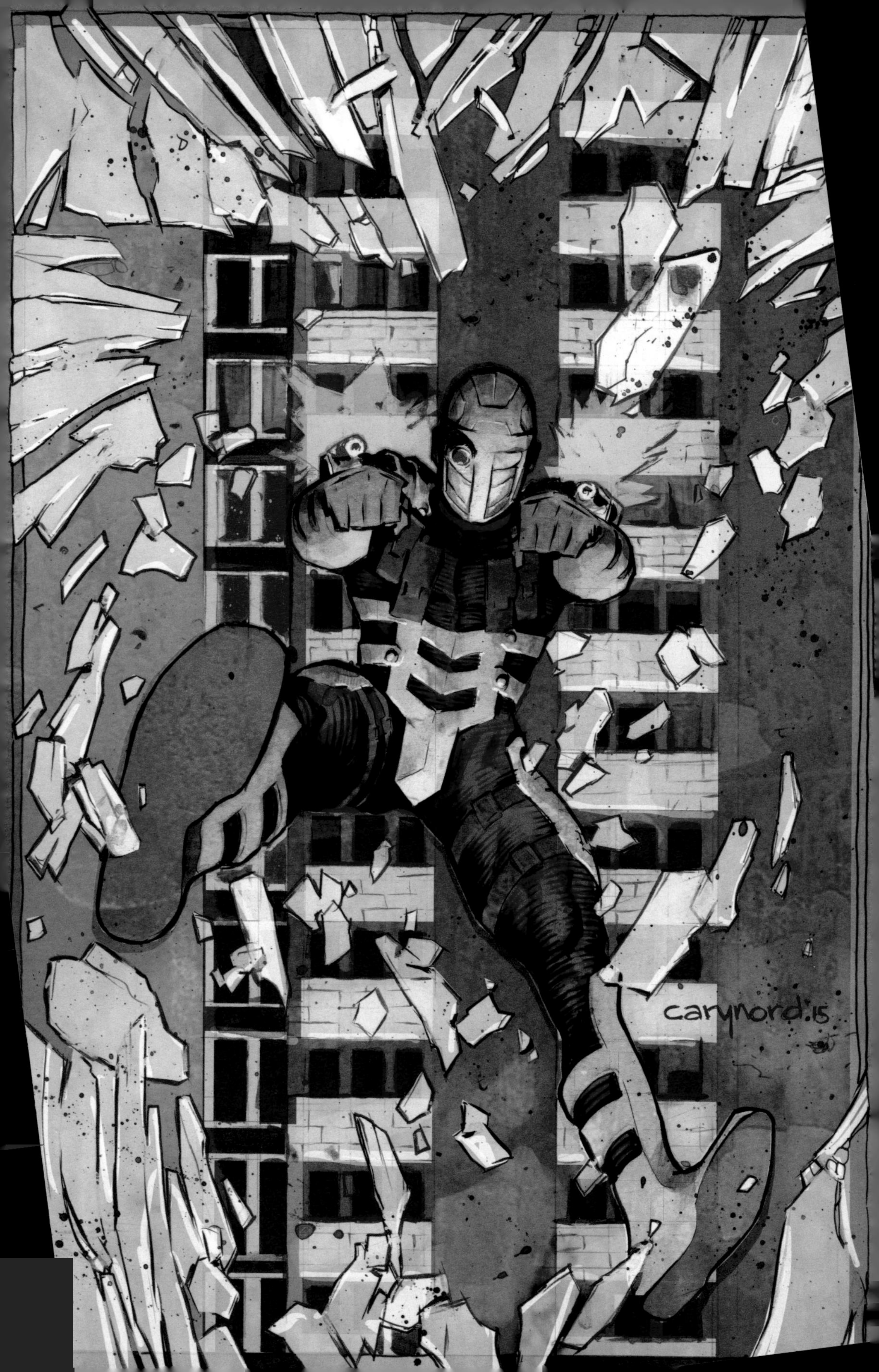
carynord.15

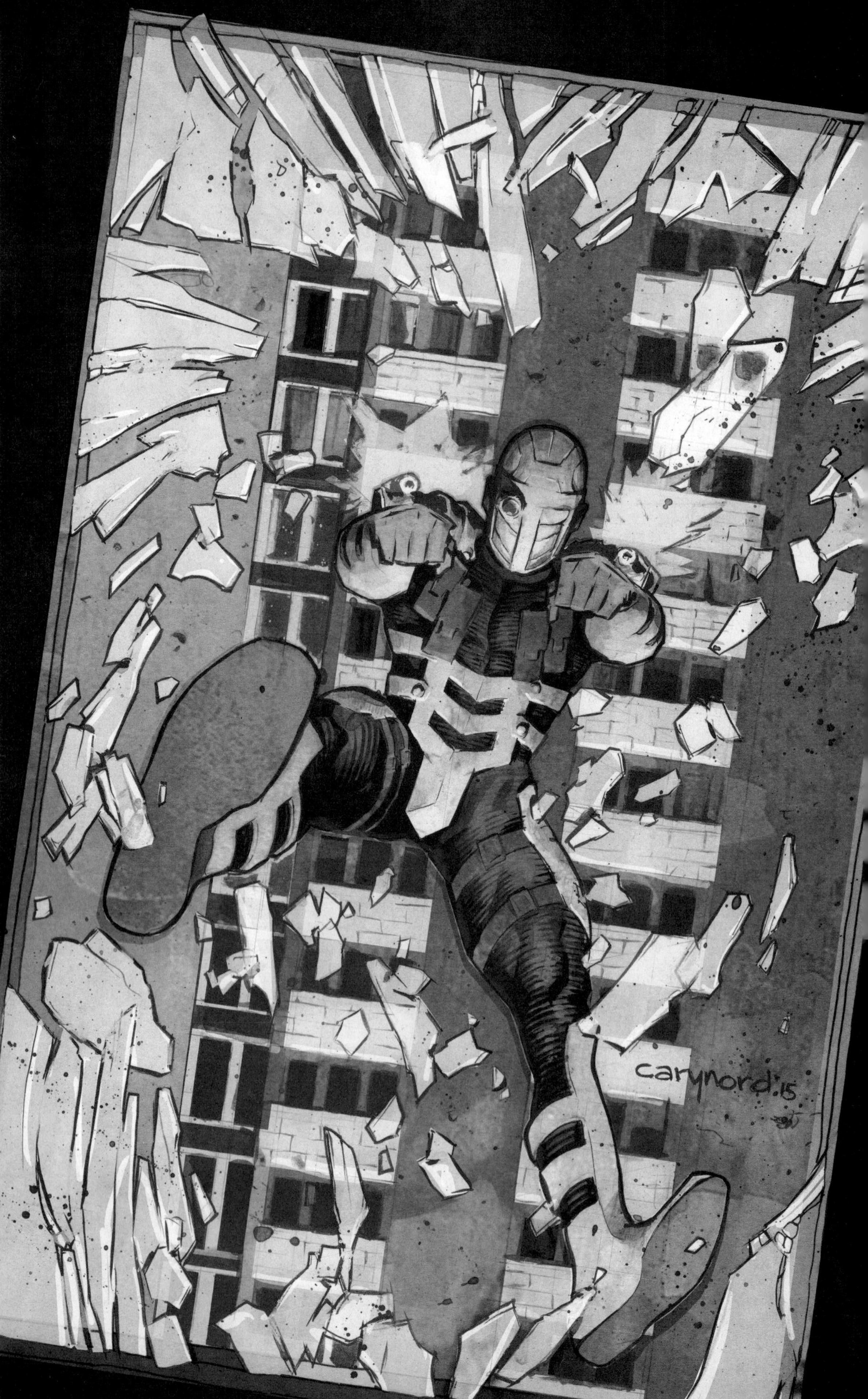
carynord.15

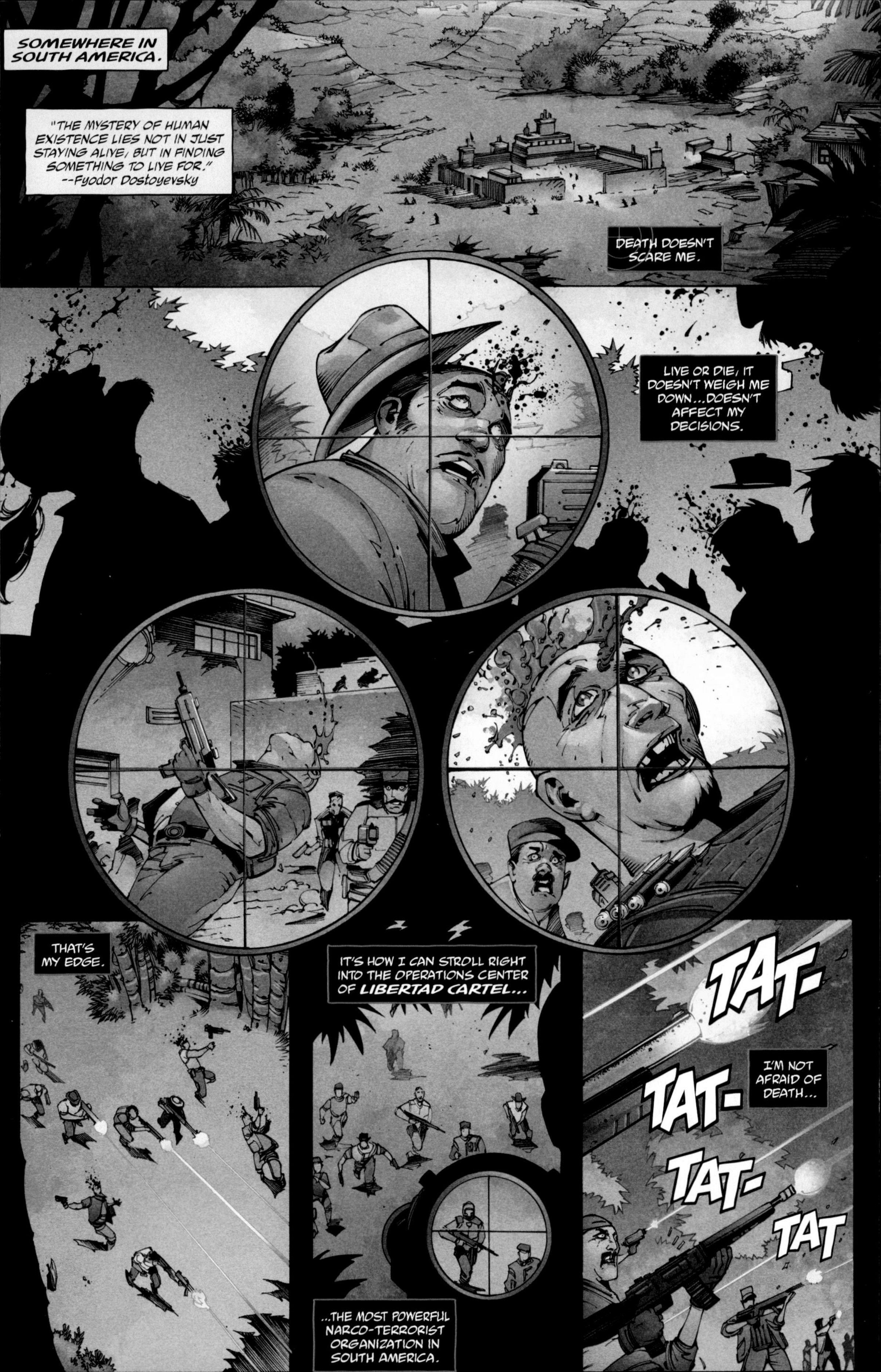
SOMEWHERE IN SOUTH AMERICA.
"THE MYSTERY OF HUMAN EXISTENCE LIES NOT IN JUST STAYING ALIVE, BUT IN FINDING SOMETHING TO LIVE FOR."
--Fyodor Dostoyevsky
DEATH DOESN'T SCARE ME.
LIVE OR DIE, IT DOESN'T WEIGH ME DOWN...DOESN'T AFFECT MY DECISIONS.
THAT'S MY EDGE.
IT'S HOW I CAN STROLL RIGHT INTO THE OPERATIONS CENTER OF LIBERTAD CARTEL...
...THE MOST POWERFUL NARCO-TERRORIST ORGANIZATION IN SOUTH AMERICA.
TAT-
TAT-
I'M NOT AFRAID OF DEATH...
TAT-
TAT

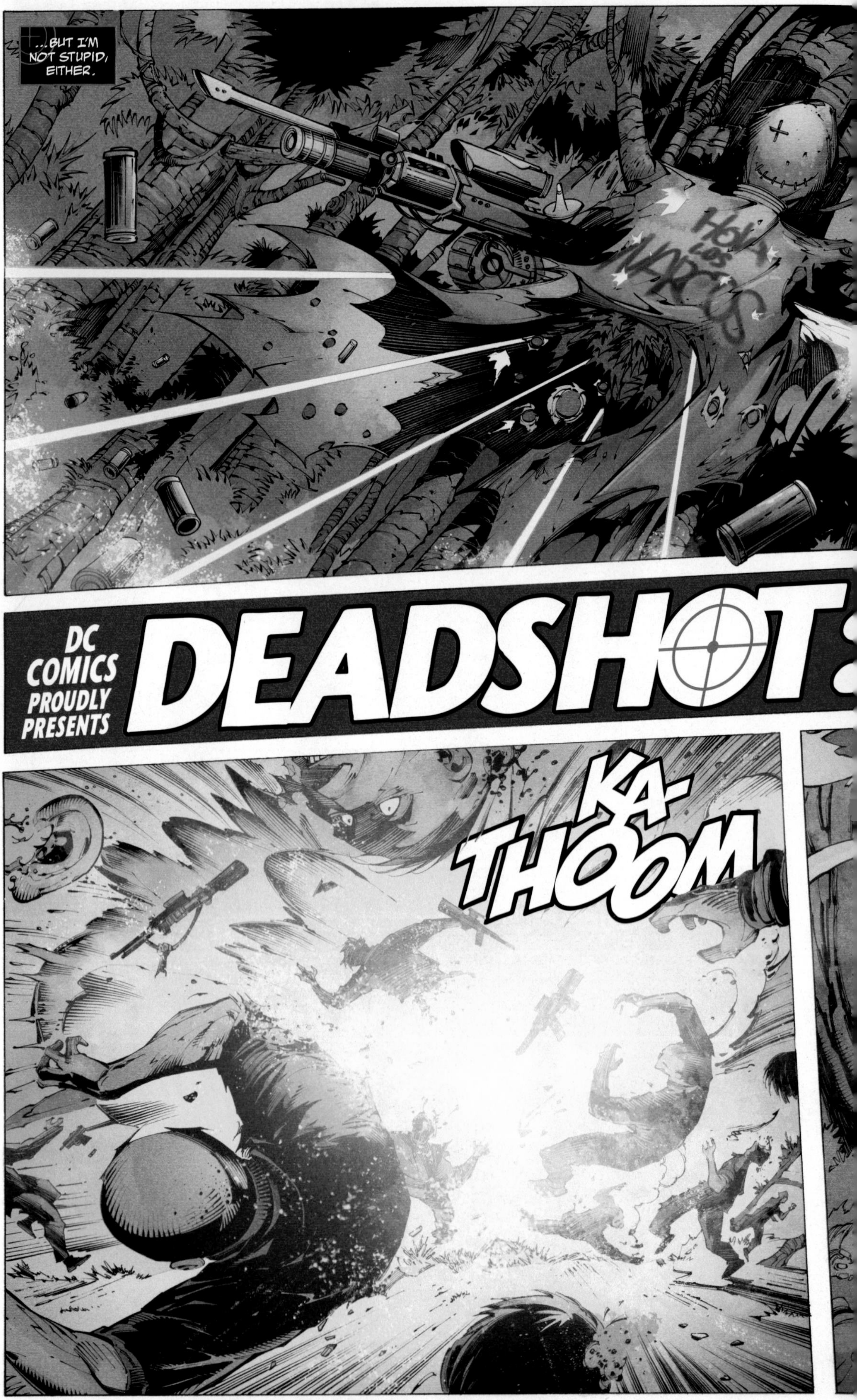
...BUT I'M NOT STUPID, EITHER.
HOLA LOS NARCOS
DC COMICS PROUDLY PRESENTS
DEADSHOT
KA-THOOM

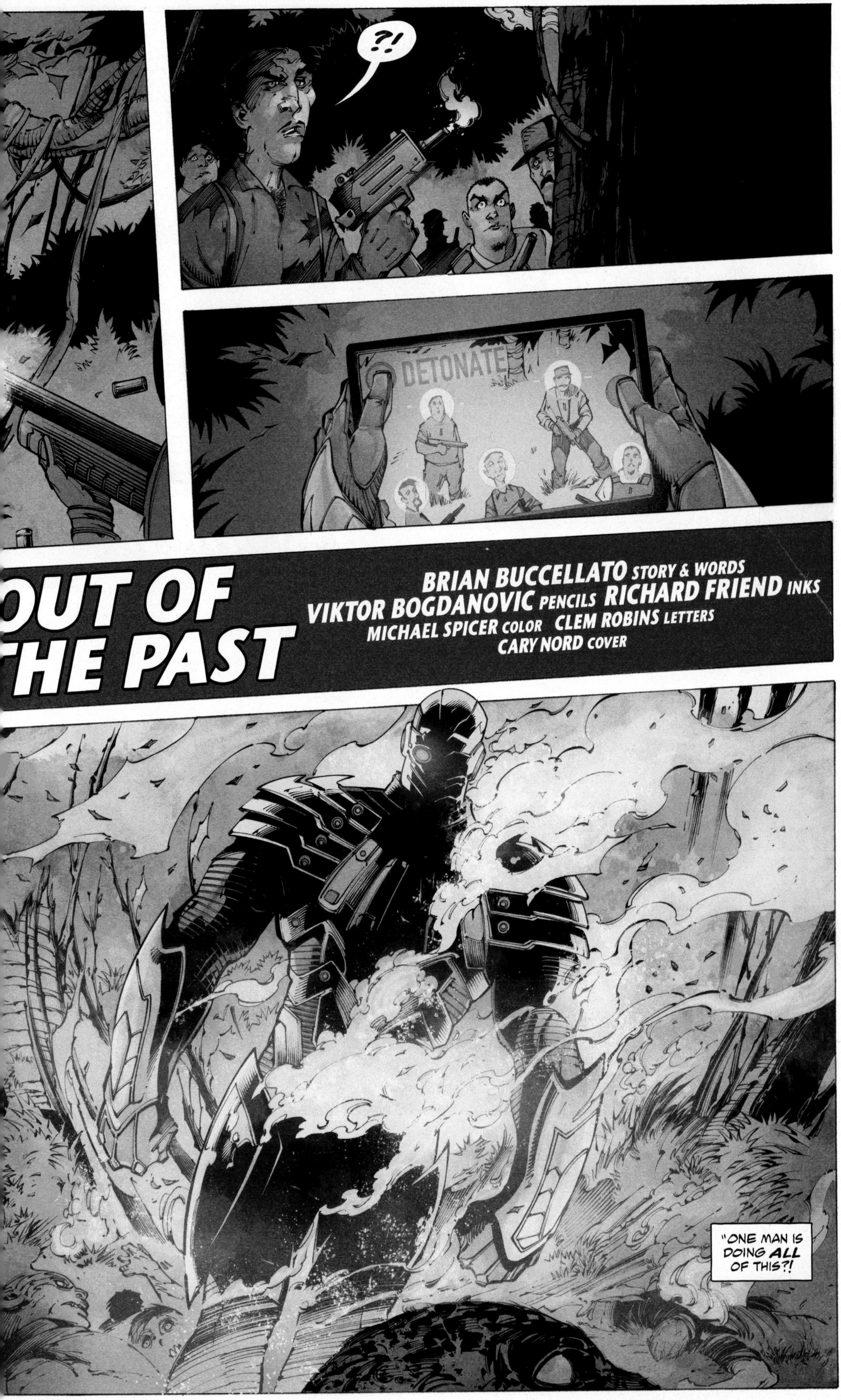
?!
DETONATE
OUT OF THE PAST
BRIAN BUCCELLATO STORY & WORDS
VIKTOR BOGDANOVIC PENCILS RICHARD FRIEND INKS
MICHAEL SPICER COLOR CLEM ROBINS LETTERS
CARY NORD COVER
"ONE MAN IS DOING ALL OF THIS?!

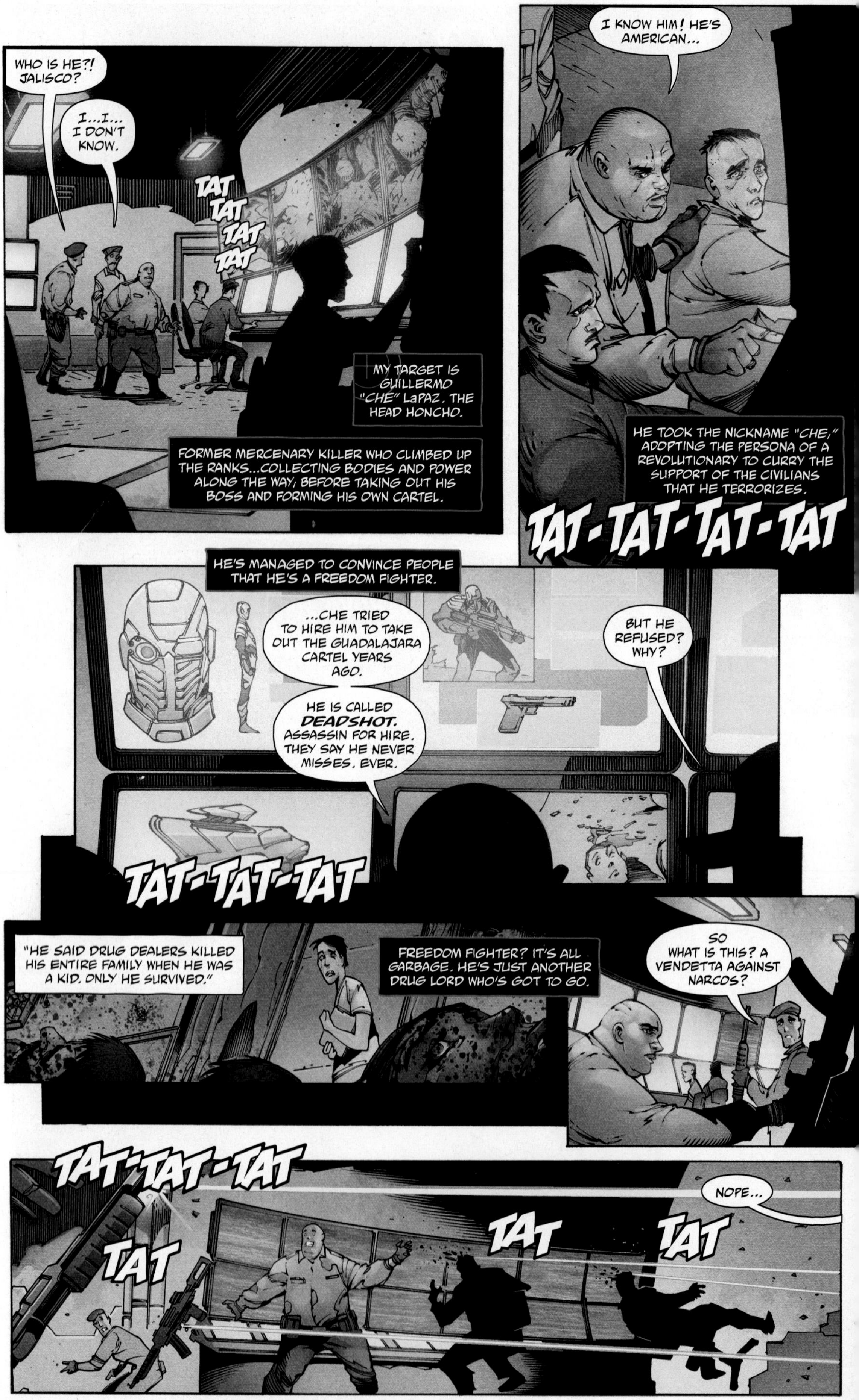
WHO IS HE?! JALISCO?
I...I... I DON'T KNOW.
TAT TAT TAT TAT
MY TARGET IS GUILLERMO "CHE" LaPAZ. THE HEAD HONCHO.
FORMER MERCENARY KILLER WHO CLIMBED UP THE RANKS...COLLECTING BODIES AND POWER ALONG THE WAY, BEFORE TAKING OUT HIS BOSS AND FORMING HIS OWN CARTEL.
I KNOW HIM! HE'S AMERICAN...
HE TOOK THE NICKNAME "CHE," ADOPTING THE PERSONA OF A REVOLUTIONARY TO CURRY THE SUPPORT OF THE CIVILIANS THAT HE TERRORIZES.
TAT-TAT-TAT-TAT
HE'S MANAGED TO CONVINCE PEOPLE THAT HE'S A FREEDOM FIGHTER.
...CHE TRIED TO HIRE HIM TO TAKE OUT THE GUADALAJARA CARTEL YEARS AGO.
HE IS CALLED DEADSHOT. ASSASSIN FOR HIRE. THEY SAY HE NEVER MISSES. EVER.
BUT HE REFUSED? WHY?
TAT-TAT-TAT
"HE SAID DRUG DEALERS KILLED HIS ENTIRE FAMILY WHEN HE WAS A KID. ONLY HE SURVIVED."
FREEDOM FIGHTER? IT'S ALL GARBAGE. HE'S JUST ANOTHER DRUG LORD WHO'S GOT TO GO.
SO WHAT IS THIS? A VENDETTA AGAINST NARCOS?
TAT-TAT-TAT
NOPE...
TAT
TAT
TAT

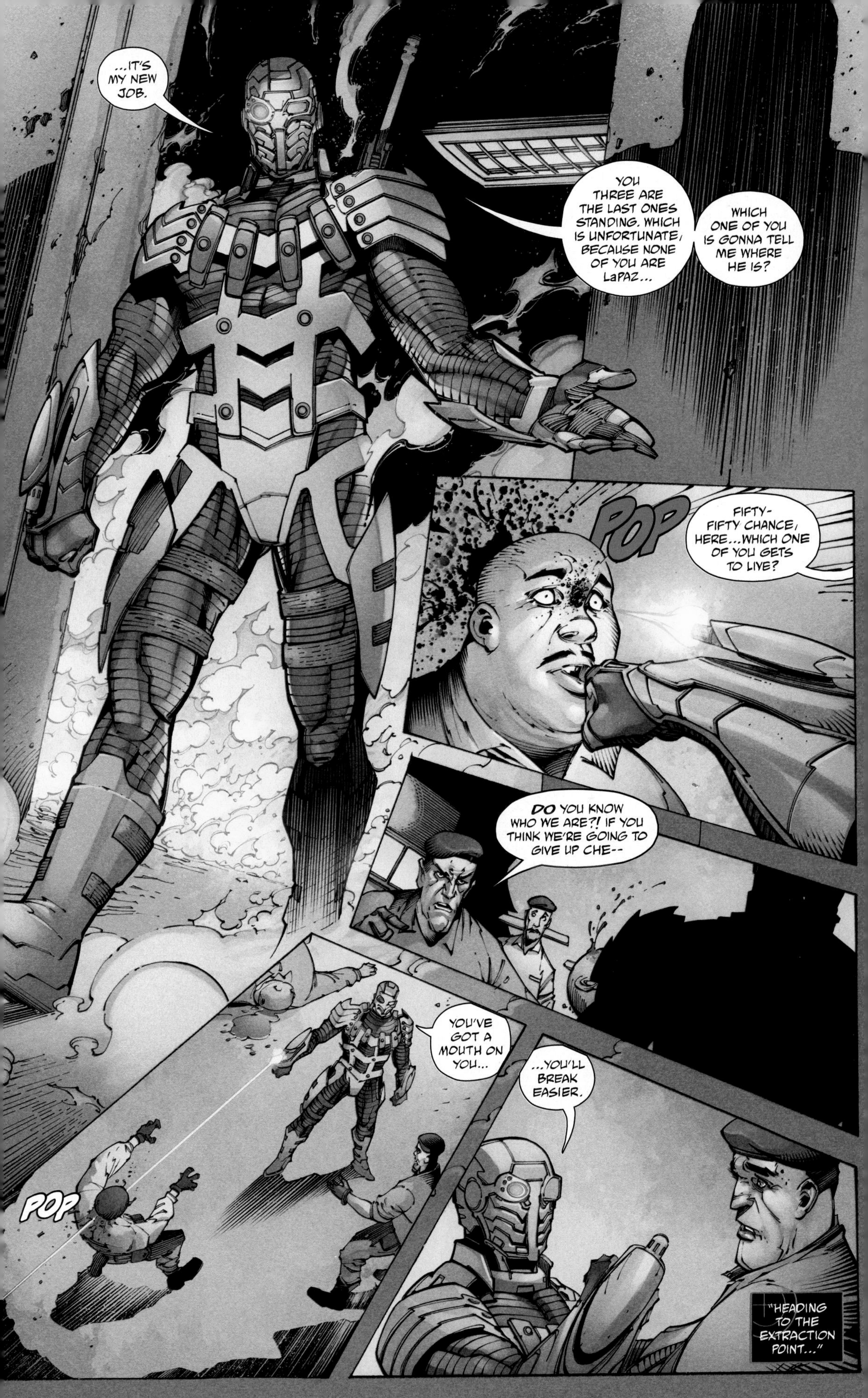
...IT'S MY NEW JOB.
YOU THREE ARE THE LAST ONES STANDING. WHICH IS UNFORTUNATE, BECAUSE NONE OF YOU ARE LaPAZ...
WHICH ONE OF YOU IS GONNA TELL ME WHERE HE IS?
POP
FIFTY-FIFTY CHANCE, HERE...WHICH ONE OF YOU GETS TO LIVE?
DO YOU KNOW WHO WE ARE?! IF YOU THINK WE'RE GOING TO GIVE UP CHE--
YOU'VE GOT A MOUTH ON YOU...
POP
...YOU'LL BREAK EASIER.
"HEADING TO THE EXTRACTION POINT..."

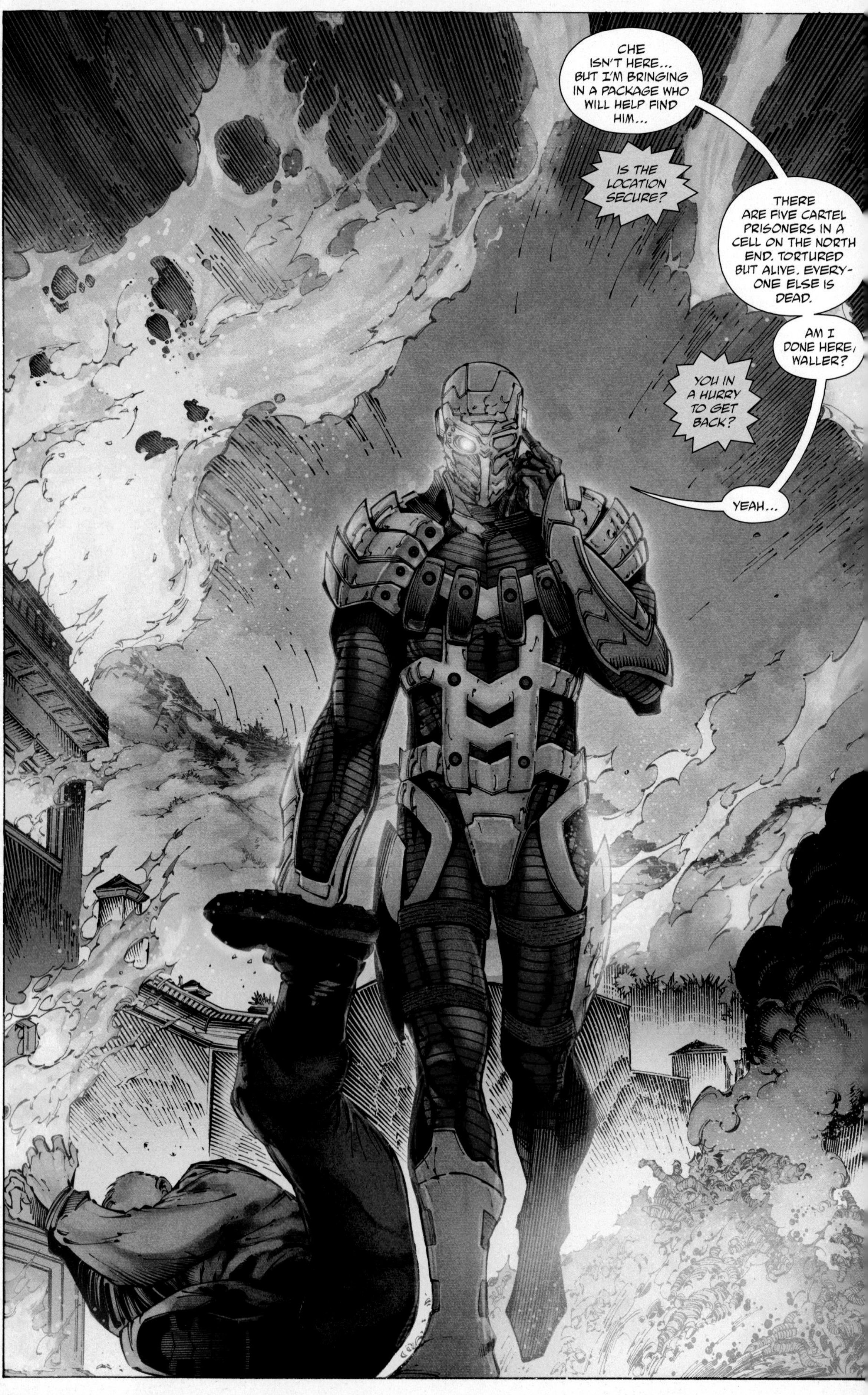
CHE ISN'T HERE... BUT I'M BRINGING IN A PACKAGE WHO WILL HELP FIND HIM...
IS THE LOCATION SECURE?
THERE ARE FIVE CARTEL PRISONERS IN A CELL ON THE NORTH END. TORTURED BUT ALIVE. EVERY-ONE ELSE IS DEAD.
AM I DONE HERE, WALLER?
YOU IN A HURRY TO GET BACK?
YEAH...

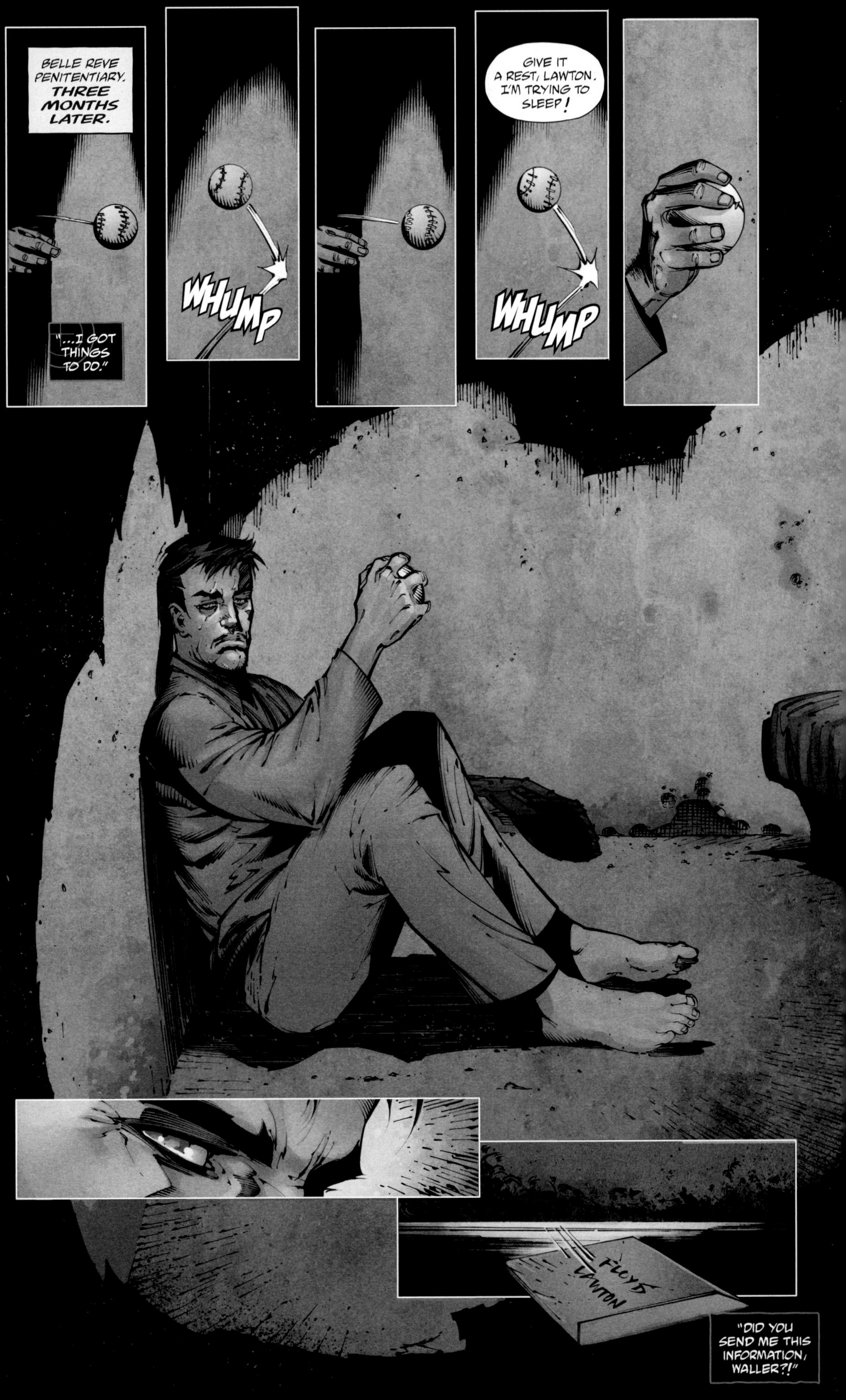
BELLE REVE PENITENTIARY. THREE MONTHS LATER.
"...I GOT THINGS TO DO."
WHUMP
GIVE IT A REST, LAWTON. I'M TRYING TO SLEEP!
WHUMP
FLOYD LAWTON
"DID YOU SEND ME THIS INFORMATION, WALLER?!"

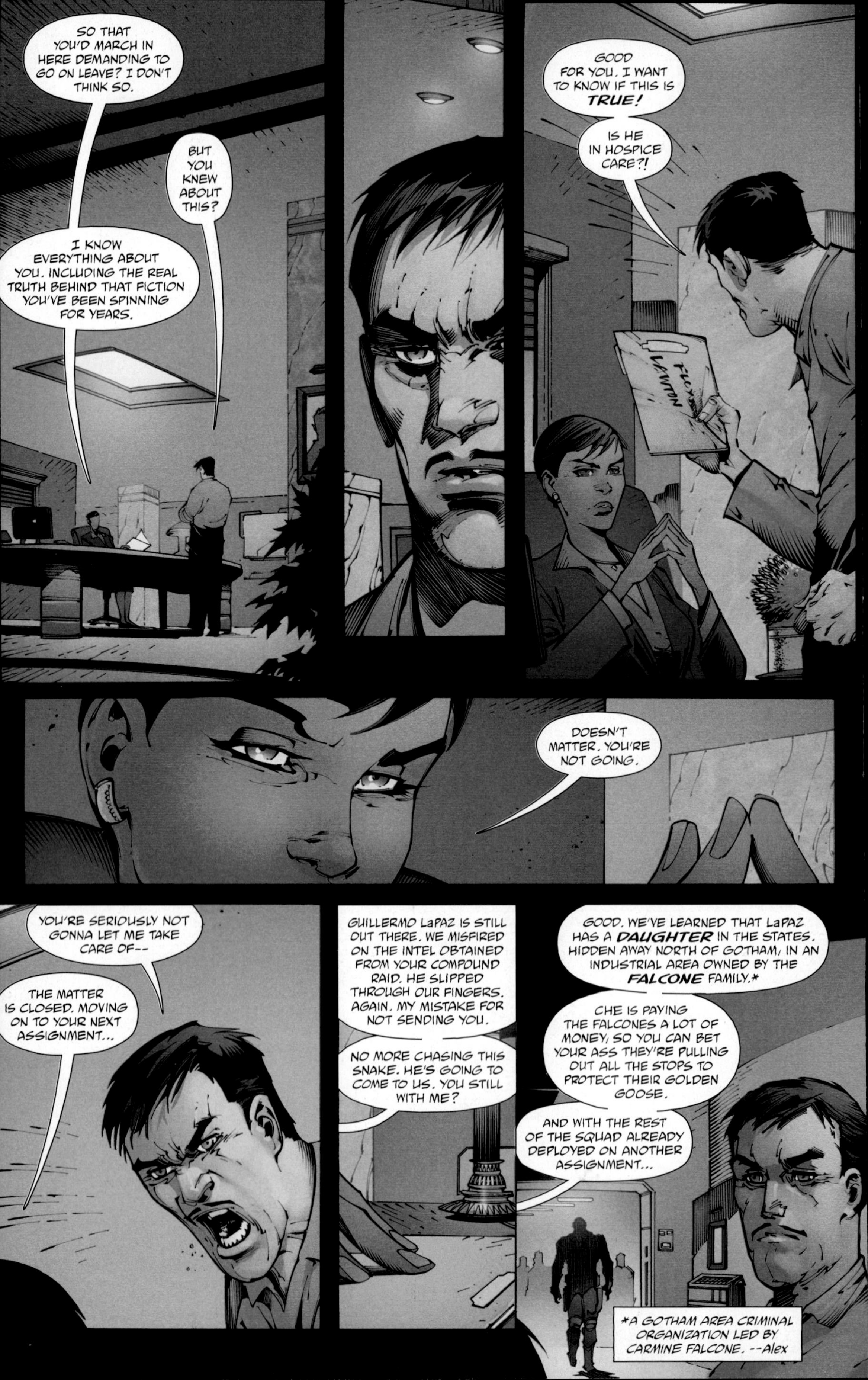
SO THAT YOU'D MARCH IN HERE DEMANDING TO GO ON LEAVE? I DON'T THINK SO.
BUT YOU KNEW ABOUT THIS?
I KNOW EVERYTHING ABOUT YOU. INCLUDING THE REAL TRUTH BEHIND THAT FICTION YOU'VE BEEN SPINNING FOR YEARS.
GOOD FOR YOU. I WANT TO KNOW IF THIS IS TRUE!
IS HE IN HOSPICE CARE?!
FLOYD LAWTON
DOESN'T MATTER. YOU'RE NOT GOING.
YOU'RE SERIOUSLY NOT GONNA LET ME TAKE CARE OF--
THE MATTER IS CLOSED. MOVING ON TO YOUR NEXT ASSIGNMENT...
GUILLERMO LaPAZ IS STILL OUT THERE. WE MISFIRED ON THE INTEL OBTAINED FROM YOUR COMPOUND RAID. HE SLIPPED THROUGH OUR FINGERS. AGAIN. MY MISTAKE FOR NOT SENDING YOU.
NO MORE CHASING THIS SNAKE. HE'S GOING TO COME TO US. YOU STILL WITH ME?
GOOD. WE'VE LEARNED THAT LaPAZ HAS A DAUGHTER IN THE STATES. HIDDEN AWAY NORTH OF GOTHAM, IN AN INDUSTRIAL AREA OWNED BY THE FALCONE FAMILY.*
CHE IS PAYING THE FALCONES A LOT OF MONEY, SO YOU CAN BET YOUR ASS THEY'RE PULLING OUT ALL THE STOPS TO PROTECT THEIR GOLDEN GOOSE.
AND WITH THE REST OF THE SQUAD ALREADY DEPLOYED ON ANOTHER ASSIGNMENT...
*A GOTHAM AREA CRIMINAL ORGANIZATION LED BY CARMINE FALCONE. --Alex

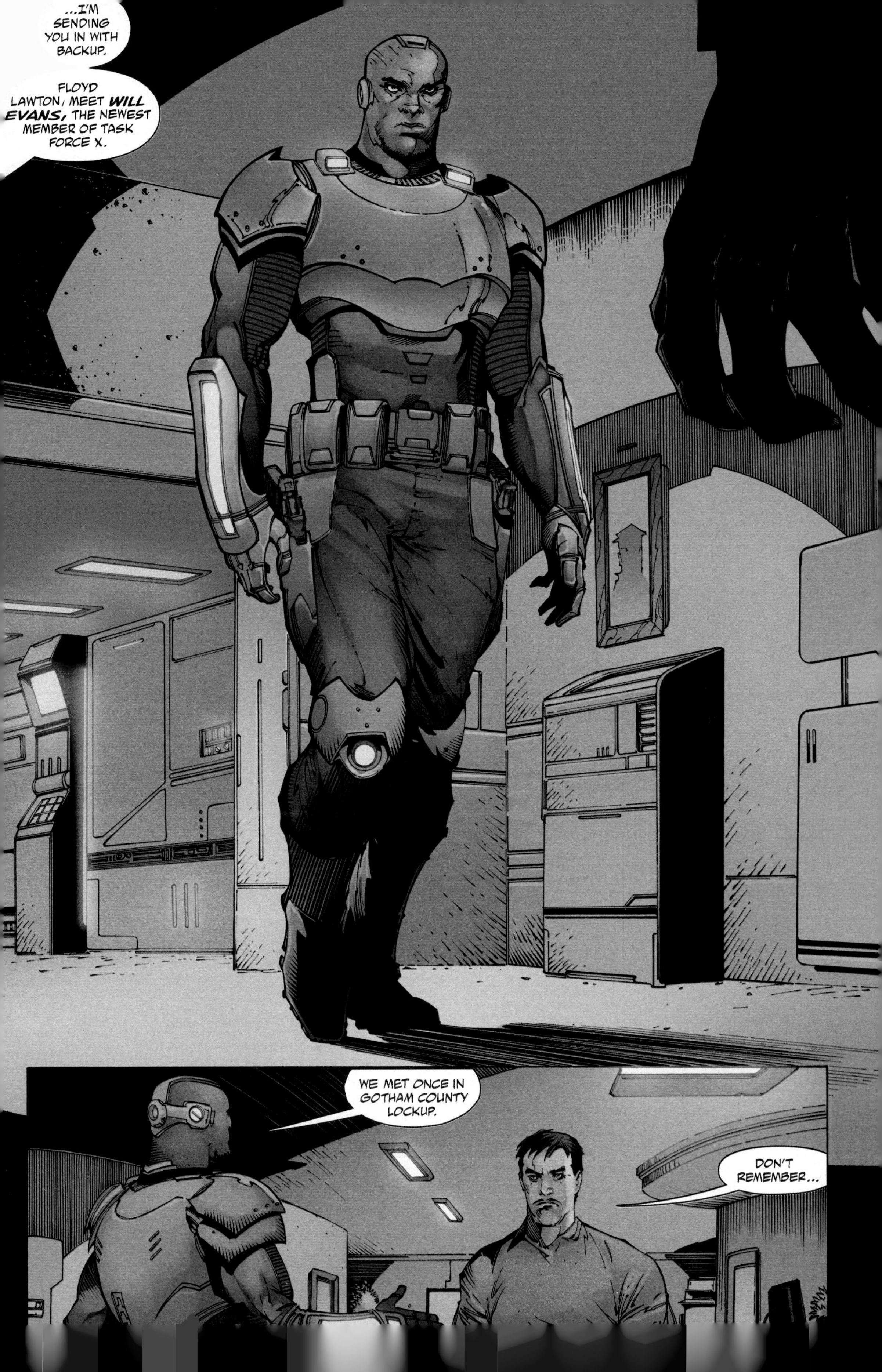
...I'M SENDING YOU IN WITH BACKUP.
FLOYD LAWTON, MEET WILL EVANS, THE NEWEST MEMBER OF TASK FORCE X.
WE MET ONCE IN GOTHAM COUNTY LOCKUP.
DON'T REMEMBER...

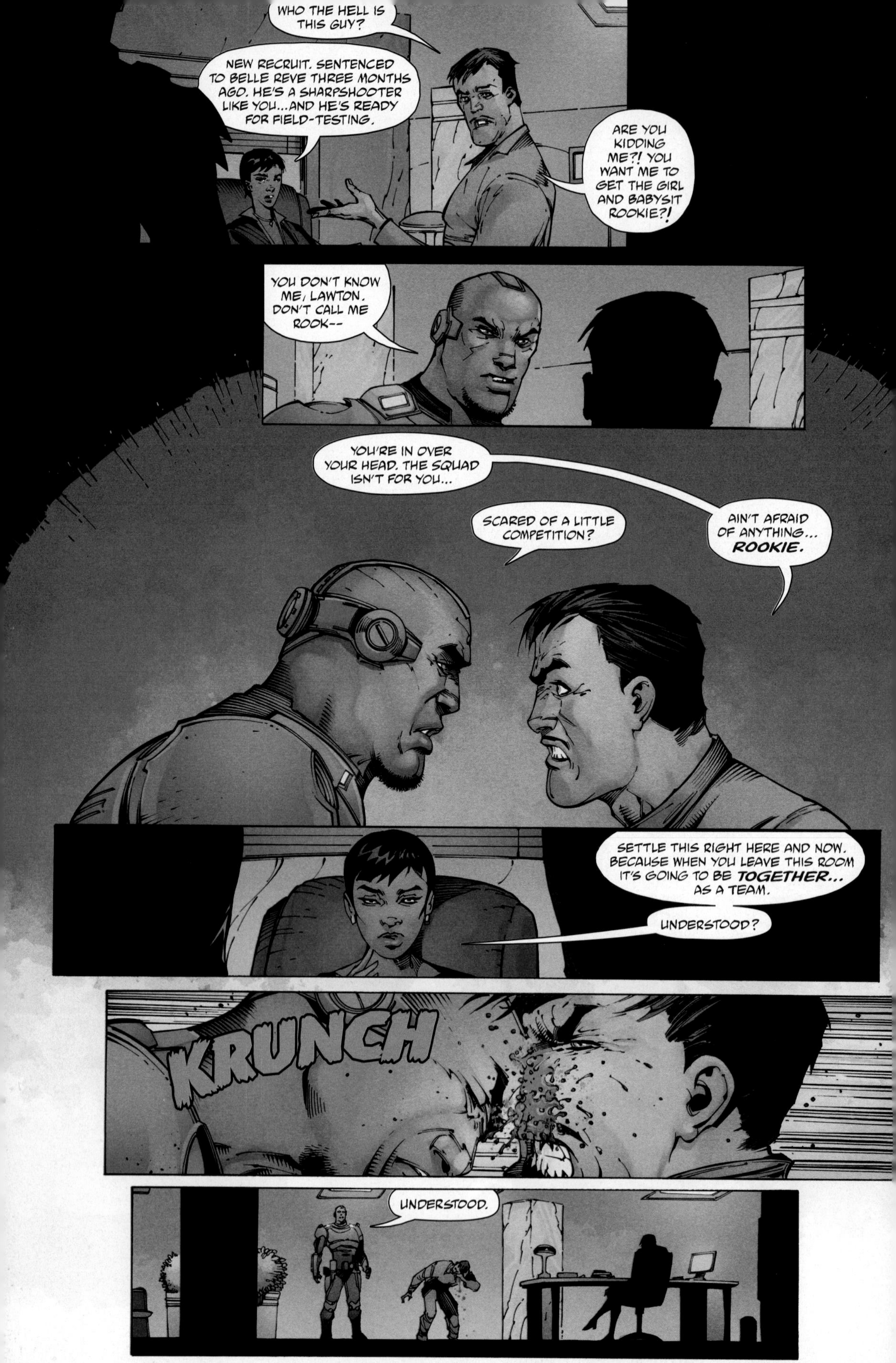
WHO THE HELL IS THIS GUY?
NEW RECRUIT. SENTENCED TO BELLE REVE THREE MONTHS AGO. HE'S A SHARPSHOOTER LIKE YOU...AND HE'S READY FOR FIELD-TESTING.
ARE YOU KIDDING ME?! YOU WANT ME TO GET THE GIRL AND BABYSIT ROOKIE?!
YOU DON'T KNOW ME, LAWTON. DON'T CALL ME ROOK--
YOU'RE IN OVER YOUR HEAD. THE SQUAD ISN'T FOR YOU...
SCARED OF A LITTLE COMPETITION?
AIN'T AFRAID OF ANYTHING... ROOKIE.
SETTLE THIS RIGHT HERE AND NOW. BECAUSE WHEN YOU LEAVE THIS ROOM IT'S GOING TO BE TOGETHER... AS A TEAM.
UNDERSTOOD?
KRUNCH
UNDERSTOOD.

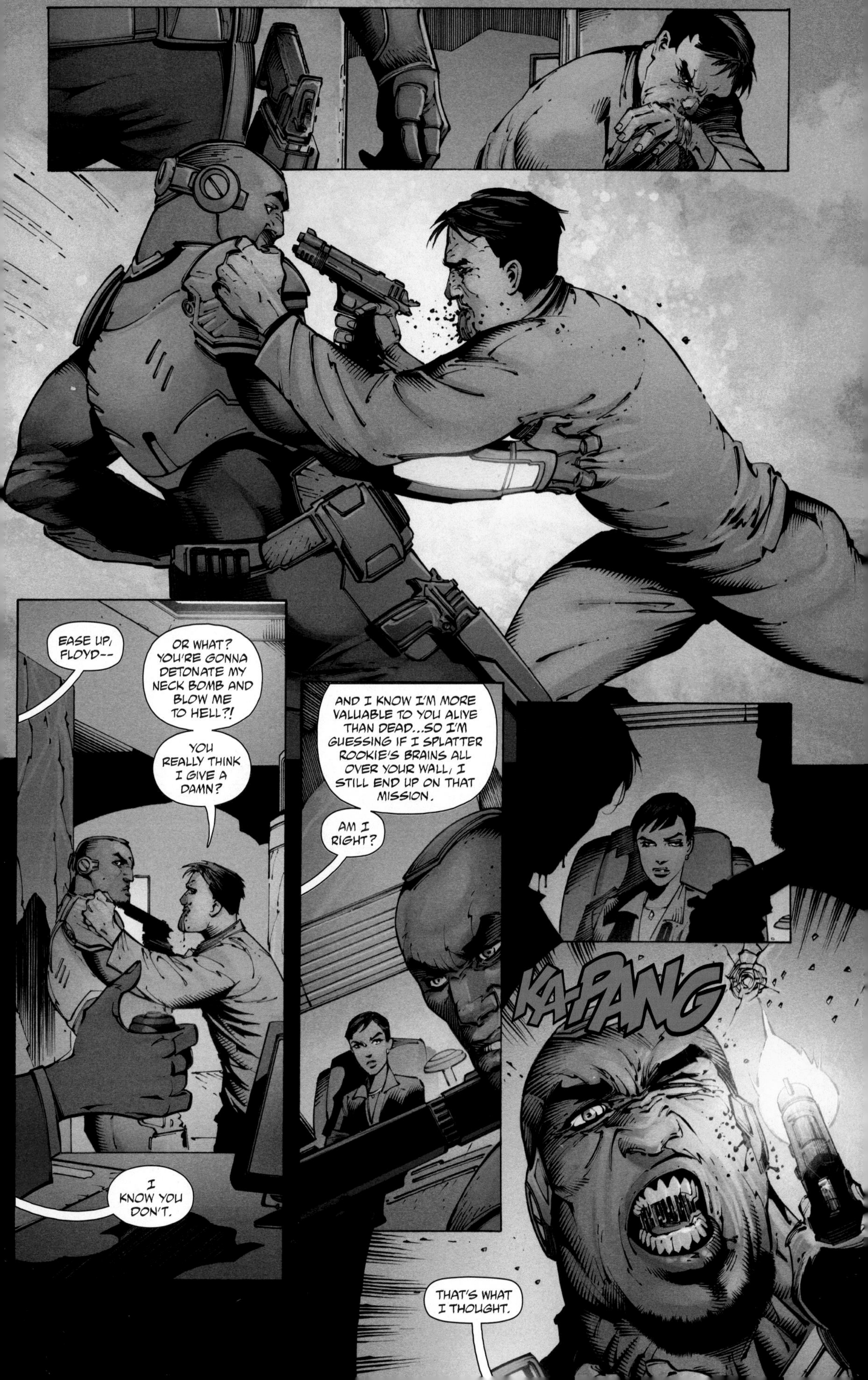

EASE UP, FLOYD--
OR WHAT? YOU'RE GONNA DETONATE MY NECK BOMB AND BLOW ME TO HELL?!
YOU REALLY THINK I GIVE A DAMN?
I KNOW YOU DON'T.
AND I KNOW I'M MORE VALUABLE TO YOU ALIVE THAN DEAD...SO I'M GUESSING IF I SPLATTER ROOKIE'S BRAINS ALL OVER YOUR WALL, I STILL END UP ON THAT MISSION.
AM I RIGHT?
KA-PANG
THAT'S WHAT I THOUGHT.

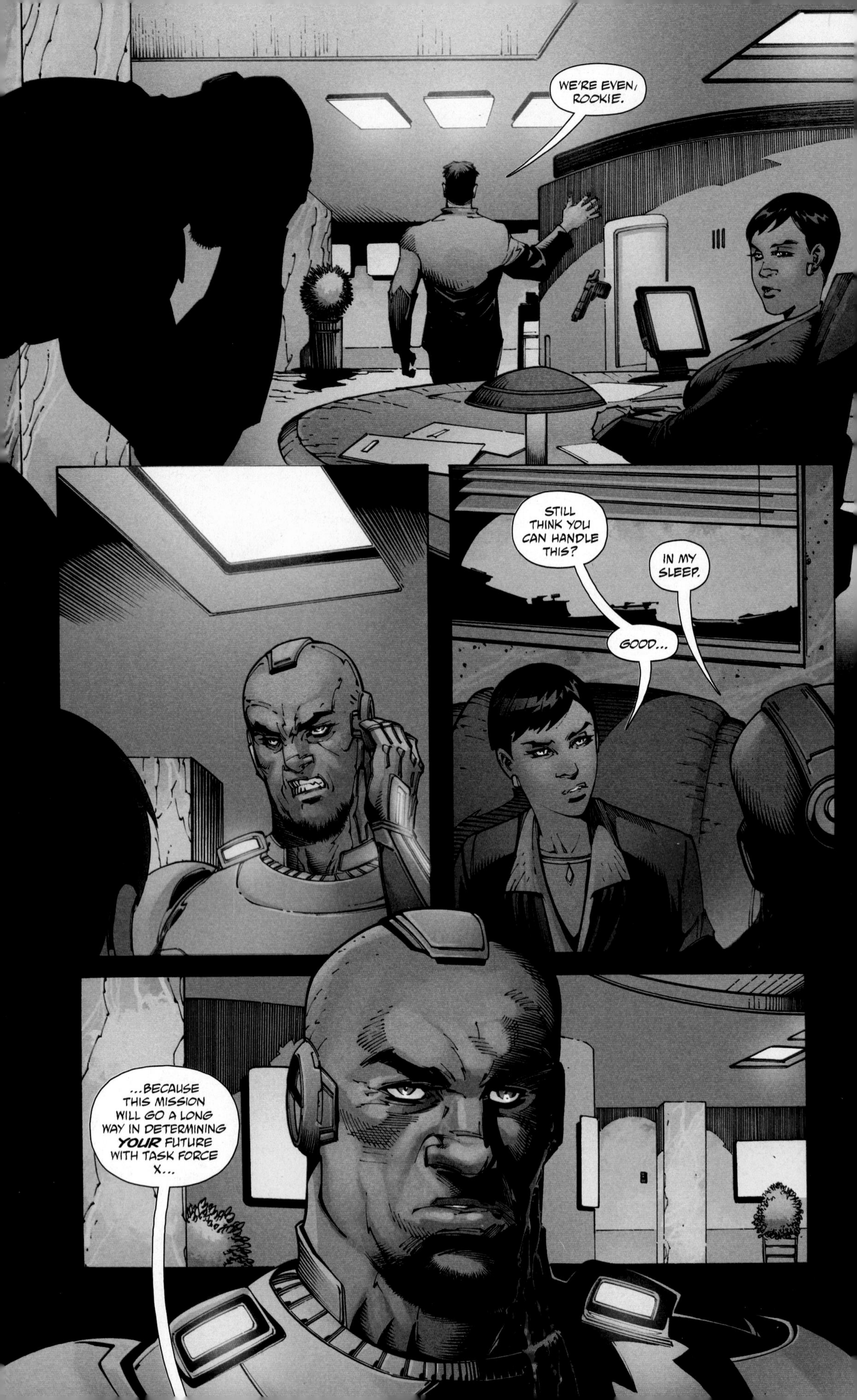
WE'RE EVEN, ROOKIE.
STILL THINK YOU CAN HANDLE THIS?
IN MY SLEEP.
GOOD...
...BECAUSE THIS MISSION WILL GO A LONG WAY IN DETERMINING YOUR FUTURE WITH TASK FORCE X...

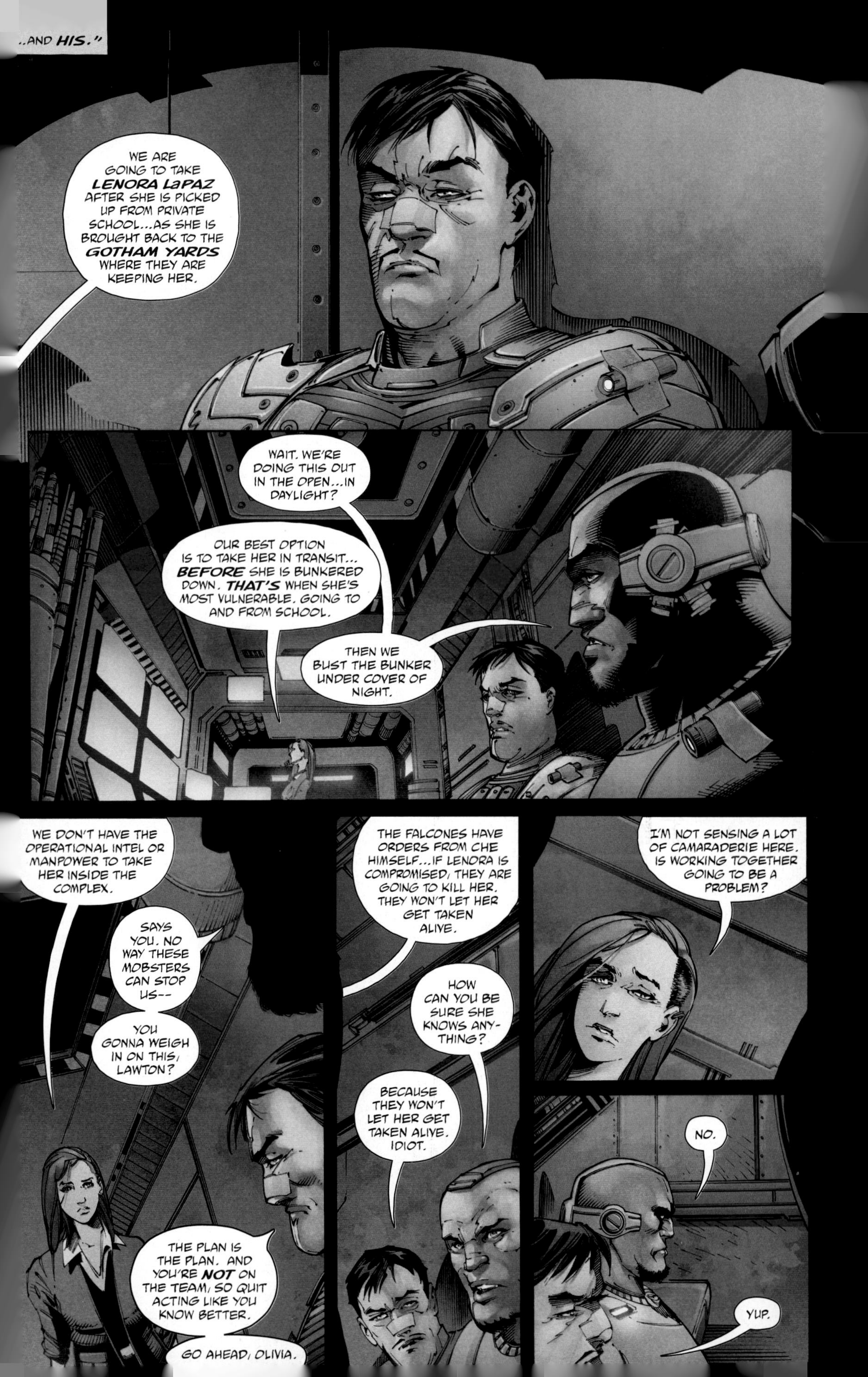
..AND HIS."
WE ARE GOING TO TAKE LENORA LaPAZ AFTER SHE IS PICKED UP FROM PRIVATE SCHOOL...AS SHE IS BROUGHT BACK TO THE GOTHAM YARDS WHERE THEY ARE KEEPING HER.
WAIT. WE'RE DOING THIS OUT IN THE OPEN...IN DAYLIGHT?
OUR BEST OPTION IS TO TAKE HER IN TRANSIT... BEFORE SHE IS BUNKERED DOWN. THAT'S WHEN SHE'S MOST VULNERABLE. GOING TO AND FROM SCHOOL.
THEN WE BUST THE BUNKER UNDER COVER OF NIGHT.
WE DON'T HAVE THE OPERATIONAL INTEL OR MANPOWER TO TAKE HER INSIDE THE COMPLEX.
SAYS YOU. NO WAY THESE MOBSTERS CAN STOP US--
YOU GONNA WEIGH IN ON THIS, LAWTON?
THE PLAN IS THE PLAN. AND YOU'RE NOT ON THE TEAM, SO QUIT ACTING LIKE YOU KNOW BETTER.
GO AHEAD, OLIVIA.
THE FALCONES HAVE ORDERS FROM CHE HIMSELF...IF LENORA IS COMPROMISED, THEY ARE GOING TO KILL HER. THEY WON'T LET HER GET TAKEN ALIVE.
HOW CAN YOU BE SURE SHE KNOWS ANYTHING?
BECAUSE THEY WON'T LET HER GET TAKEN ALIVE. IDIOT.
I'M NOT SENSING A LOT OF CAMARADERIE HERE. IS WORKING TOGETHER GOING TO BE A PROBLEM?
NO.
YUP.

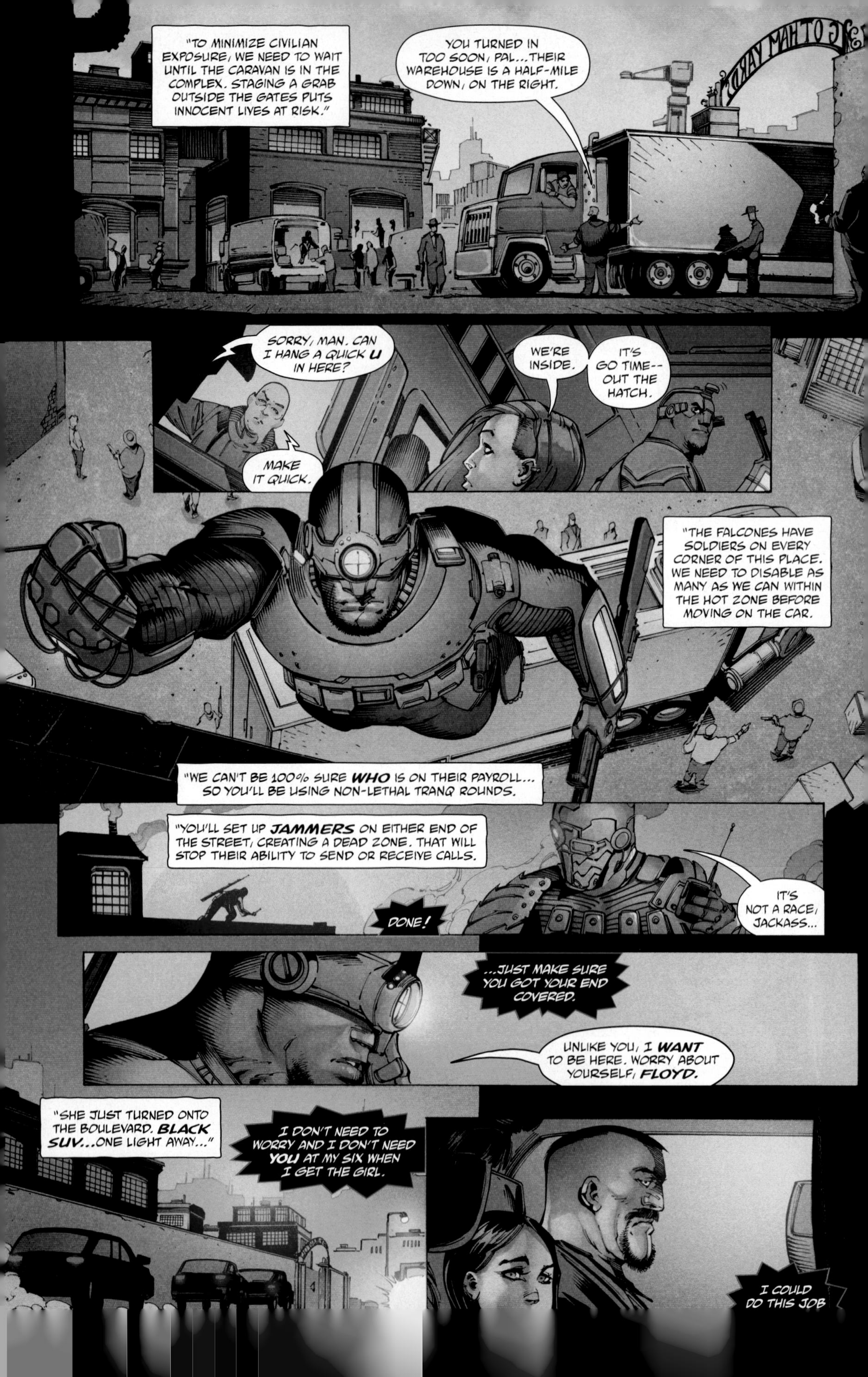

GOTHAM YARDS
"TO MINIMIZE CIVILIAN EXPOSURE, WE NEED TO WAIT UNTIL THE CARAVAN IS IN THE COMPLEX. STAGING A GRAB OUTSIDE THE GATES PUTS INNOCENT LIVES AT RISK."
YOU TURNED IN TOO SOON, PAL...THEIR WAREHOUSE IS A HALF-MILE DOWN, ON THE RIGHT.
SORRY, MAN. CAN I HANG A QUICK U IN HERE?
MAKE IT QUICK.
WE'RE INSIDE.
IT'S GO TIME--OUT THE HATCH.
"THE FALCONES HAVE SOLDIERS ON EVERY CORNER OF THIS PLACE. WE NEED TO DISABLE AS MANY AS WE CAN WITHIN THE HOT ZONE BEFORE MOVING ON THE CAR.
"WE CAN'T BE 100% SURE WHO IS ON THEIR PAYROLL... SO YOU'LL BE USING NON-LETHAL TRANQ ROUNDS.
"YOU'LL SET UP JAMMERS ON EITHER END OF THE STREET, CREATING A DEAD ZONE. THAT WILL STOP THEIR ABILITY TO SEND OR RECEIVE CALLS.
DONE!
IT'S NOT A RACE, JACKASS...
...JUST MAKE SURE YOU GOT YOUR END COVERED.
UNLIKE YOU, I WANT TO BE HERE. WORRY ABOUT YOURSELF, FLOYD.
"SHE JUST TURNED ONTO THE BOULEVARD. BLACK SUV...ONE LIGHT AWAY..."
I DON'T NEED TO WORRY AND I DON'T NEED YOU AT MY SIX WHEN I GET THE GIRL.
I COULD DO THIS JOB

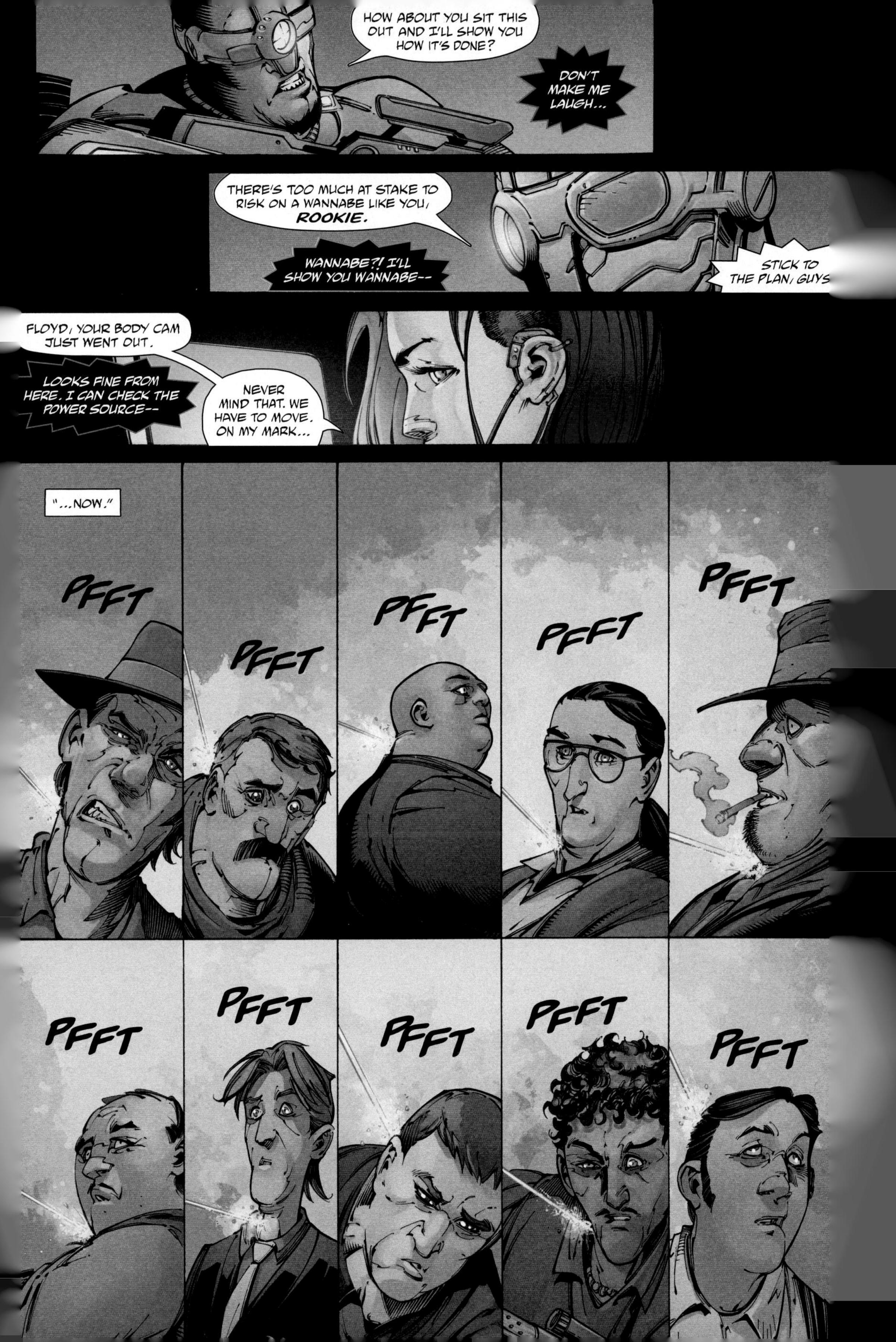
HOW ABOUT YOU SIT THIS OUT AND I'LL SHOW YOU HOW IT'S DONE?
DON'T MAKE ME LAUGH...
THERE'S TOO MUCH AT STAKE TO RISK ON A WANNABE LIKE YOU, ROOKIE.
WANNABE?! I'LL SHOW YOU WANNABE--
STICK TO THE PLAN, GUYS
FLOYD, YOUR BODY CAM JUST WENT OUT.
LOOKS FINE FROM HERE. I CAN CHECK THE POWER SOURCE--
NEVER MIND THAT. WE HAVE TO MOVE. ON MY MARK...
"...NOW."
PFFT
PFFT
PFFT
PFFT
PFFT
PFFT
PFFT
PFFT
PFFT
PFFT

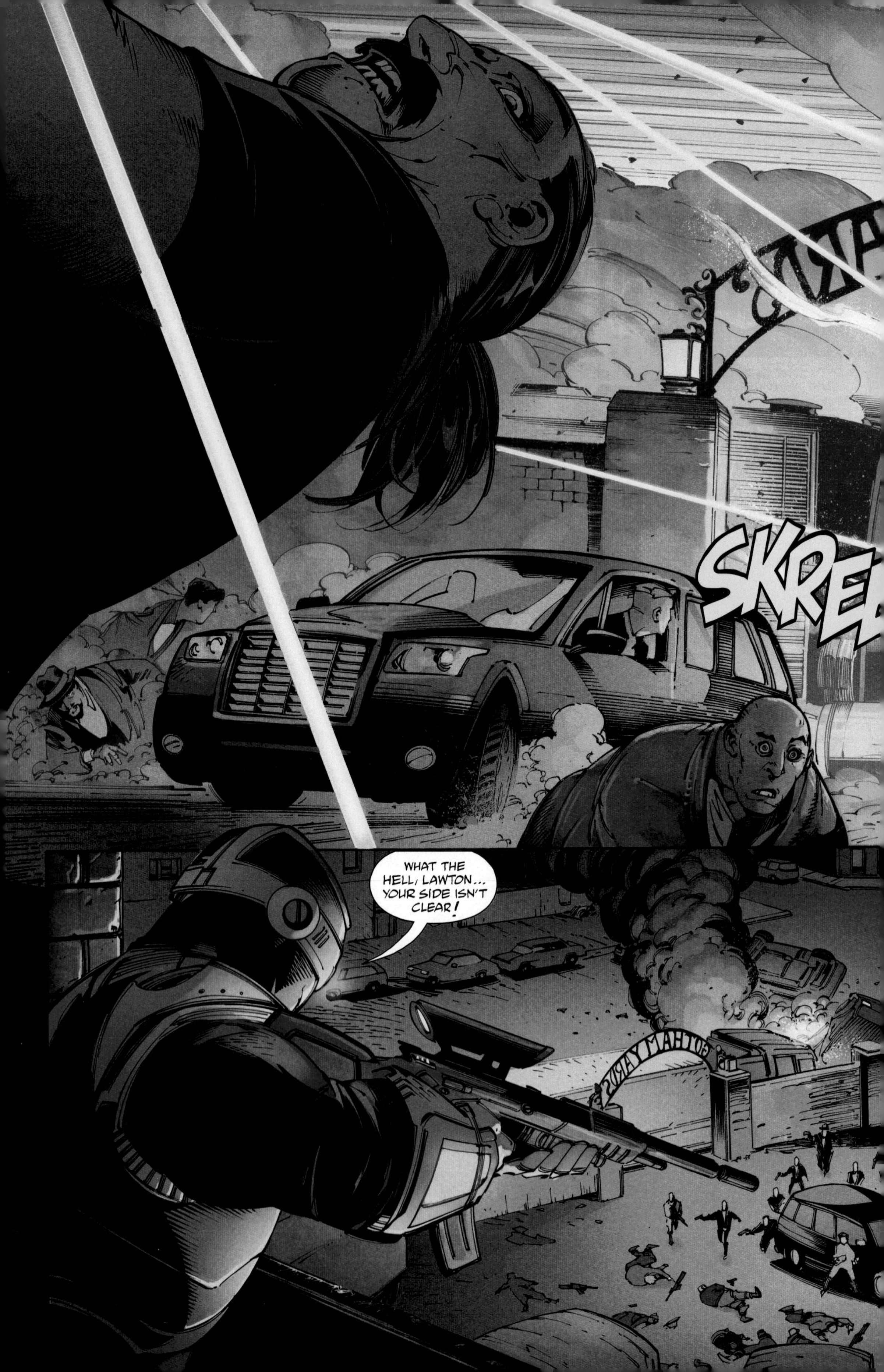
SKREE
WHAT THE HELL, LAWTON... YOUR SIDE ISN'T CLEAR!
GOTHAM YARDS

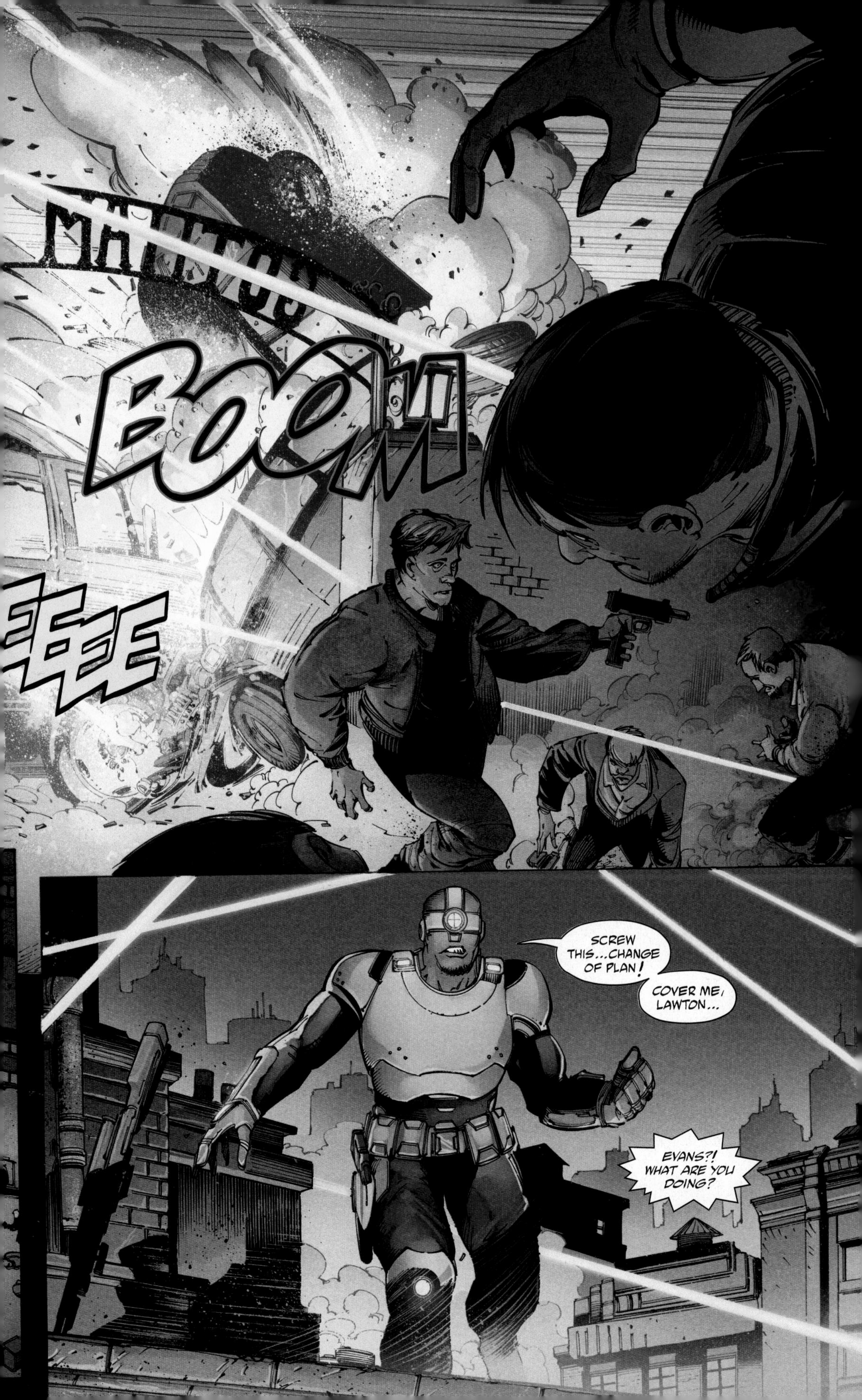
BOOM
EEEE
SCREW THIS...CHANGE OF PLAN!
COVER ME, LAWTON...
EVANS?! WHAT ARE YOU DOING?

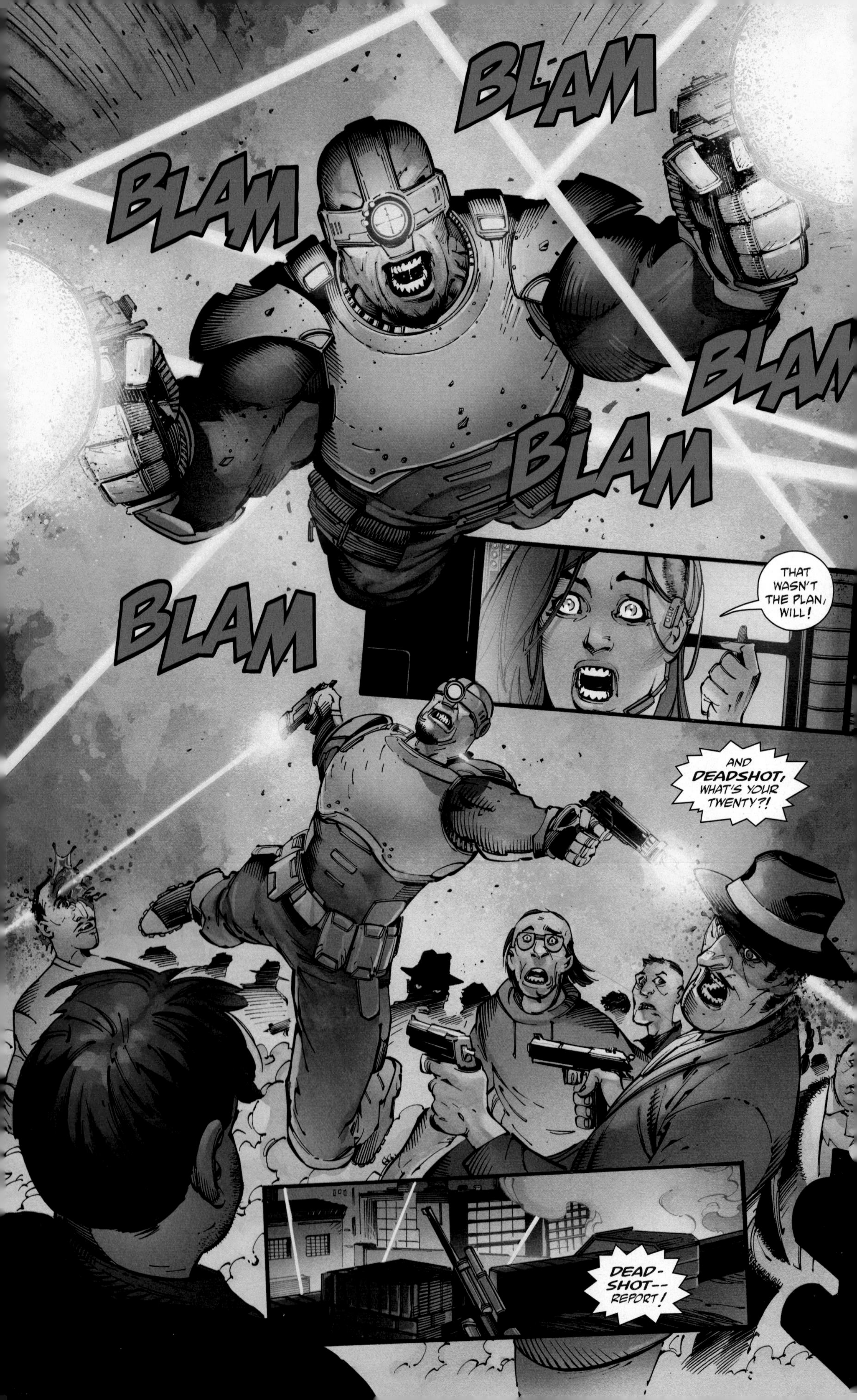
BLAM
BLAM
BLAM
BLAM
BLAM
THAT WASN'T THE PLAN, WILL!
AND DEADSHOT, WHAT'S YOUR TWENTY?!
DEAD-SHOT-- REPORT!

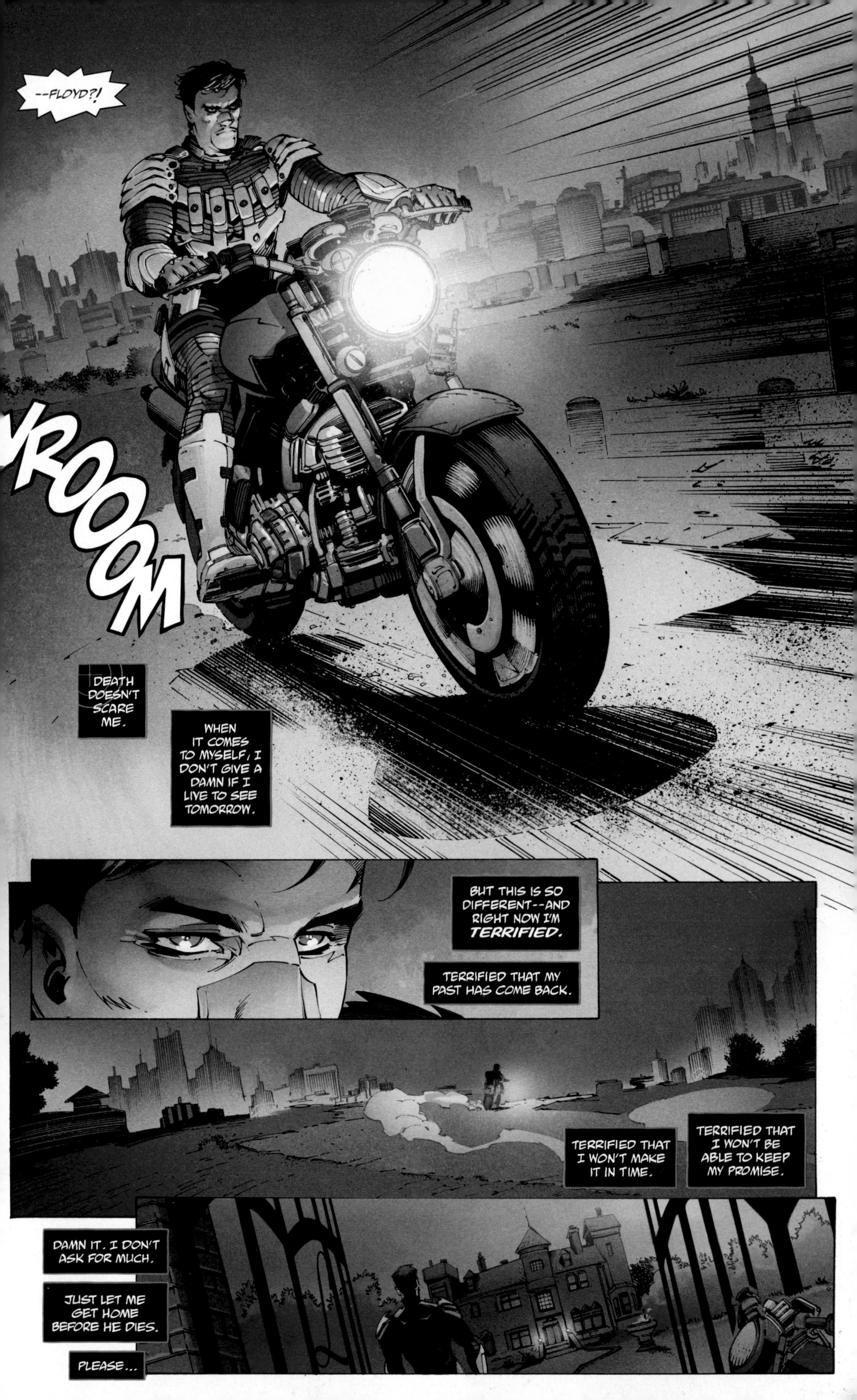
--FLOYD?!
VROOOOM
DEATH DOESN'T SCARE ME.
WHEN IT COMES TO MYSELF, I DON'T GIVE A DAMN IF I LIVE TO SEE TOMORROW.
BUT THIS IS SO DIFFERENT--AND RIGHT NOW I'M *TERRIFIED.*
TERRIFIED THAT MY PAST HAS COME BACK.
TERRIFIED THAT I WON'T MAKE IT IN TIME.
TERRIFIED THAT I WON'T BE ABLE TO KEEP MY PROMISE.
DAMN IT. I DON'T ASK FOR MUCH.
JUST LET ME GET HOME BEFORE HE DIES.
PLEASE...

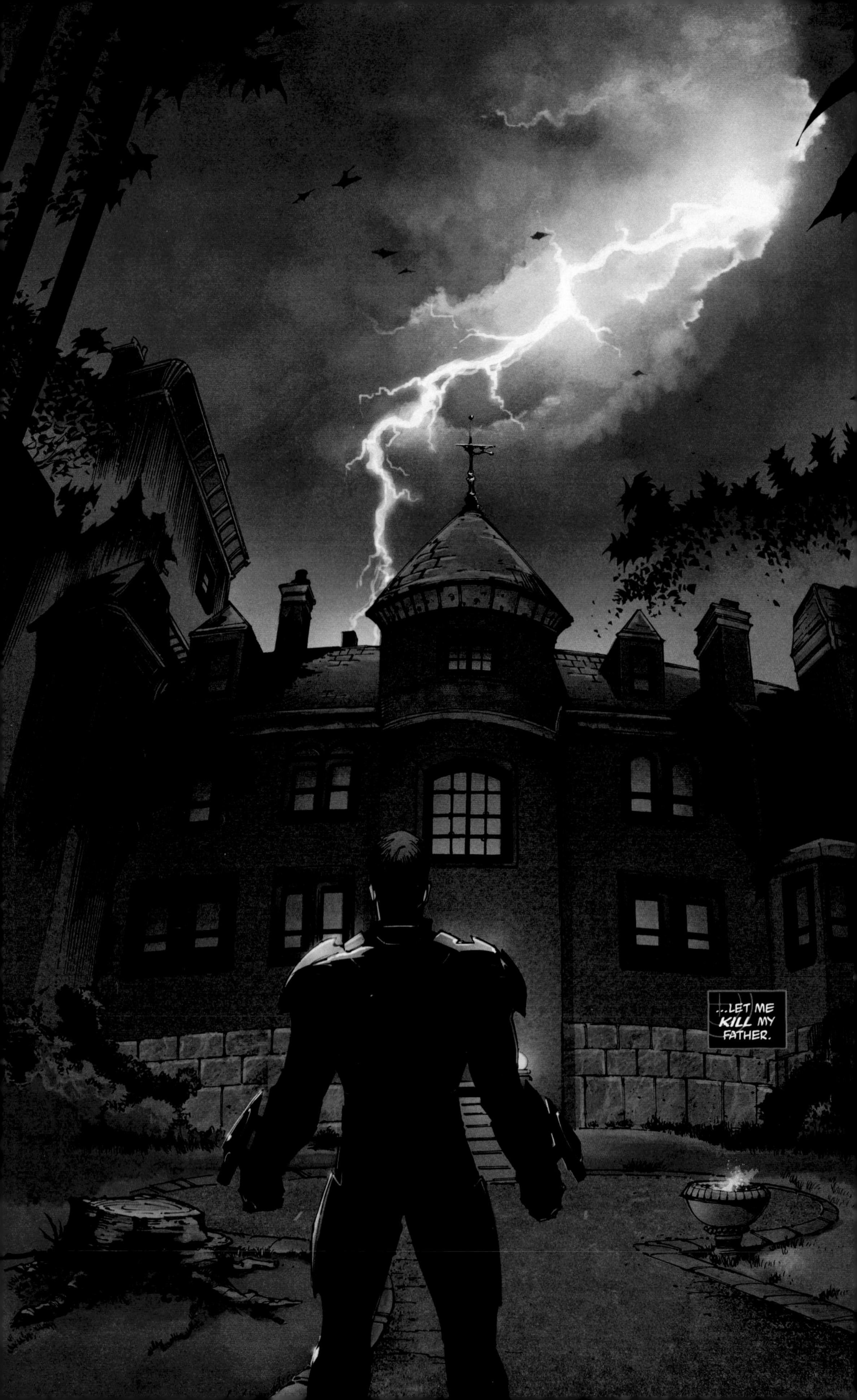
...LET ME KILL MY FATHER.

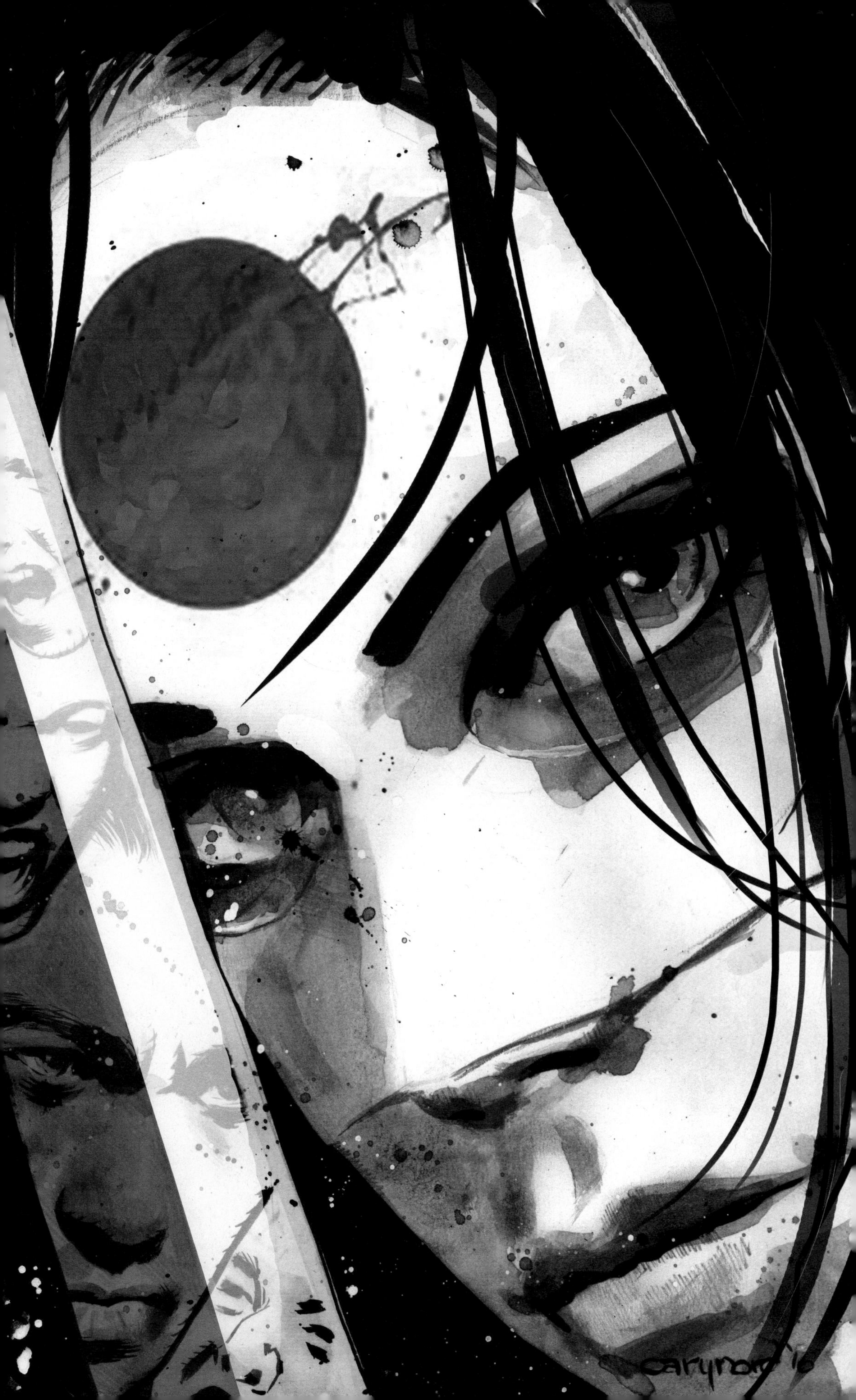

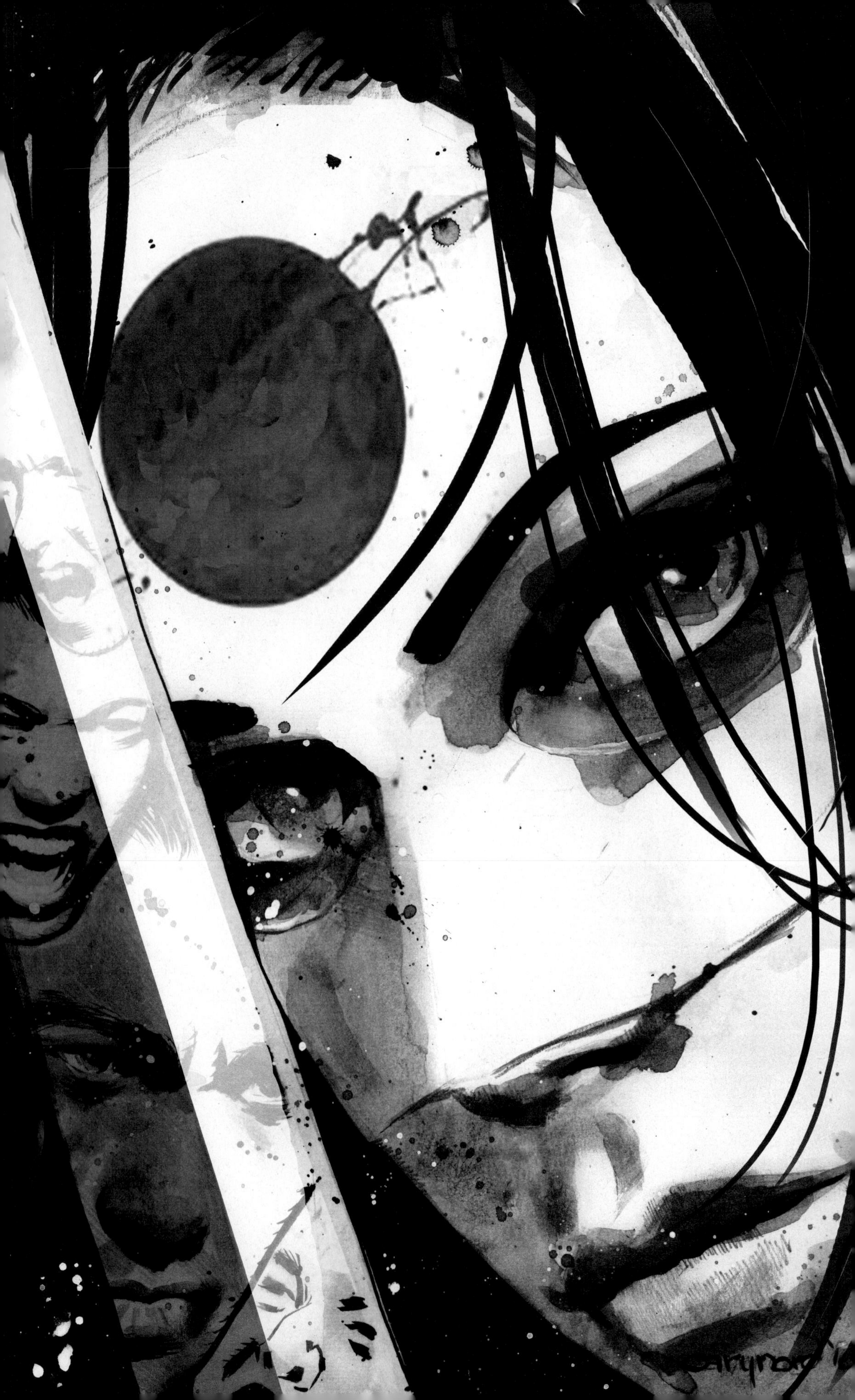

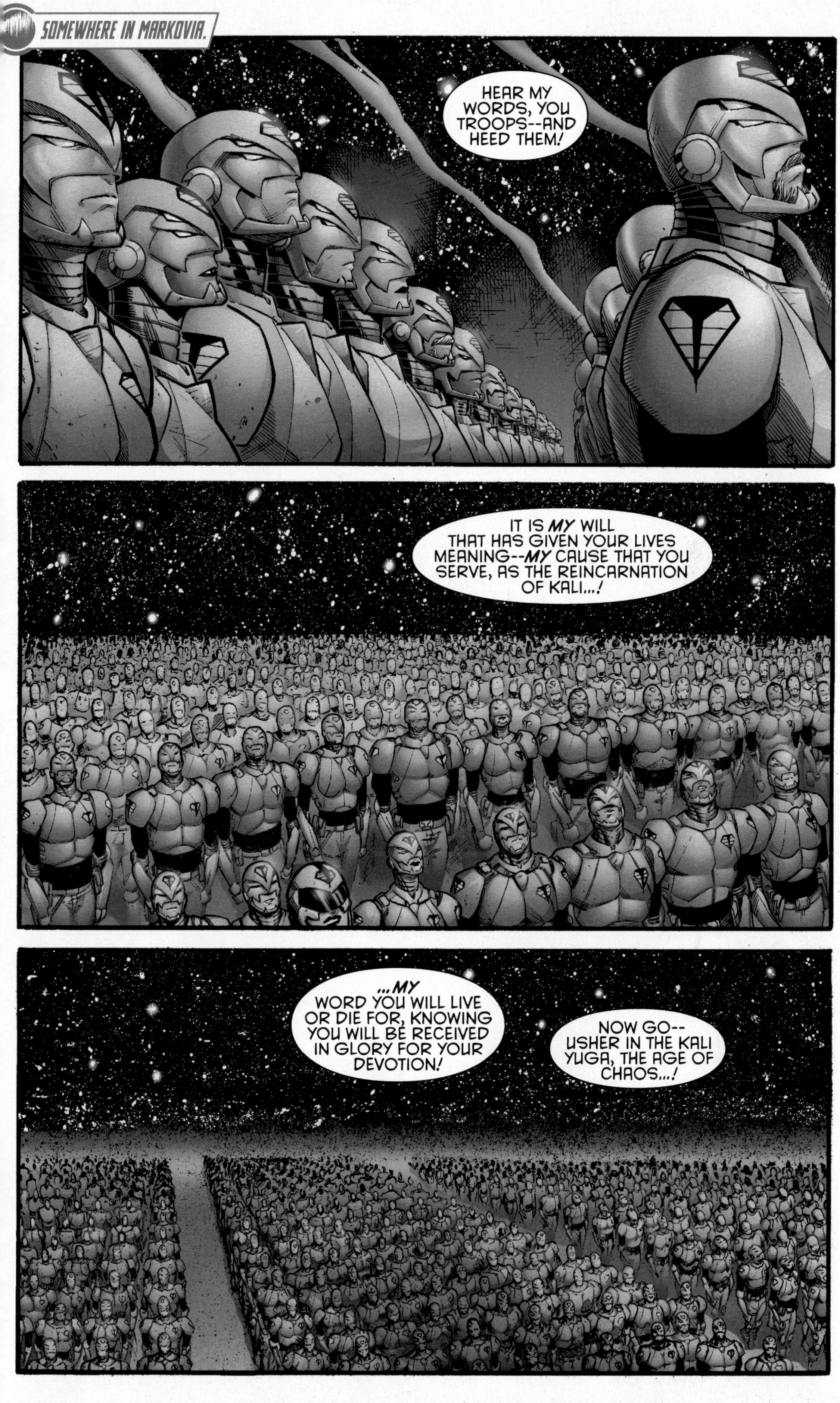
SOMEWHERE IN MARKOVIA.
HEAR MY WORDS, YOU TROOPS--AND HEED THEM!
IT IS MY WILL THAT HAS GIVEN YOUR LIVES MEANING--MY CAUSE THAT YOU SERVE, AS THE REINCARNATION OF KALI...!
...MY WORD YOU WILL LIVE OR DIE FOR, KNOWING YOU WILL BE RECEIVED IN GLORY FOR YOUR DEVOTION!
NOW GO--USHER IN THE KALI YUGA, THE AGE OF CHAOS...!

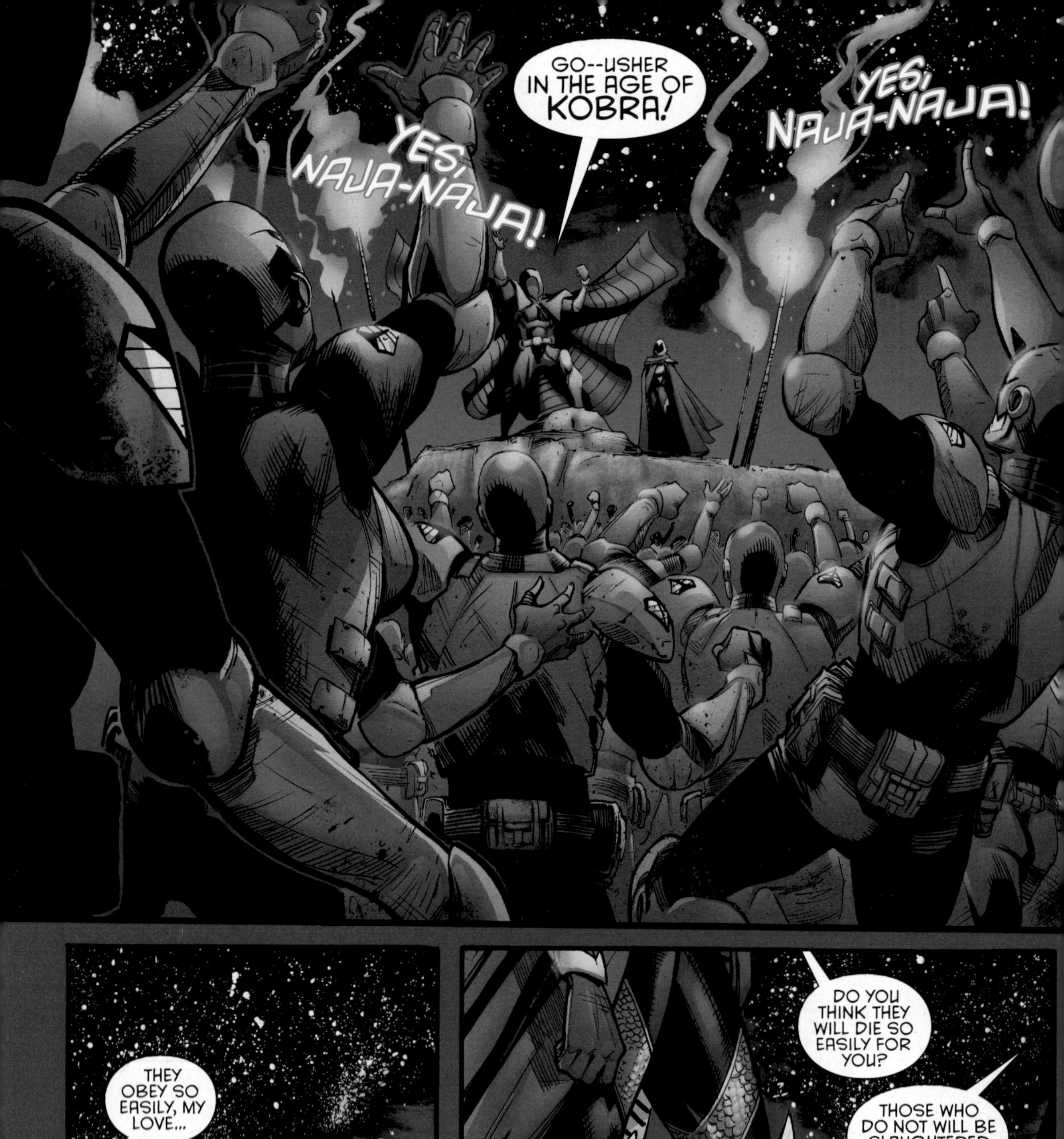
YES, NAJA-NAJA!
GO--USHER IN THE AGE OF KOBRA!
YES, NAJA-NAJA!

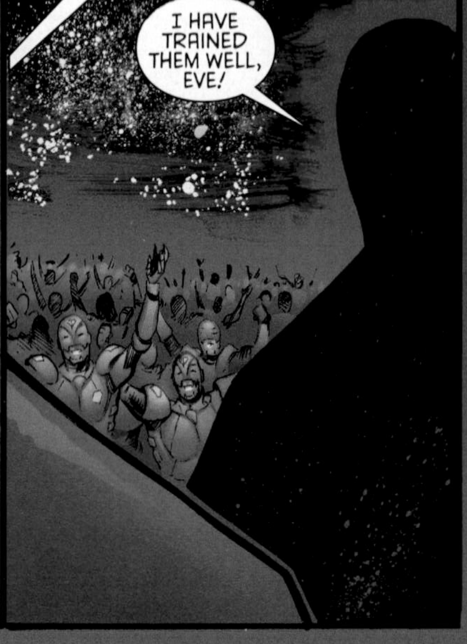
THEY OBEY SO EASILY, MY LOVE...
I HAVE TRAINED THEM WELL, EVE!

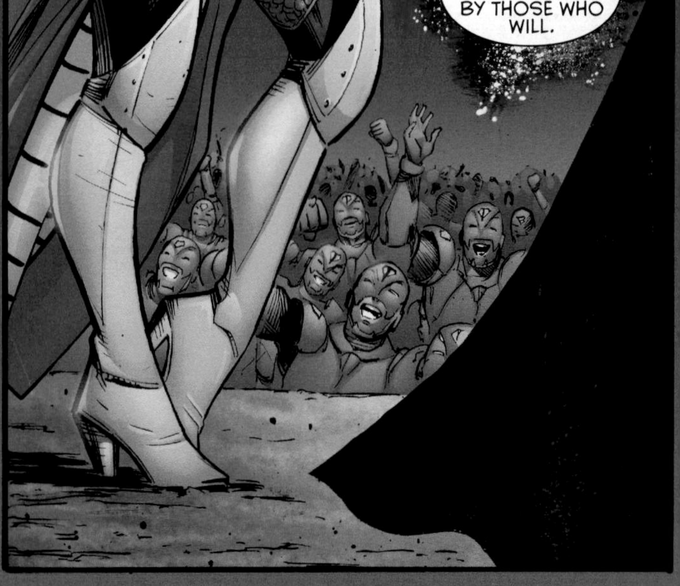
DO YOU THINK THEY WILL DIE SO EASILY FOR YOU?
THOSE WHO DO NOT WILL BE SLAUGHTERED BY THOSE WHO WILL.

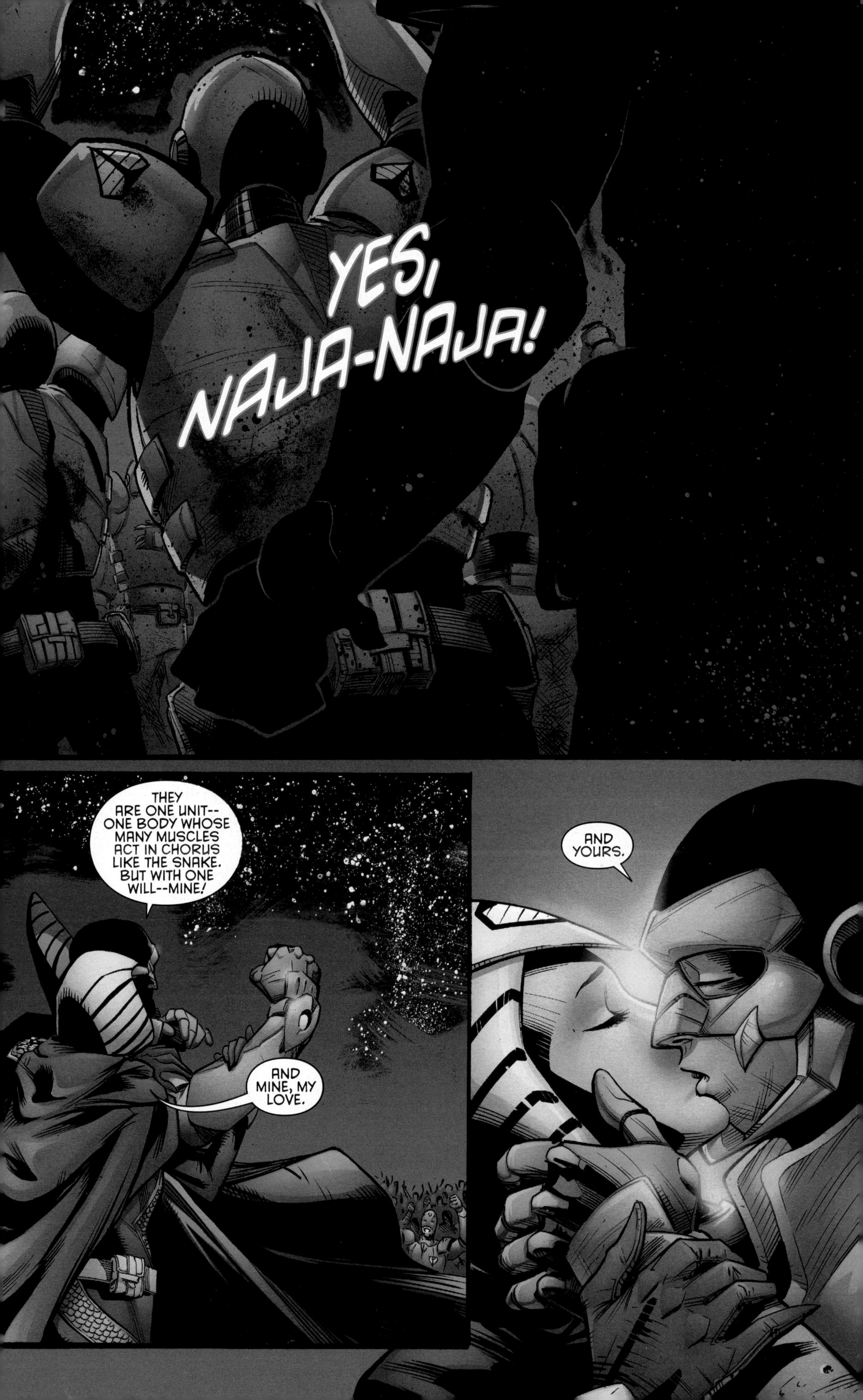
YES, NAJA-NAJA!
THEY ARE ONE UNIT-- ONE BODY WHOSE MANY MUSCLES ACT IN CHORUS LIKE THE SNAKE. BUT WITH ONE WILL--MINE!
AND MINE, MY LOVE.
AND YOURS.

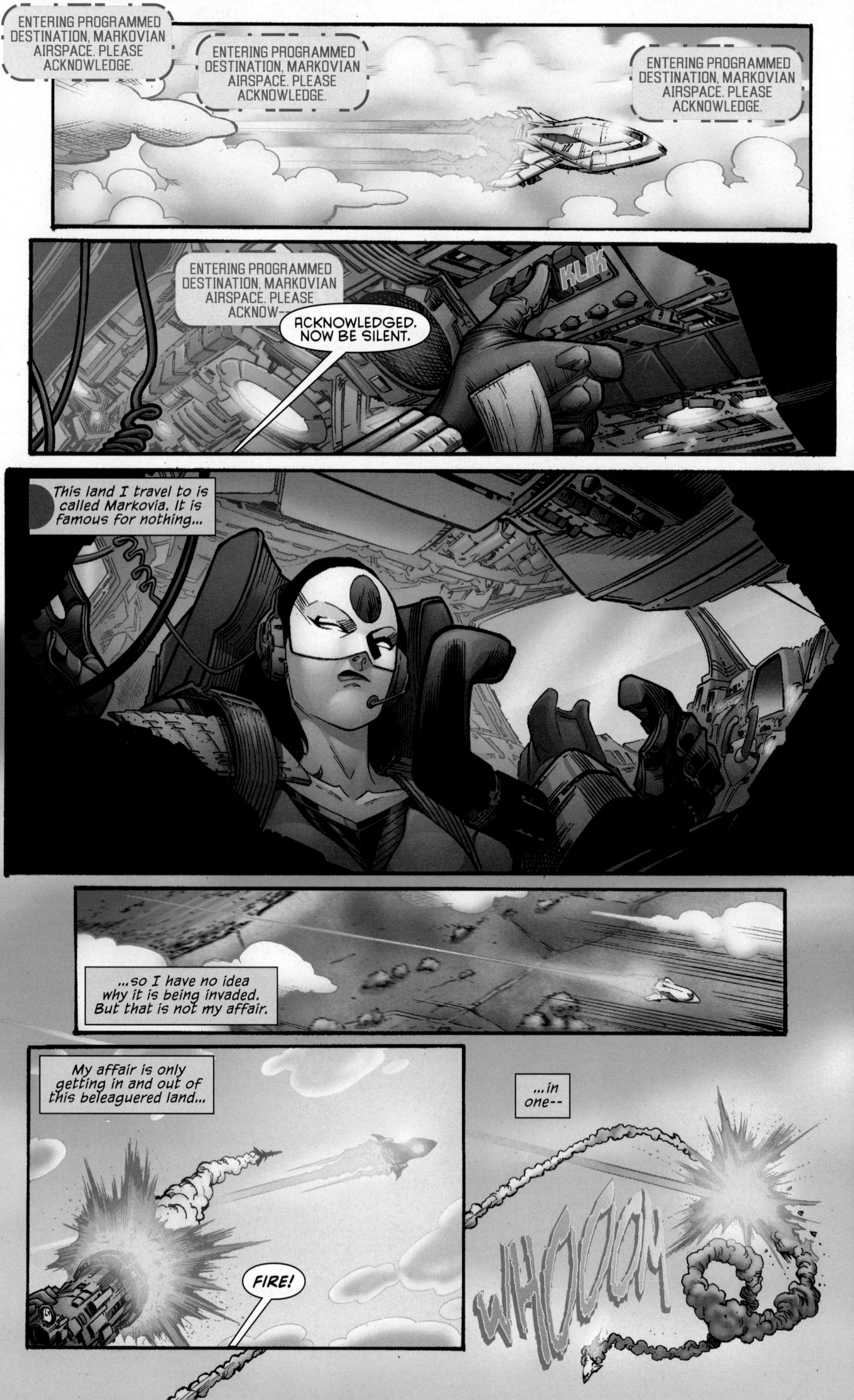
ENTERING PROGRAMMED DESTINATION, MARKOVIAN AIRSPACE. PLEASE ACKNOWLEDGE.
ENTERING PROGRAMMED DESTINATION, MARKOVIAN AIRSPACE. PLEASE ACKNOWLEDGE.
ENTERING PROGRAMMED DESTINATION, MARKOVIAN AIRSPACE. PLEASE ACKNOWLEDGE.
ENTERING PROGRAMMED DESTINATION, MARKOVIAN AIRSPACE. PLEASE ACKNOW--
KLIK
ACKNOWLEDGED. NOW BE SILENT.
This land I travel to is called Markovia. It is famous for nothing...
...so I have no idea why it is being invaded. But that is not my affair.
My affair is only getting in and out of this beleaguered land...
FIRE!
...in one--
WHOOOM

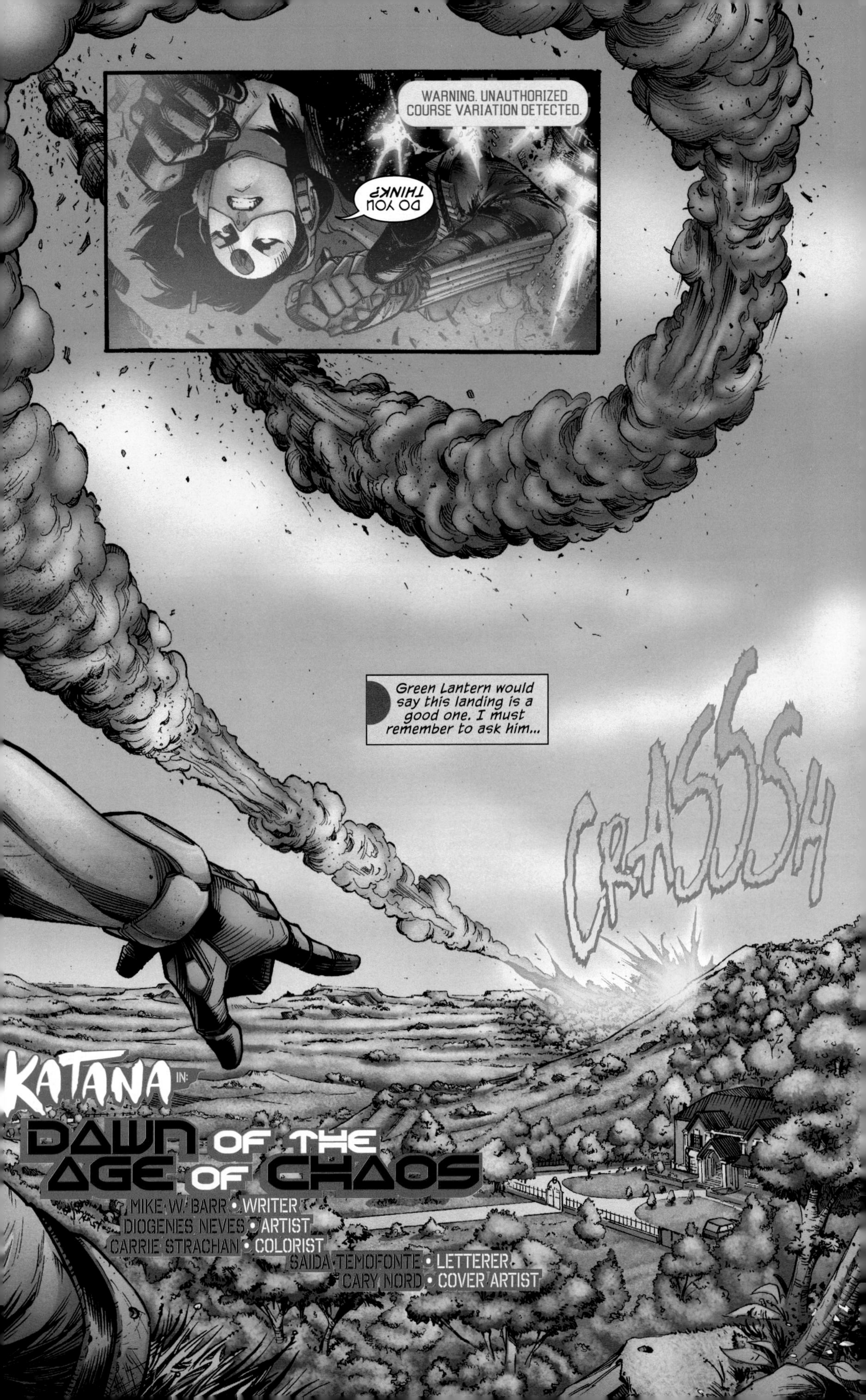
WARNING. UNAUTHORIZED COURSE VARIATION DETECTED.
DO YOU THINK?
Green Lantern would say this landing is a good one. I must remember to ask him...
CRASSSH
KATANA IN:
DAWN OF THE AGE OF CHAOS
MIKE W. BARR • WRITER
DIOGENES NEVES • ARTIST
CARRIE STRACHAN • COLORIST
SAIDA TEMOFONTE • LETTERER
CARY NORD • COVER ARTIST

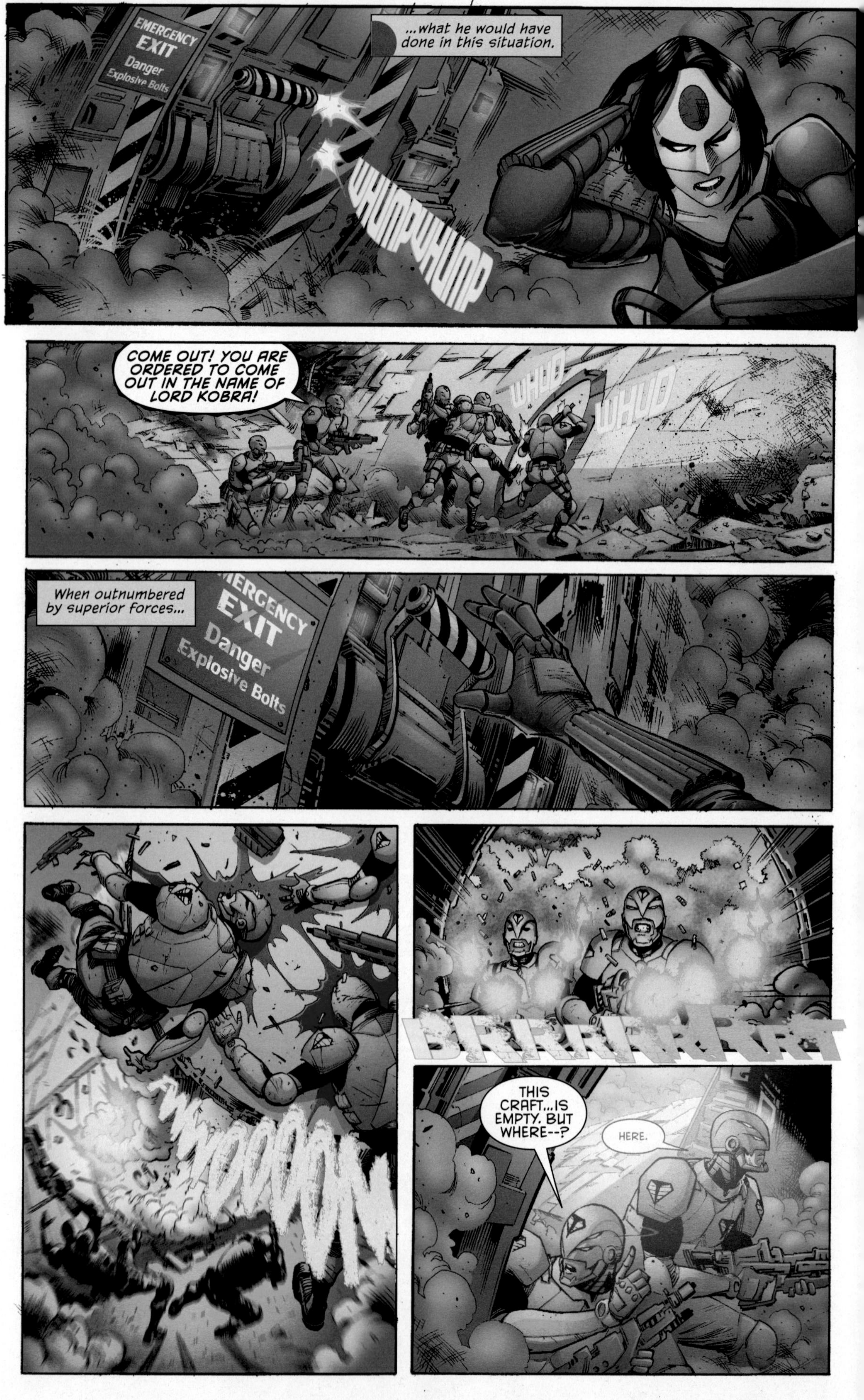
...what he would have done in this situation.
EMERGENCY EXIT Danger Explosive Bolts
WHUMPWHUMP
COME OUT! YOU ARE ORDERED TO COME OUT IN THE NAME OF LORD KOBRA!
WHUD
WHUD
When outnumbered by superior forces...
EMERGENCY EXIT Danger Explosive Bolts
BRRRRRRAT
THIS CRAFT...IS EMPTY. BUT WHERE--?
HERE.

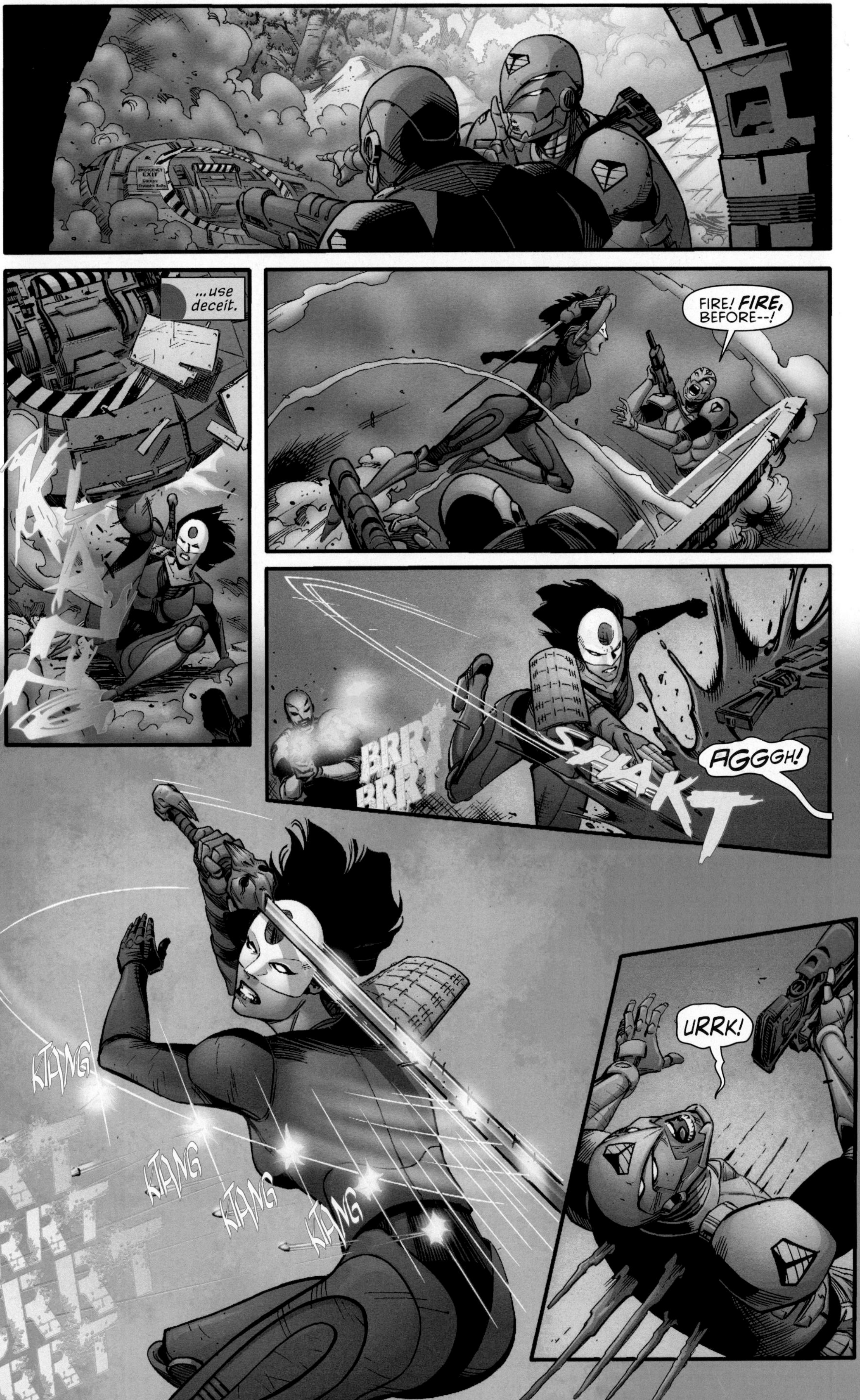

...use deceit.
FIRE! FIRE, BEFORE--!
BRRT BRRT BRRT
SHAKT
AGGGH!
KTANG
KTANG
KTANG
KTANG
URRK!

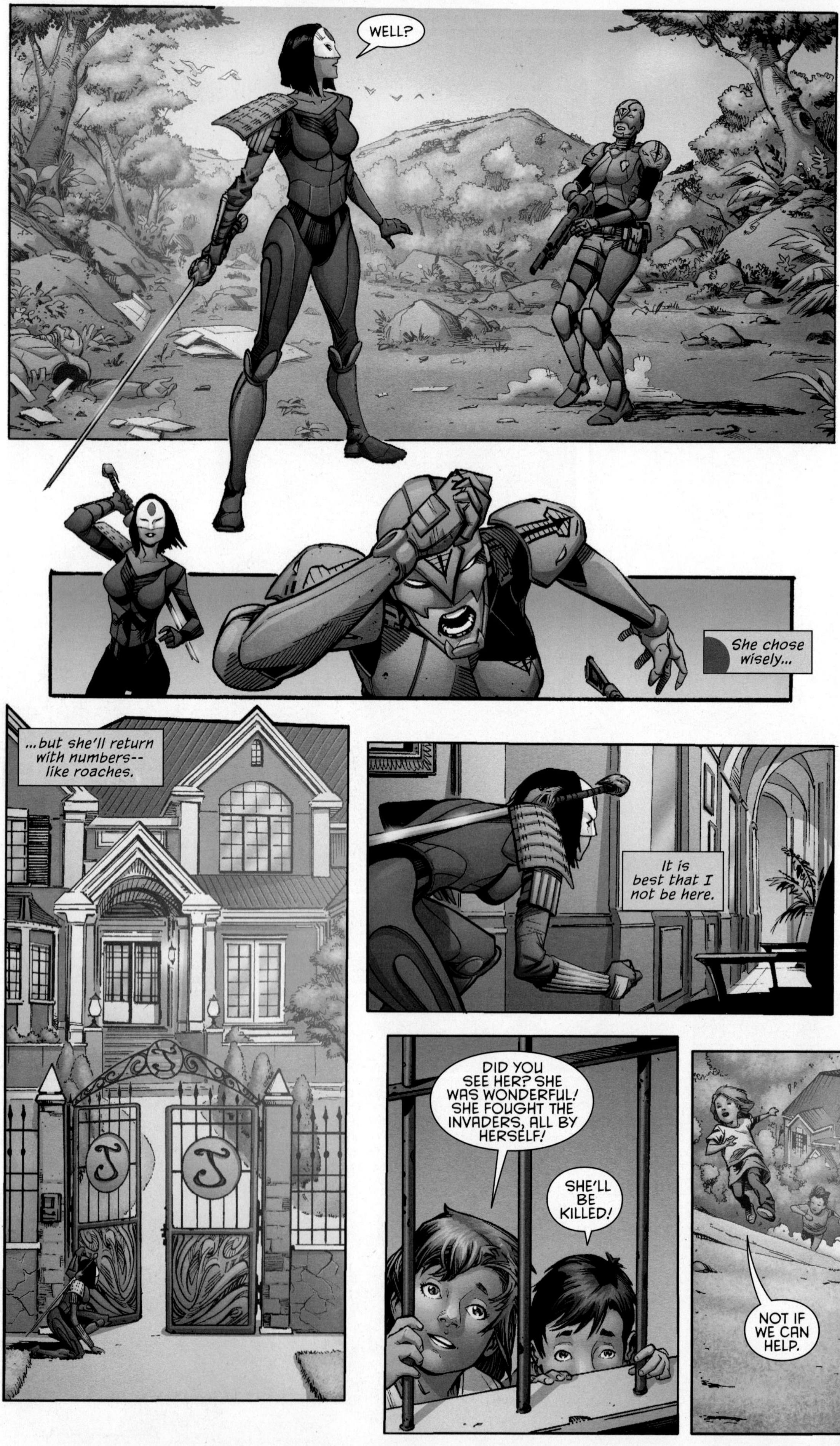
WELL?
She chose wisely...
...but she'll return with numbers-- like roaches.
It is best that I not be here.
DID YOU SEE HER? SHE WAS WONDERFUL! SHE FOUGHT THE INVADERS, ALL BY HERSELF!
SHE'LL BE KILLED!
NOT IF WE CAN HELP.

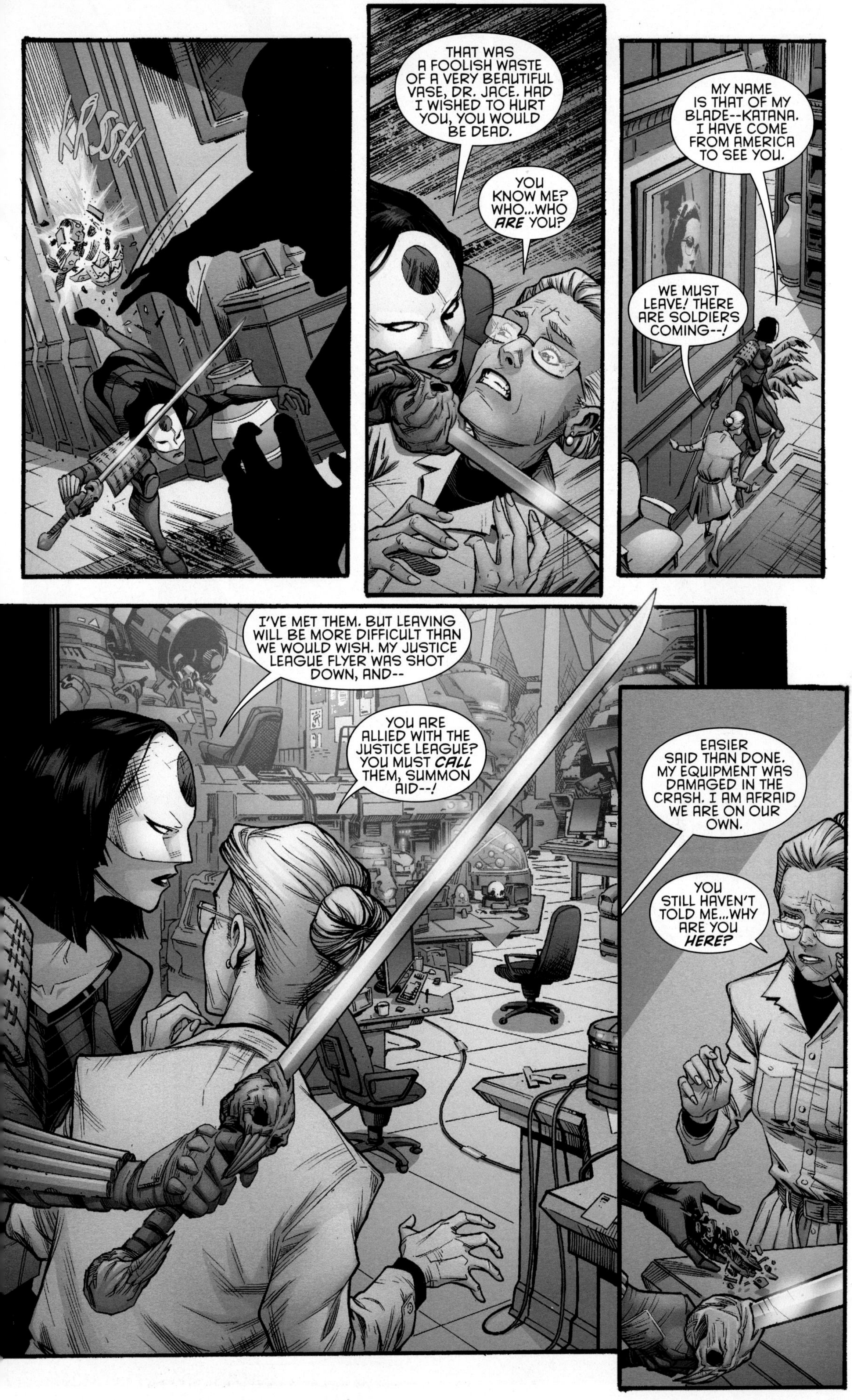
KRSSH
THAT WAS A FOOLISH WASTE OF A VERY BEAUTIFUL VASE, DR. JACE. HAD I WISHED TO HURT YOU, YOU WOULD BE DEAD.
YOU KNOW ME? WHO...WHO *ARE* YOU?
MY NAME IS THAT OF MY BLADE--KATANA. I HAVE COME FROM AMERICA TO SEE YOU.
WE MUST LEAVE! THERE ARE SOLDIERS COMING--!
I'VE MET THEM. BUT LEAVING WILL BE MORE DIFFICULT THAN WE WOULD WISH. MY JUSTICE LEAGUE FLYER WAS SHOT DOWN, AND--
YOU ARE ALLIED WITH THE JUSTICE LEAGUE? YOU MUST *CALL* THEM, SUMMON AID--!
EASIER SAID THAN DONE. MY EQUIPMENT WAS DAMAGED IN THE CRASH. I AM AFRAID WE ARE ON OUR OWN.
YOU STILL HAVEN'T TOLD ME...WHY ARE YOU *HERE?*

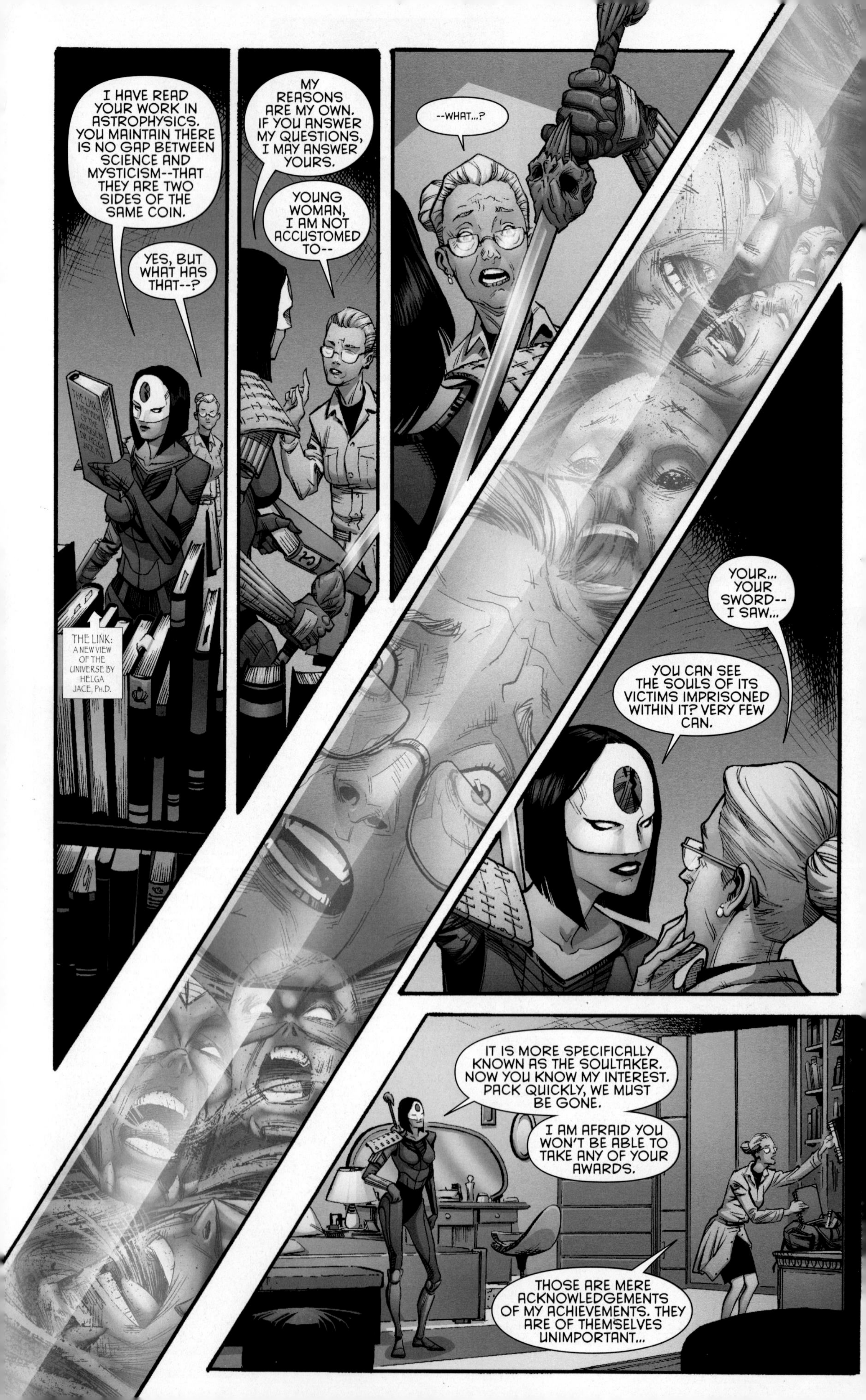
I HAVE READ YOUR WORK IN ASTROPHYSICS. YOU MAINTAIN THERE IS NO GAP BETWEEN SCIENCE AND MYSTICISM--THAT THEY ARE TWO SIDES OF THE SAME COIN.
YES, BUT WHAT HAS THAT--?
THE LINK: A NEW VIEW OF THE UNIVERSE BY HELGA JACE, PH.D.
MY REASONS ARE MY OWN. IF YOU ANSWER MY QUESTIONS, I MAY ANSWER YOURS.
YOUNG WOMAN, I AM NOT ACCUSTOMED TO--
--WHAT...?
YOUR... YOUR SWORD-- I SAW...
YOU CAN SEE THE SOULS OF ITS VICTIMS IMPRISONED WITHIN IT? VERY FEW CAN.
IT IS MORE SPECIFICALLY KNOWN AS THE SOULTAKER. NOW YOU KNOW MY INTEREST. PACK QUICKLY, WE MUST BE GONE.
I AM AFRAID YOU WON'T BE ABLE TO TAKE ANY OF YOUR AWARDS.
THOSE ARE MERE ACKNOWLEDGEMENTS OF MY ACHIEVEMENTS. THEY ARE OF THEMSELVES UNIMPORTANT...

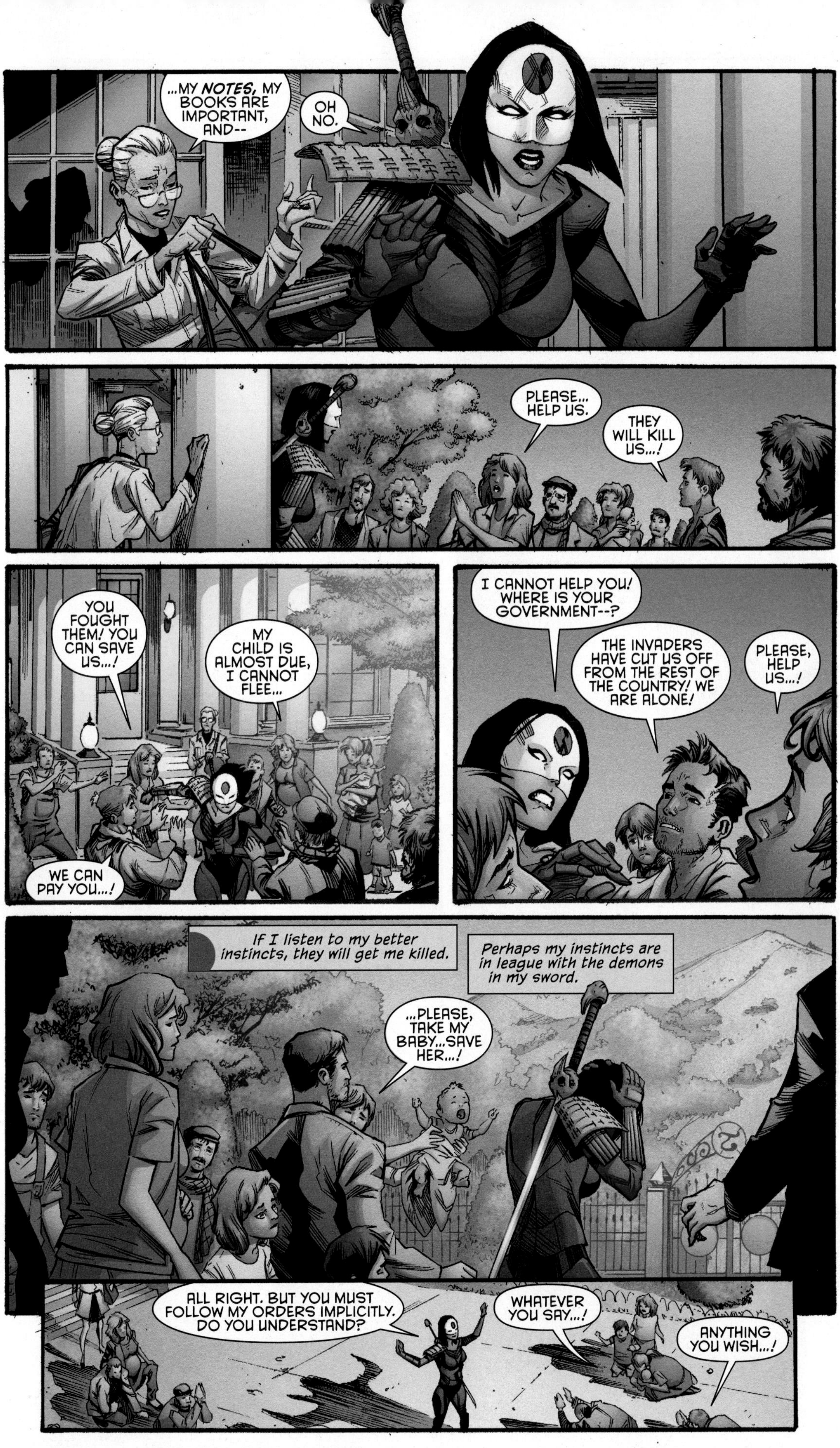

...MY NOTES, MY BOOKS ARE IMPORTANT, AND--
OH NO.
PLEASE... HELP US.
THEY WILL KILL US...!
YOU FOUGHT THEM! YOU CAN SAVE US...!
MY CHILD IS ALMOST DUE, I CANNOT FLEE...
WE CAN PAY YOU...!
I CANNOT HELP YOU! WHERE IS YOUR GOVERNMENT--?
THE INVADERS HAVE CUT US OFF FROM THE REST OF THE COUNTRY! WE ARE ALONE!
PLEASE, HELP US...!
If I listen to my better instincts, they will get me killed.
Perhaps my instincts are in league with the demons in my sword.
...PLEASE, TAKE MY BABY...SAVE HER...!
ALL RIGHT. BUT YOU MUST FOLLOW MY ORDERS IMPLICITLY. DO YOU UNDERSTAND?
WHATEVER YOU SAY...!
ANYTHING YOU WISH...!

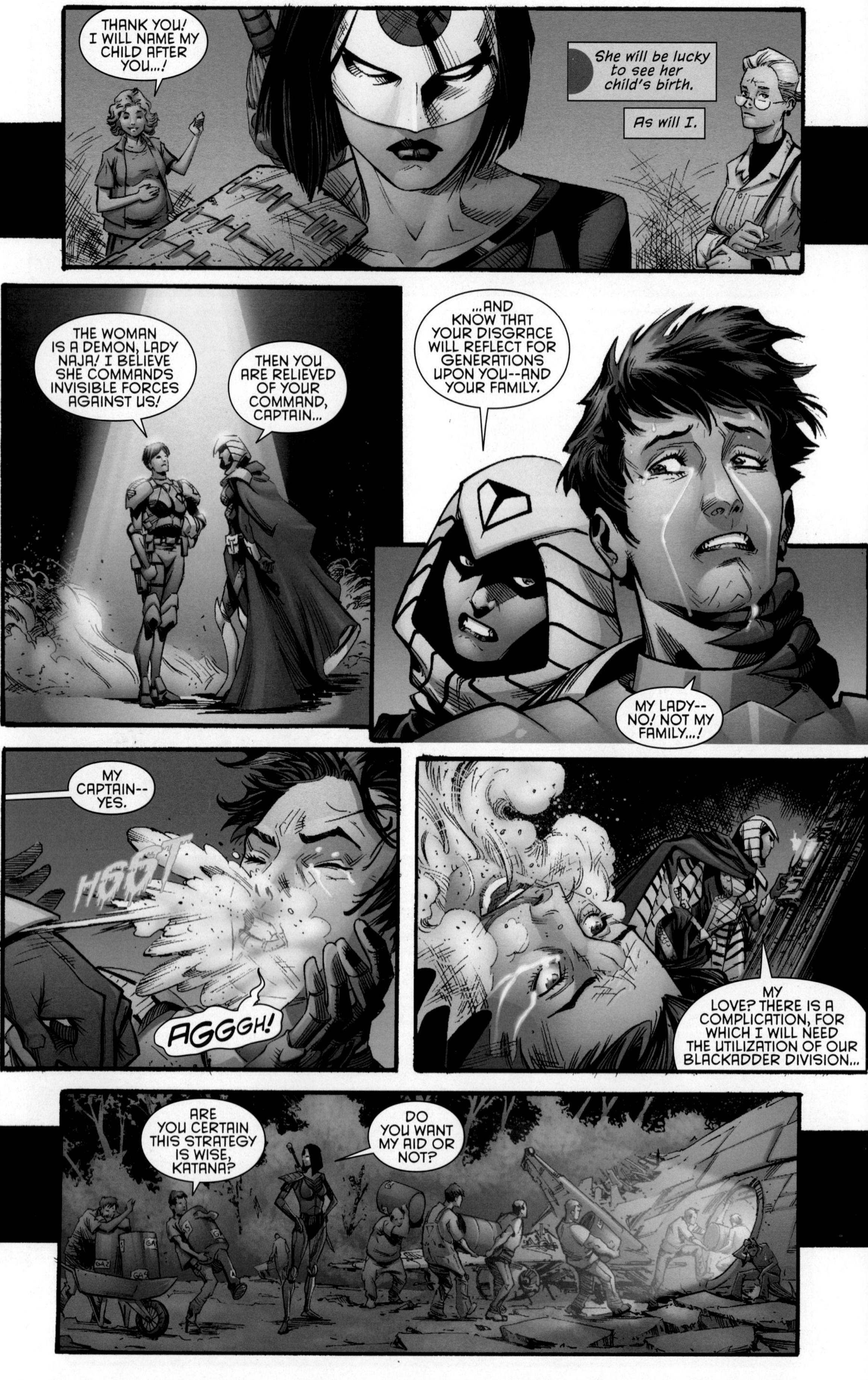
THANK YOU! I WILL NAME MY CHILD AFTER YOU...!
She will be lucky to see her child's birth.
As will I.
THE WOMAN IS A DEMON, LADY NAJA! I BELIEVE SHE COMMANDS INVISIBLE FORCES AGAINST US!
THEN YOU ARE RELIEVED OF YOUR COMMAND, CAPTAIN...
...AND KNOW THAT YOUR DISGRACE WILL REFLECT FOR GENERATIONS UPON YOU--AND YOUR FAMILY.
MY LADY-- NO! NOT MY FAMILY...!
MY CAPTAIN-- YES.
HSST
AGGGH!
MY LOVE? THERE IS A COMPLICATION, FOR WHICH I WILL NEED THE UTILIZATION OF OUR BLACKADDER DIVISION...
ARE YOU CERTAIN THIS STRATEGY IS WISE, KATANA?
DO YOU WANT MY AID OR NOT?

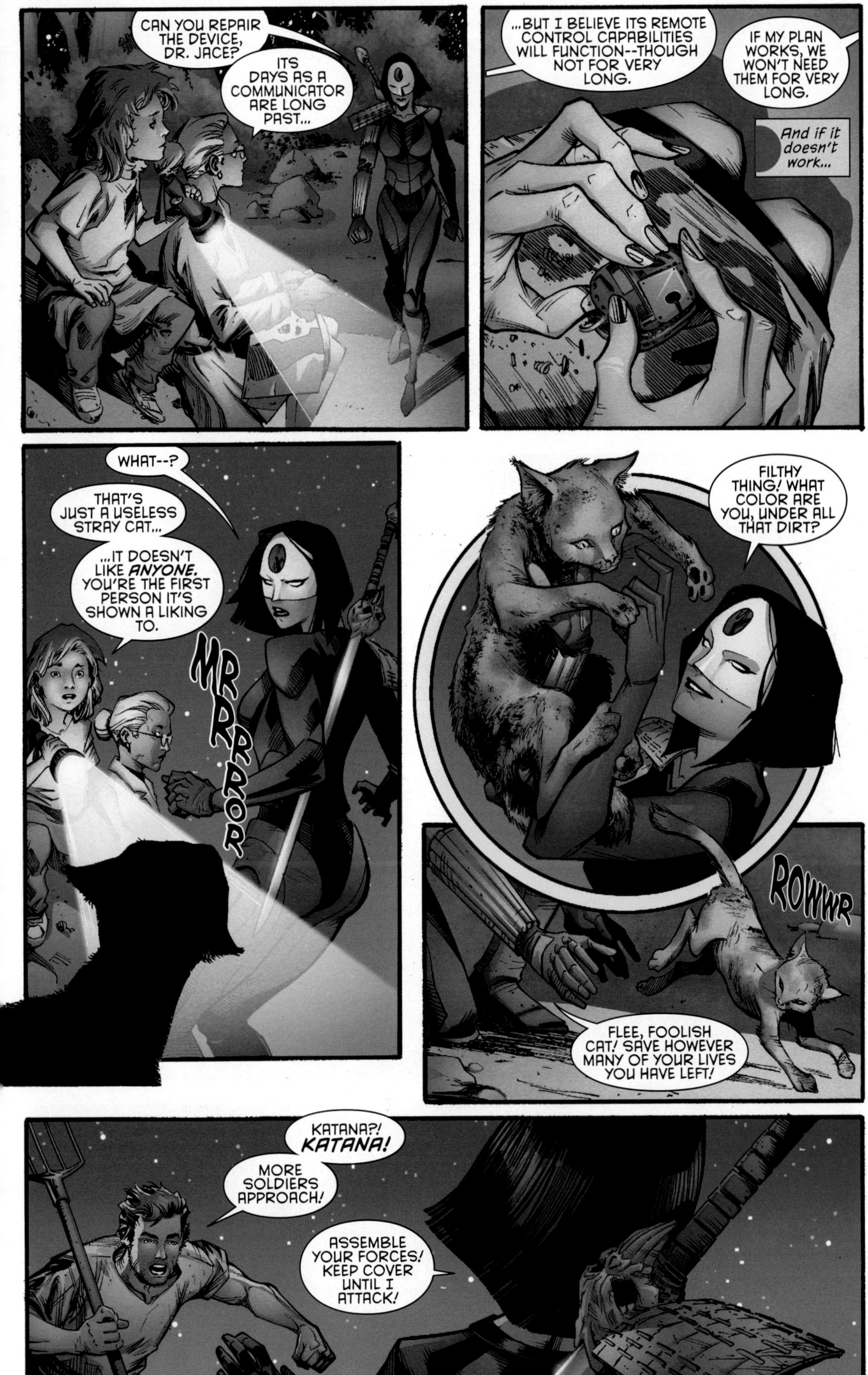
CAN YOU REPAIR THE DEVICE, DR. JACE?
ITS DAYS AS A COMMUNICATOR ARE LONG PAST...
...BUT I BELIEVE ITS REMOTE CONTROL CAPABILITIES WILL FUNCTION--THOUGH NOT FOR VERY LONG.
IF MY PLAN WORKS, WE WON'T NEED THEM FOR VERY LONG.
And if it doesn't work...
WHAT--?
THAT'S JUST A USELESS STRAY CAT...
...IT DOESN'T LIKE ANYONE. YOU'RE THE FIRST PERSON IT'S SHOWN A LIKING TO.
MRRRRROR
FILTHY THING! WHAT COLOR ARE YOU, UNDER ALL THAT DIRT?
ROWWR
FLEE, FOOLISH CAT! SAVE HOWEVER MANY OF YOUR LIVES YOU HAVE LEFT!
KATANA?! KATANA!
MORE SOLDIERS APPROACH!
ASSEMBLE YOUR FORCES! KEEP COVER UNTIL I ATTACK!

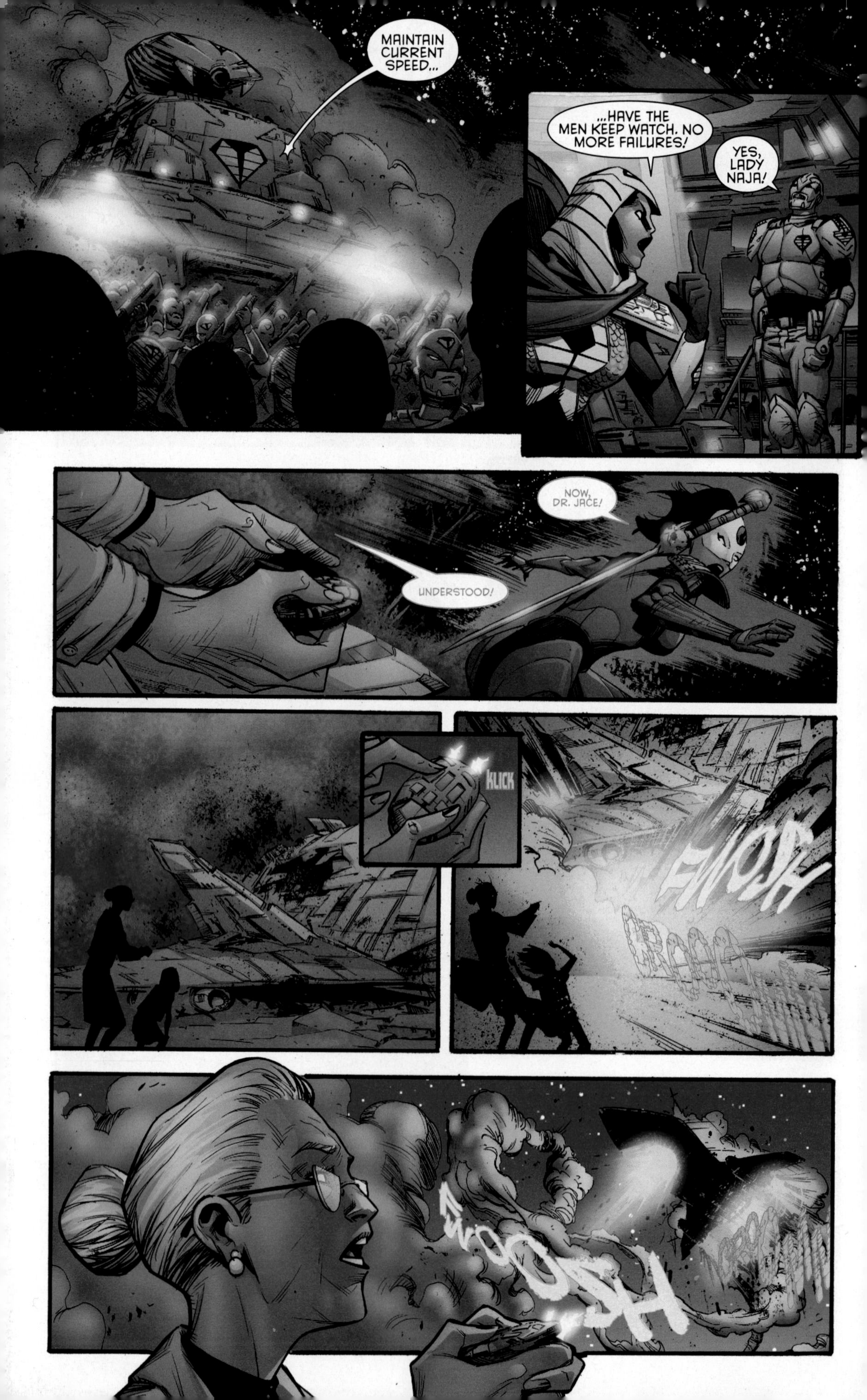
MAINTAIN CURRENT SPEED...
...HAVE THE MEN KEEP WATCH. NO MORE FAILURES!
YES, LADY NAJA!
NOW, DR. JACE!
UNDERSTOOD!
KLICK

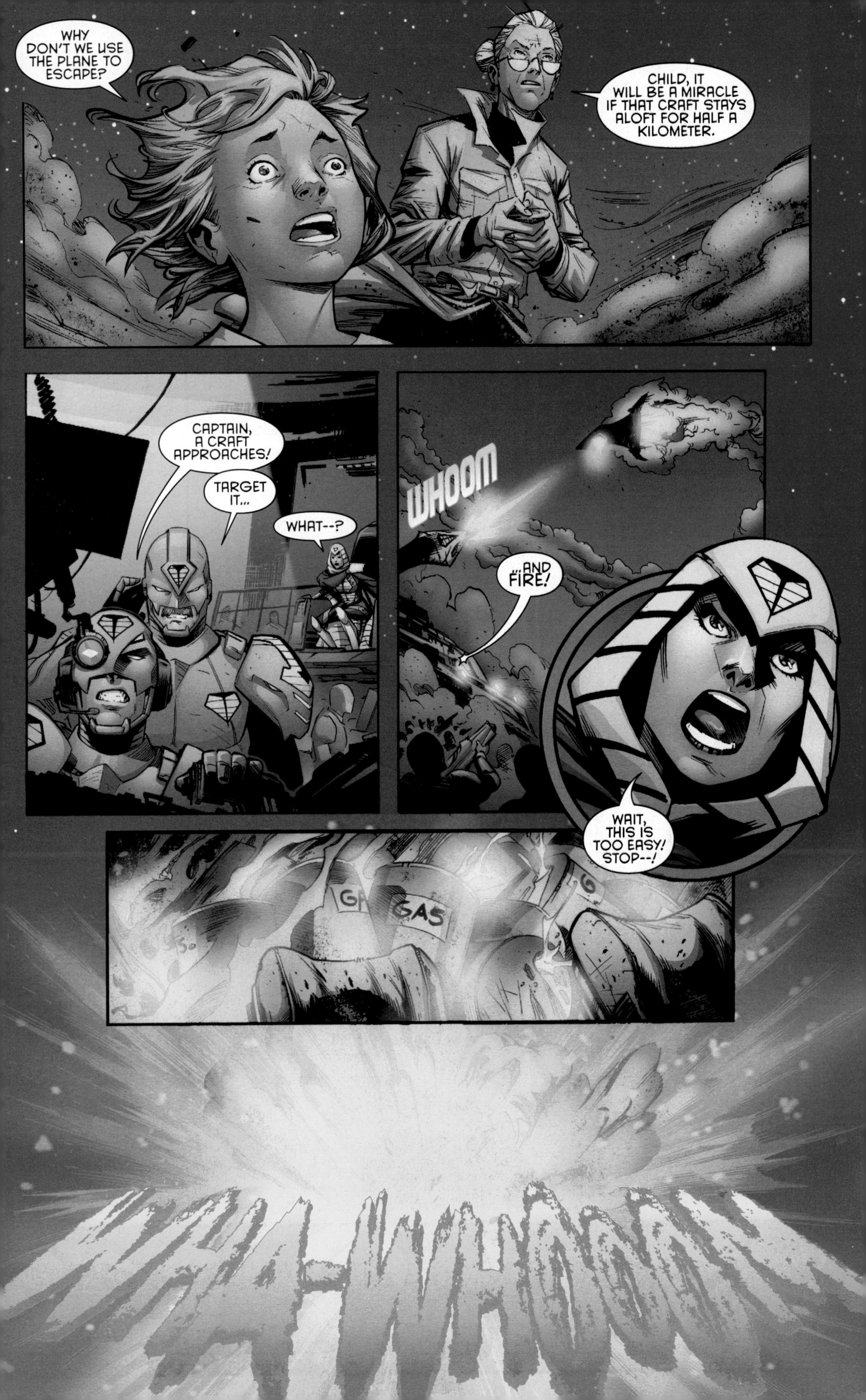
WHY DON'T WE USE THE PLANE TO ESCAPE?
CHILD, IT WILL BE A MIRACLE IF THAT CRAFT STAYS ALOFT FOR HALF A KILOMETER.
CAPTAIN, A CRAFT APPROACHES!
TARGET IT...
WHAT--?
WHOOM
...AND FIRE!
WAIT, THIS IS TOO EASY! STOP--!
GAS

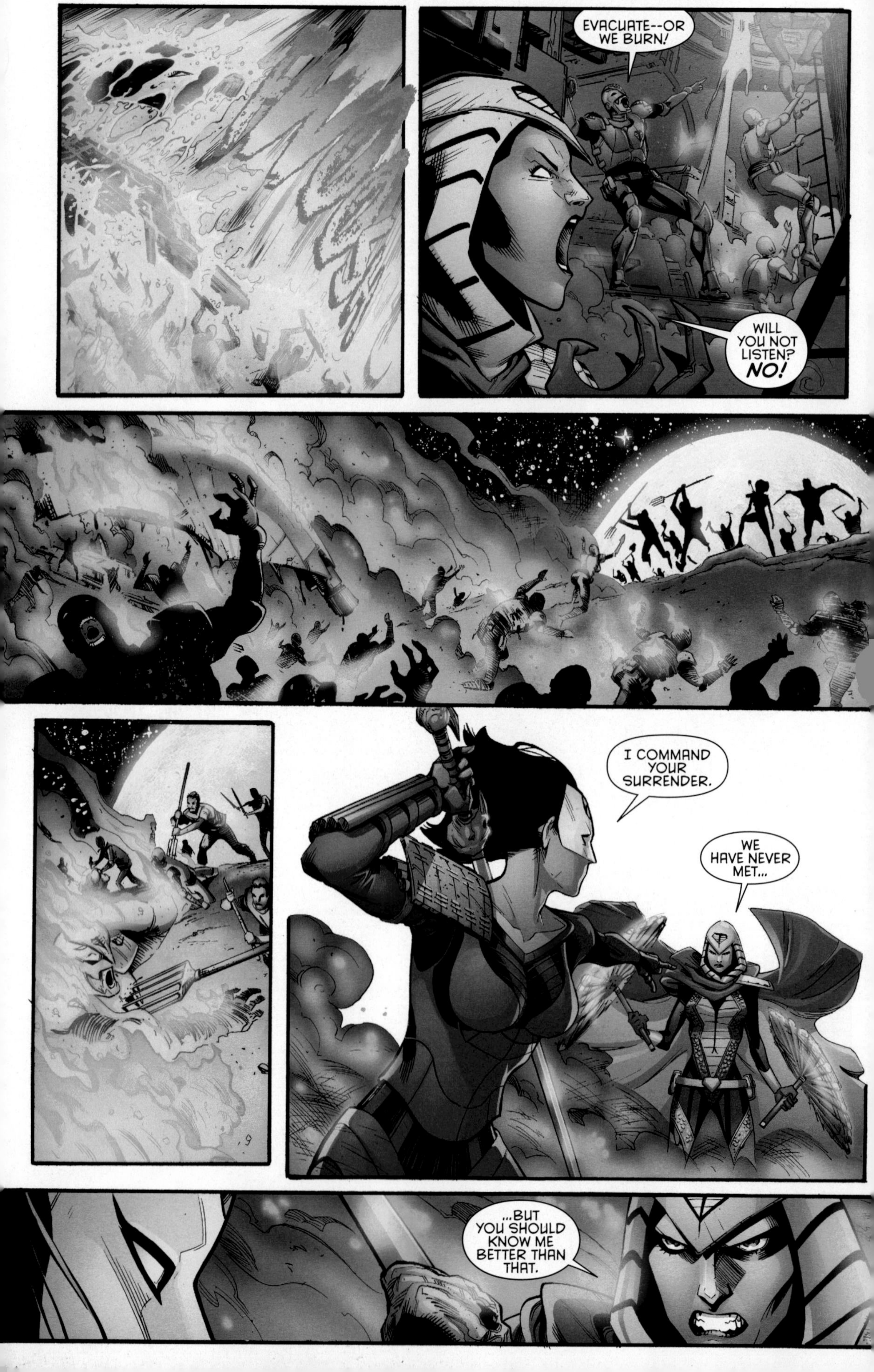
EVACUATE--OR WE BURN!
WILL YOU NOT LISTEN? NO!
I COMMAND YOUR SURRENDER.
WE HAVE NEVER MET...
...BUT YOU SHOULD KNOW ME BETTER THAN THAT.

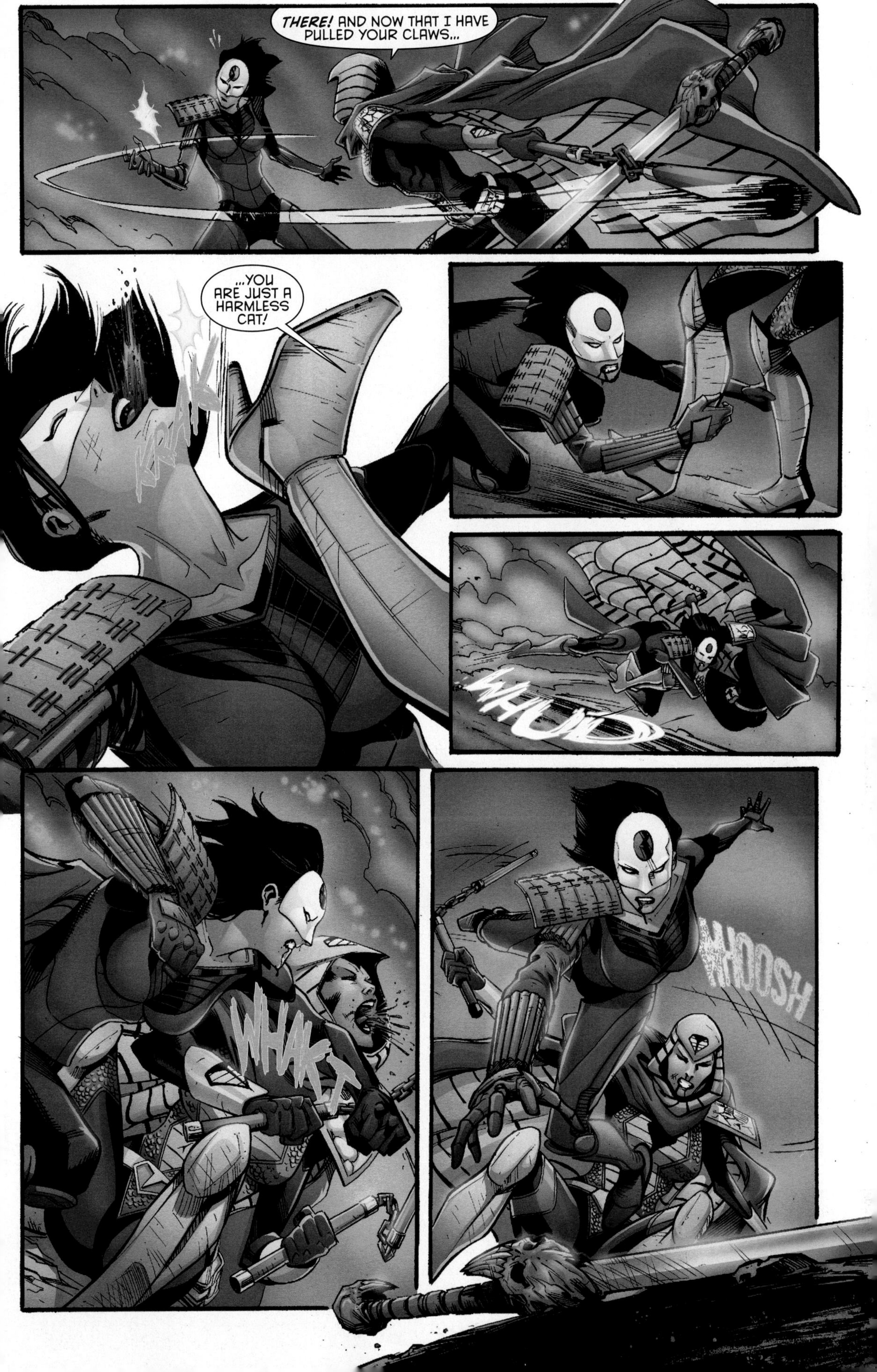
THERE! AND NOW THAT I HAVE PULLED YOUR CLAWS...
...YOU ARE JUST A HARMLESS CAT!
KRAK
WHUD
WHAK
WHOOSH

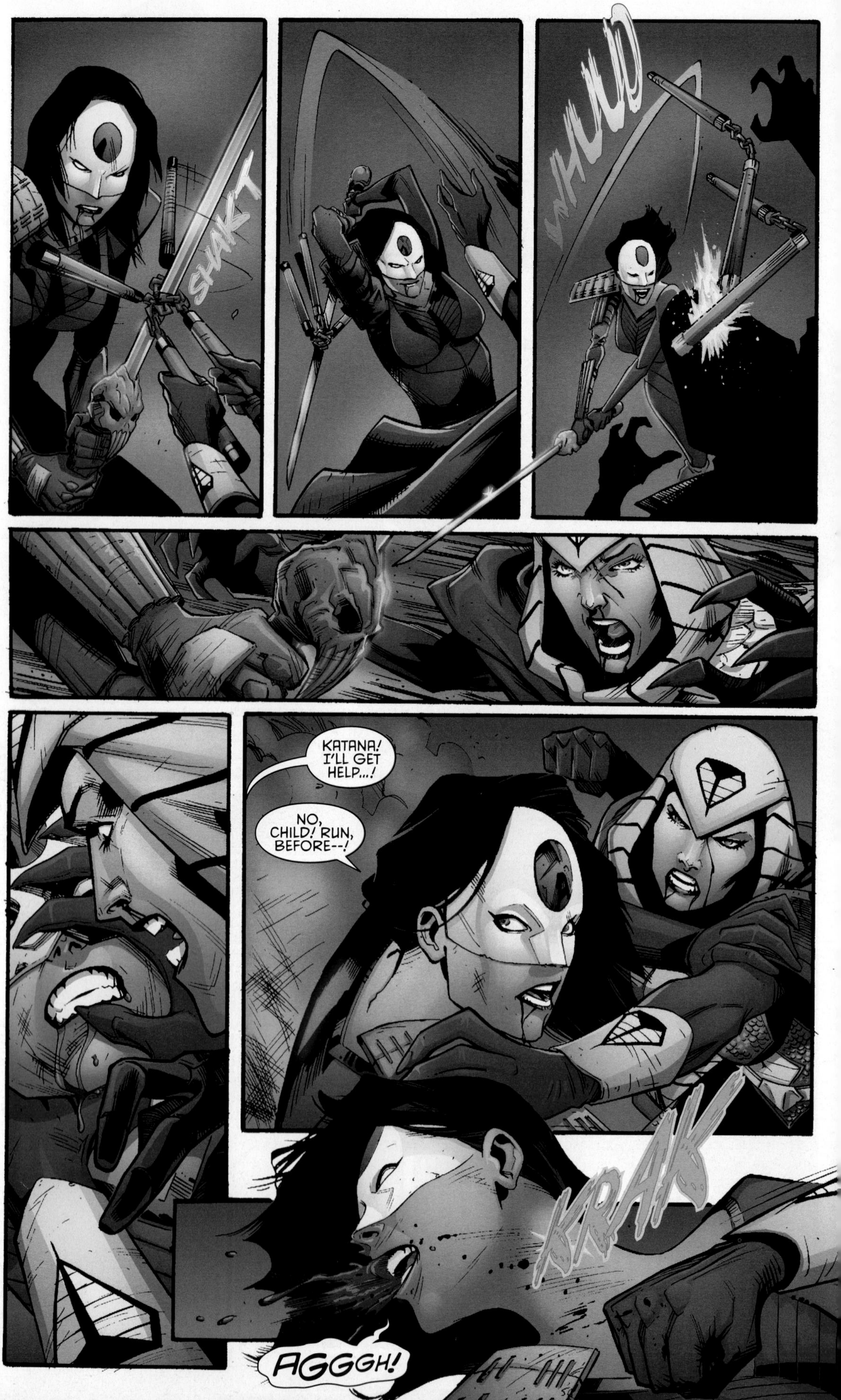
SHAK'T
WHUD
KATANA! I'LL GET HELP...!
NO, CHILD! RUN, BEFORE--!
KRAK
AGGGH!

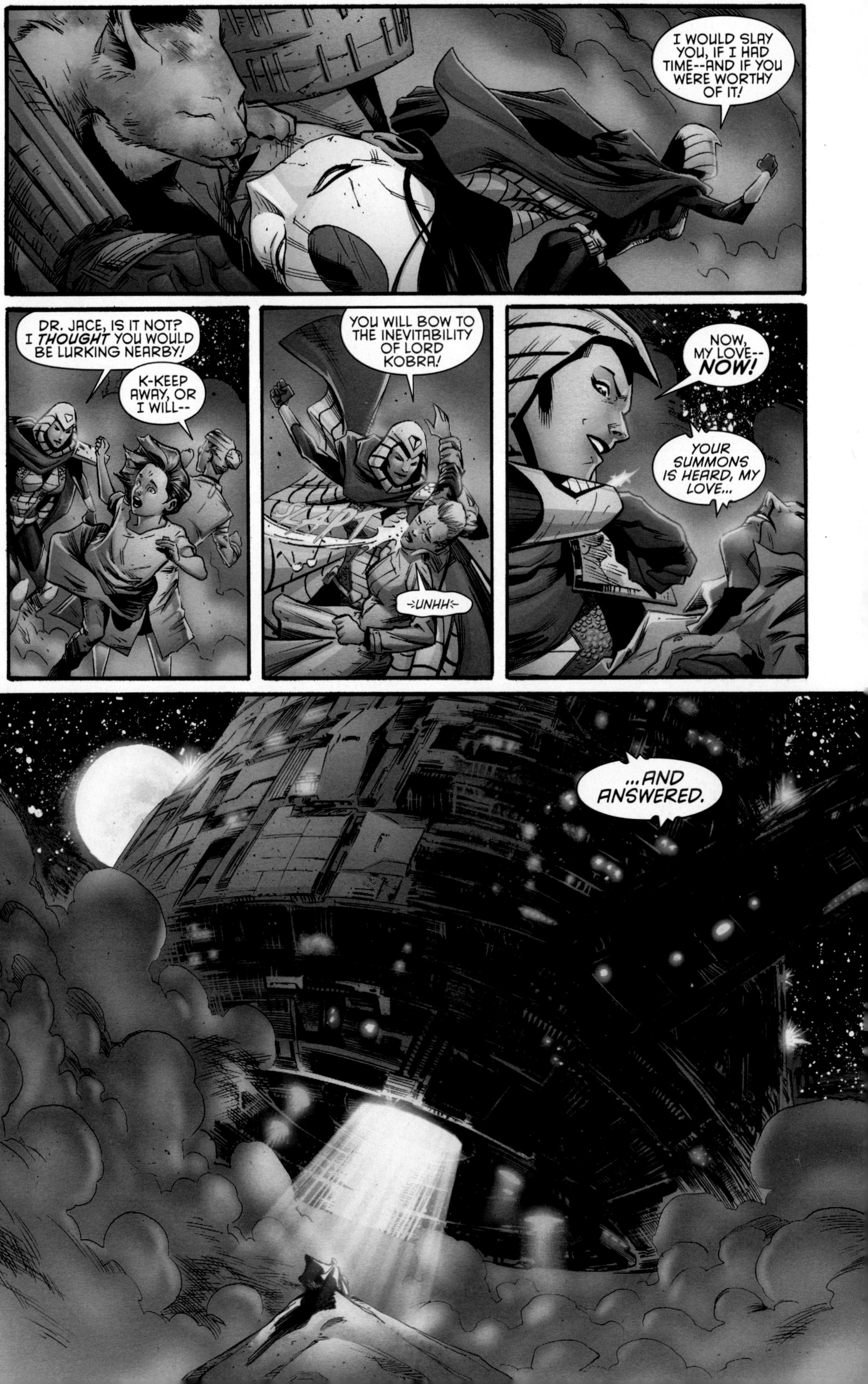
I WOULD SLAY YOU, IF I HAD TIME--AND IF YOU WERE WORTHY OF IT!
DR. JACE, IS IT NOT? I *THOUGHT* YOU WOULD BE LURKING NEARBY!
K-KEEP AWAY, OR I WILL--
YOU WILL BOW TO THE INEVITABILITY OF LORD KOBRA!
SLAP!
-UNHH-
NOW, MY LOVE-- ***NOW!***
YOUR SUMMONS IS HEARD, MY LOVE...
...AND ANSWERED.

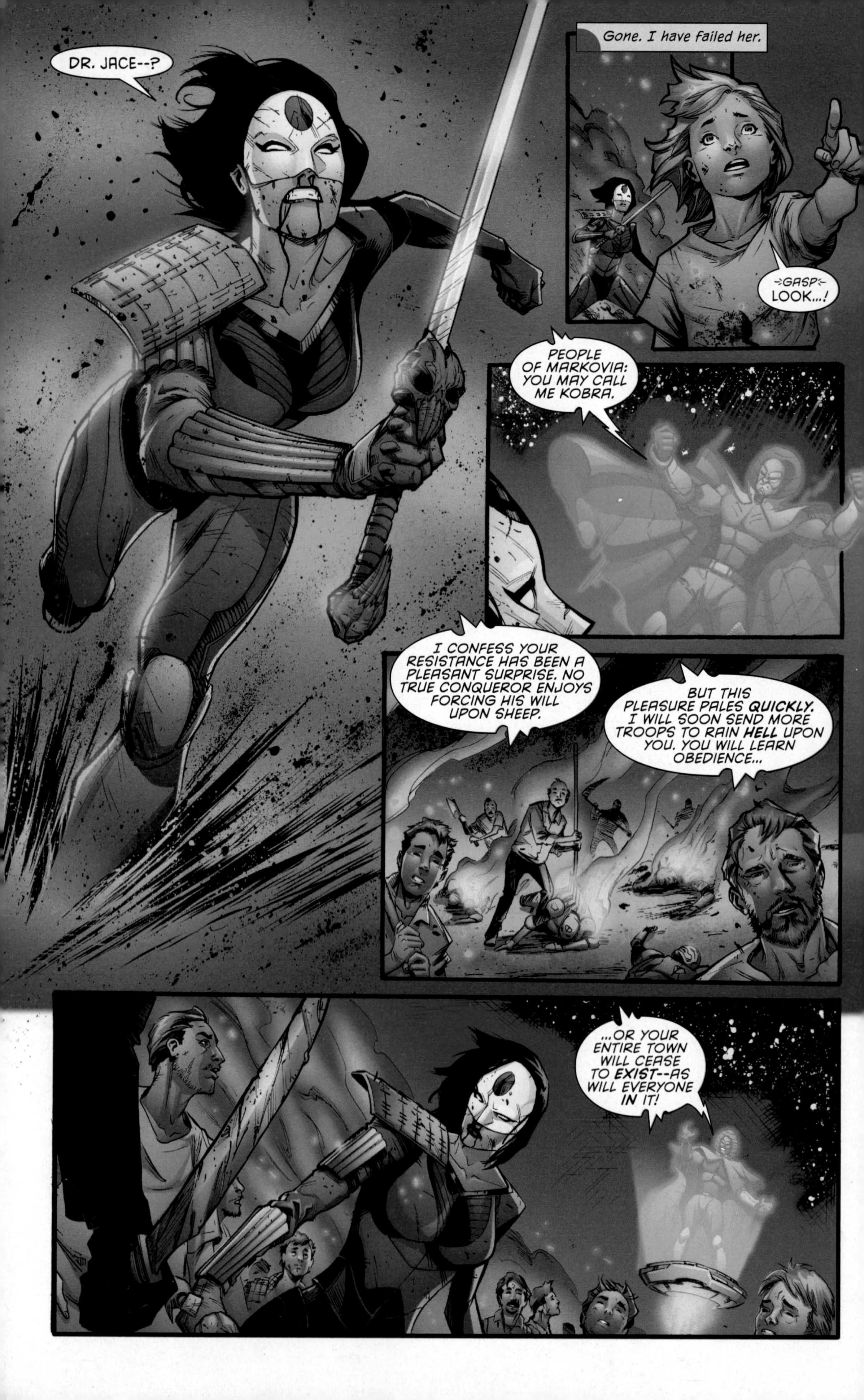
DR. JACE--?
Gone. I have failed her.
GASP
LOOK...!
PEOPLE OF MARKOVIA: YOU MAY CALL ME KOBRA.
I CONFESS YOUR RESISTANCE HAS BEEN A PLEASANT SURPRISE. NO TRUE CONQUEROR ENJOYS FORCING HIS WILL UPON SHEEP.
BUT THIS PLEASURE PALES QUICKLY. I WILL SOON SEND MORE TROOPS TO RAIN HELL UPON YOU. YOU WILL LEARN OBEDIENCE...
...OR YOUR ENTIRE TOWN WILL CEASE TO EXIST--AS WILL EVERYONE IN IT!

NEW SUICIDE SQUAD #13 variant cover by **CARY NORD**

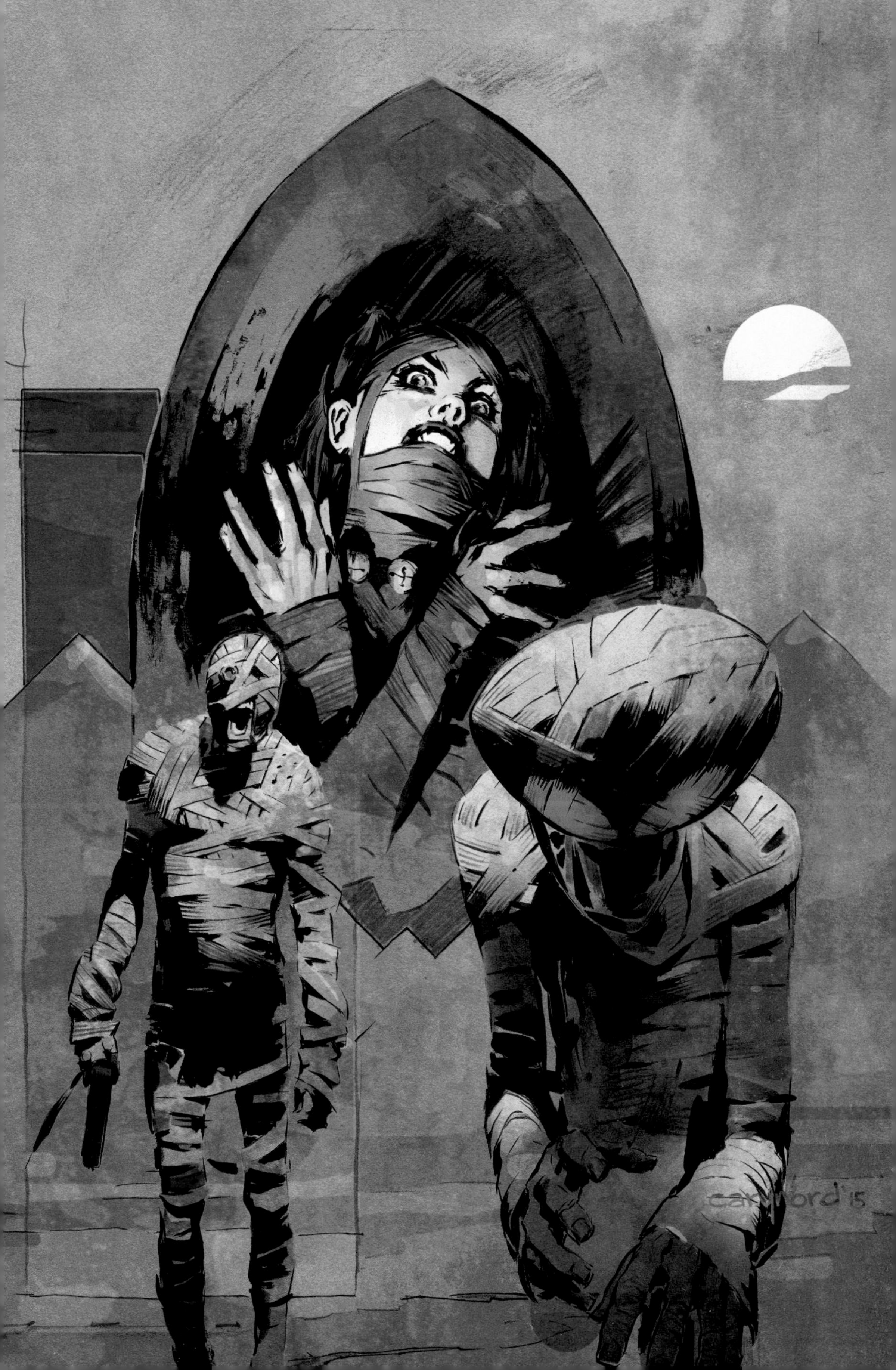

NEW SUICIDE SQUAD #14 Looney Tunes variant cover by
BILL SIENKIEWICZ and **SPIKE BRANDT**

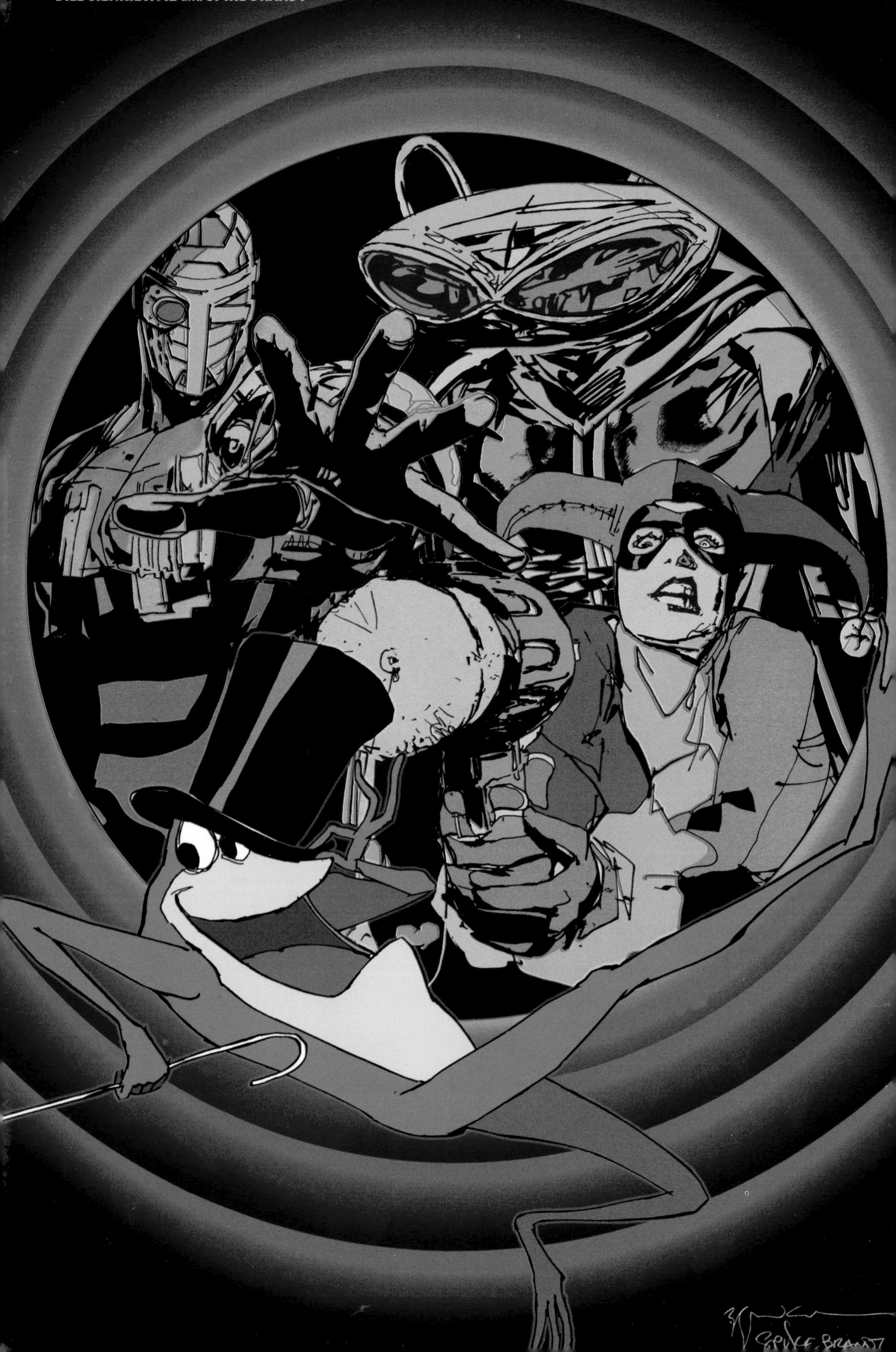

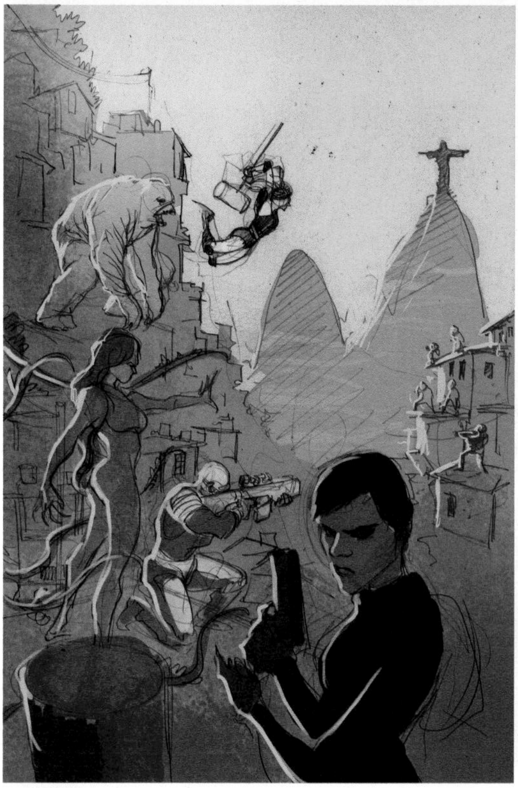

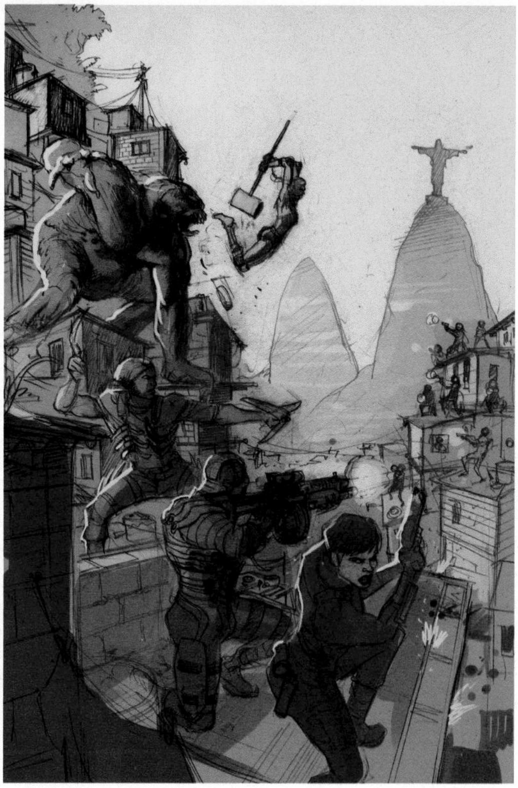

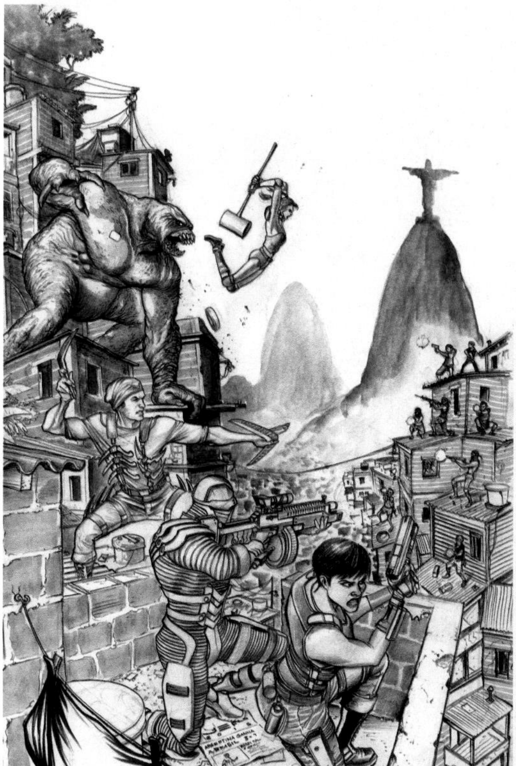

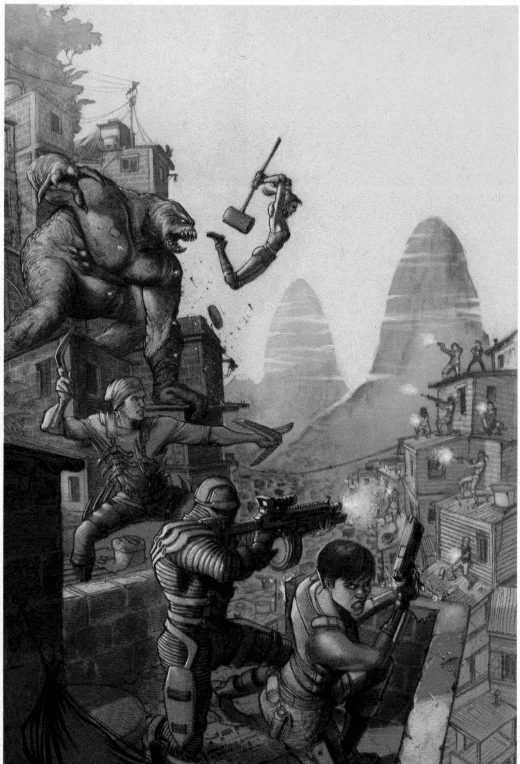

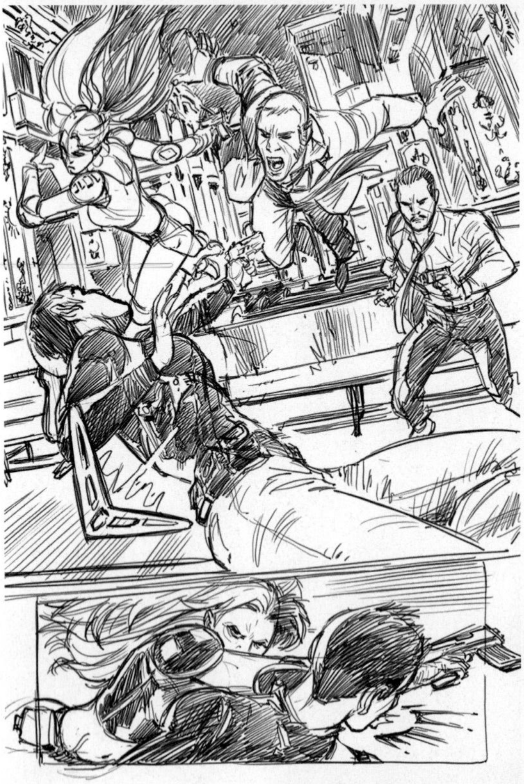

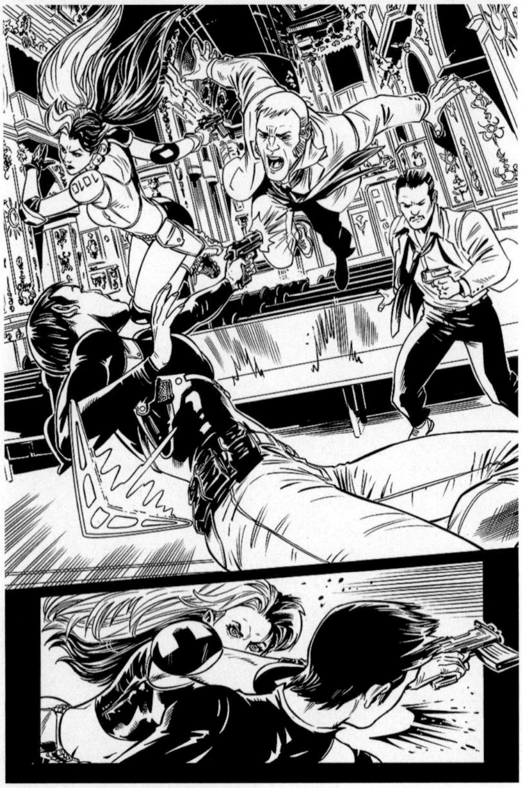

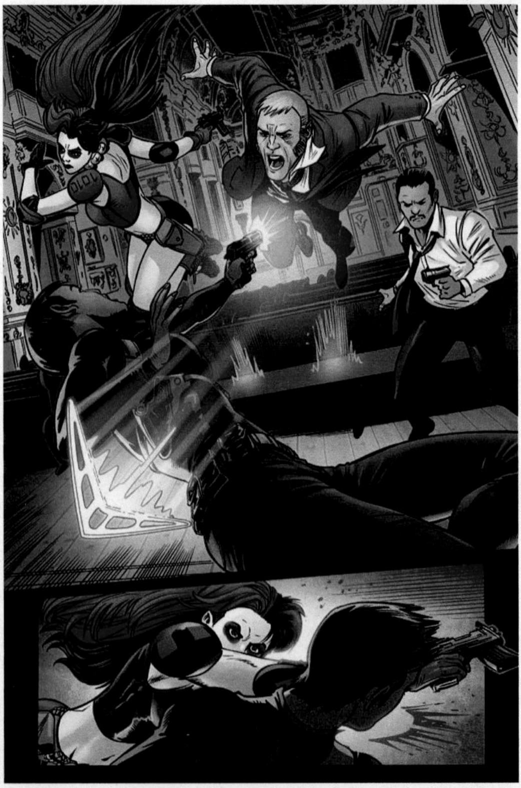

DC COMICS™

"A pretty irresistible hook. What if the good guys assembled a bunch of bad guys to work as a Dirty Dozen-like superteam and do the dirty work traditional heroes would never touch (or want to know about)?"—THE ONION/AV CLUB

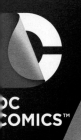

START AT THE BEGINNING!

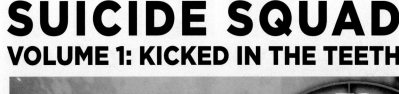

SUICIDE SQUAD
VOLUME 1: KICKED IN THE TEETH

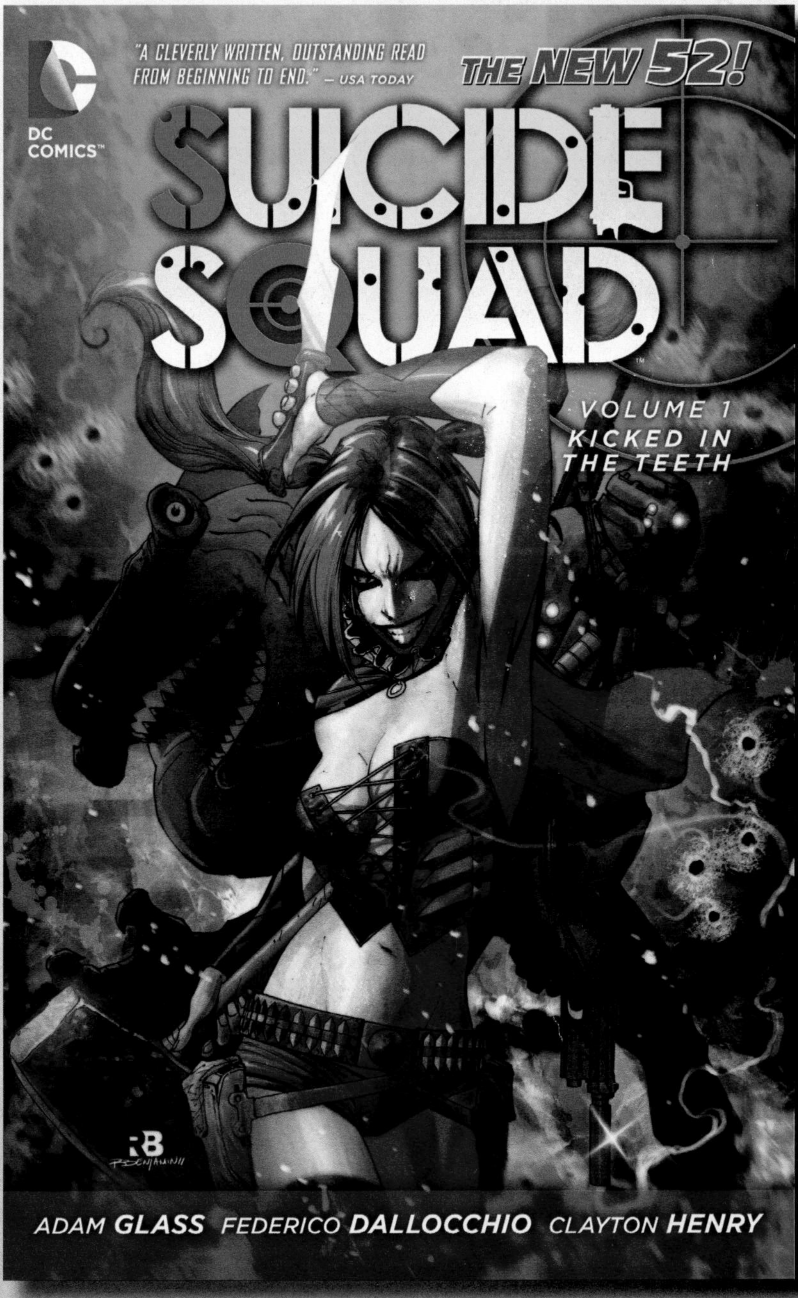

"A CLEVERLY WRITTEN, OUTSTANDING READ FROM BEGINNING TO END." — USA TODAY
THE NEW 52!
DC COMICS™
SUICIDE SQUAD
VOLUME 1 KICKED IN THE TEETH
ADAM GLASS FEDERICO DALLOCCHIO CLAYTON HENRY

SUICIDE SQUAD VOL. 2: BASILISK RISING

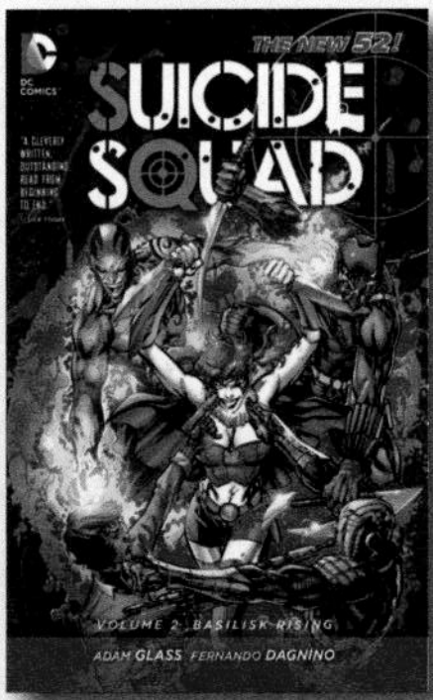

THE NEW 52!
SUICIDE SQUAD
VOLUME 2: BASILISK RISING
ADAM GLASS FERNANDO DAGNINO

SUICIDE SQUAD VOL. 3: DEATH IS FOR SUCKERS

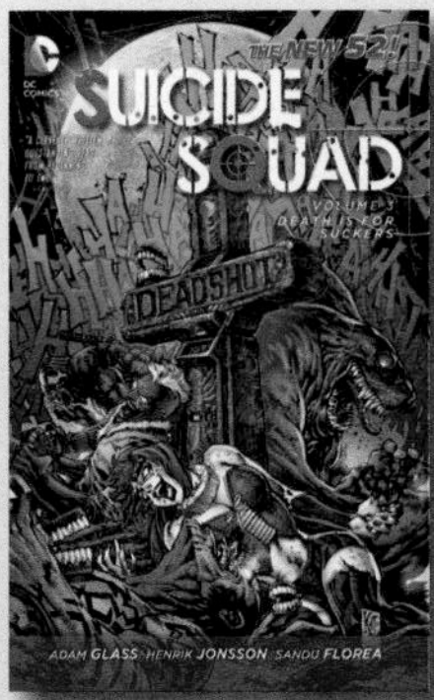

THE NEW 52!
SUICIDE SQUAD
DEADSHOT
ADAM GLASS HENRIK JONSSON SANDU FLOREA

DEATHSTROKE VOL. 1: LEGACY

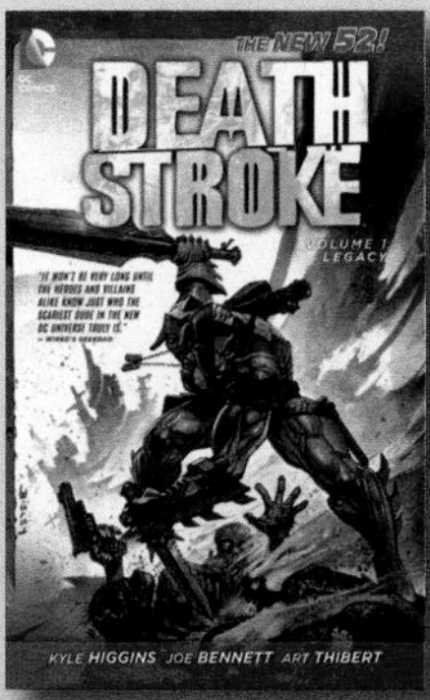

THE NEW 52!
DEATHSTROKE
VOLUME 1 LEGACY
KYLE HIGGINS JOE BENNETT ART THIBERT

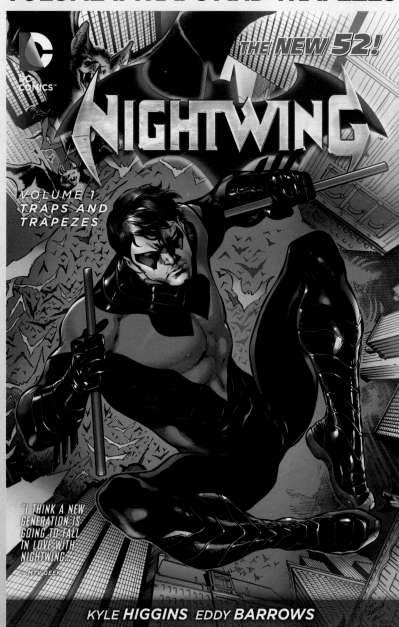

HARLEY QUINN

VOLUME 1: HOT IN THE CITY

SUICIDE SQUAD VOL. 1: KICKED IN THE TEETH

with ADAM GLASS and FEDERICO DALLOCCHIO

HARLEY QUINN: PRELUDES AND KNOCK-KNOCK JOKES

with KARL KESEL and TERRY DODSON

BATMAN: MAD LOVE AND OTHER STORIES

with PAUL DINI and BRUCE TIMM

AMANDA **CONNER** JIMMY **PALMIOTTI** CHAD **HARDIN**
STEPHANE **ROUX** ALEX **SINCLAIR** PAUL **MOUNTS**

DC COMICS™

"Chaotic and unabashedly fun."—IGN

"I'm enjoying HARLEY QUINN a great deal; it's silly, it's funny, it's irreverent."
—COMIC BOOK RESOURCES

HARLEY QUINN

VOLUME 1: PRELUDES AND KNOCK-KNOCK JOKES

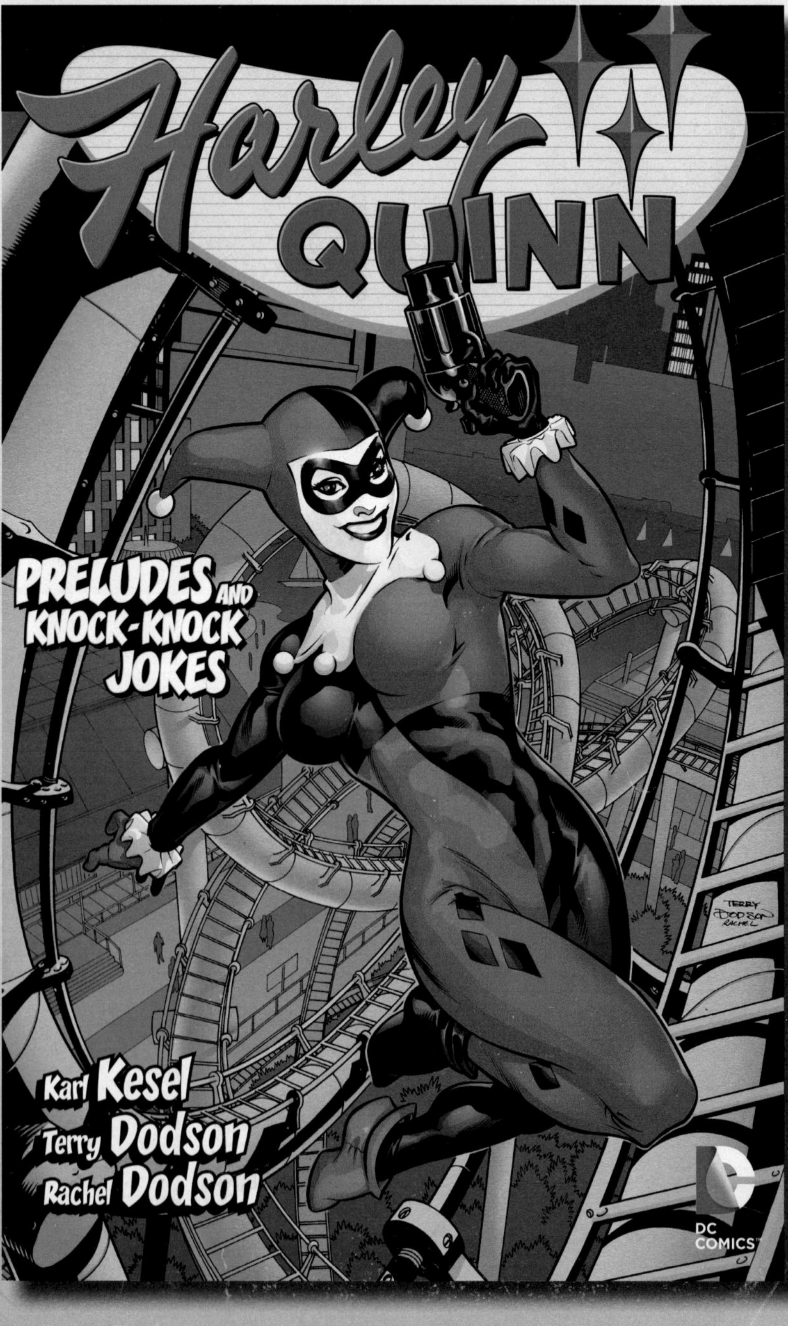

Harley
QUINN
PRELUDES AND KNOCK-KNOCK JOKES
Karl Kesel
Terry Dodson
Rachel Dodson
DC COMICS

HARLEY QUINN VOL. 2: NIGHT AND DAY

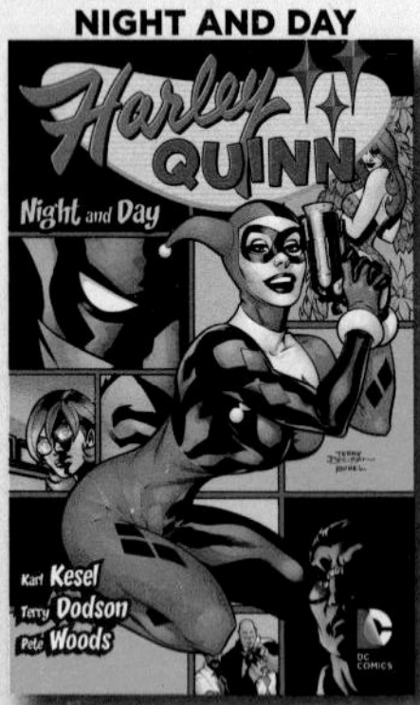

Harley
QUINN
Night and Day
Karl Kesel
Terry Dodson
Pete Woods

with KARL KESEL, TERRY DODSON, and PETE WOODS

HARLEY QUINN VOL. 3: WELCOME TO METROPOLIS

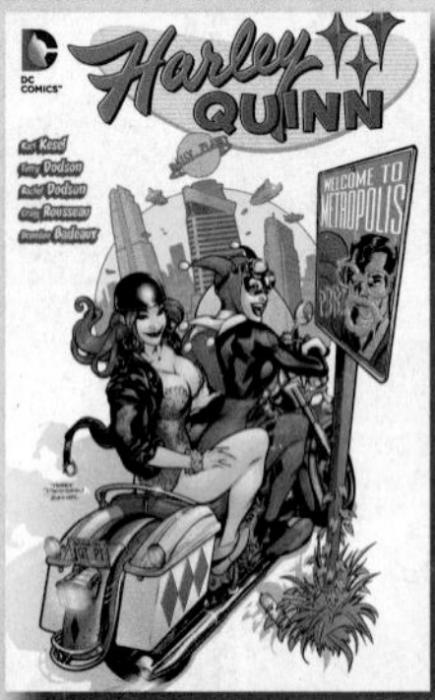

DC COMICS
Harley
QUINN
WELCOME TO METROPOLIS

with KARL KESEL, TERRY DODSON and CRAIG ROUSSEAU

HARLEY QUINN VOL. 4: VENGEANCE UNLIMITED

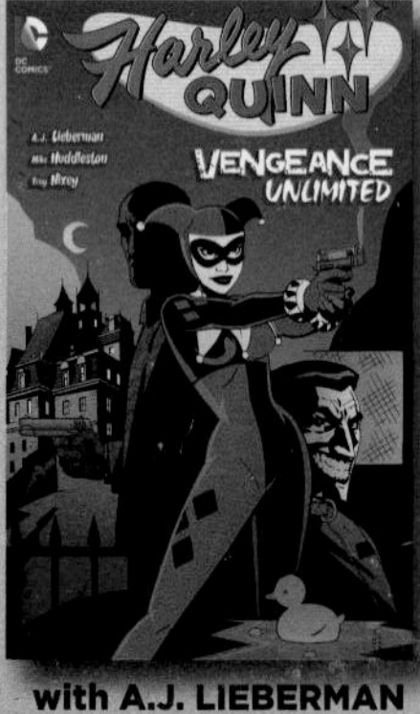

DC COMICS
Harley
QUINN
VENGEANCE UNLIMITED

with A.J. LIEBERMAN and MIKE HUDDLESTON